A passion for DANCE

MICHELLE POTTER

NATIONAL LIBRARY OF AUSTRALIA
CANBERRA 1997

Front cover: Mia Mason and Shaun Parker in *Furioso*, 1993
Meryl Tankard Australian Dance Theatre
Photograph by Régis Lansac
National Library of Australia Pictorial Collection

Back cover: Lea Francis in *Bonehead*, 1997
Chunky Move
Photograph by Kiren Chang
Photograph courtesy of Chunky Move

Published by the National Library of Australia
Canberra ACT 2600

© National Library of Australia and Michelle Potter, 1997

Every reasonable endeavour has been made to contact copyright holders of photographic material. Where this has not proved possible, the copyright holders are invited to contact the publisher.

National Library of Australia Cataloguing-in-Publication entry

Potter, Michelle, 1944– .
    A passion for dance.

    Includes index.
    ISBN 0 642 10685 1.

    1. Dancers—Australia—Interviews.
    2. Choreographers—Australia—Interviews.
    I. National Library of Australia. II. Title.

792.80280994

Editor: Julie Stokes
Designer: Beverly Swifte
Printed by Goanna Print, Canberra
Scanning and film separations by Trendsetting Pty Ltd

Contents

Introduction: Vibrant Encounters … v

Acknowledgements … xi

Stephen Baynes: Contemporary Classicist … 1

Maina Gielgud: Remarkable Years … 15

Padma Menon: Dance Reborn … 35

Paul Mercurio: Wild Card … 49

Graeme Murphy: Humanity Revealed … 61

Gideon Obarzanek: Daring Dance … 79

Stephen Page: Feet to the Earth … 93

Meryl Tankard: Touching the Heart … 105

Natalie Weir: Textures and Layers … 123

Stanton Welch: Boundless Dreams … 135

Appendix: Oral history interviews relating to dance in the collection of the National Library of Australia … 144

List of Illustrations … 145

Name Index … 146

For Neville, Timothy, James and Nick—the men in my life

Introduction
Vibrant Encounters

What is it like being a dancer, a choreographer, a director of a dance company working in Australia in the 1990s?

In the rehearsal studio, in the classroom, on stage, a host of images jostle for attention in the mind of the outsider: visions of athleticism, virtuosity, exoticism, romanticism, glamour, professionalism, passion, commitment, drama, daring, pain, injury, sweat, obsession, engagement, pleasure, sorrow, support, transformation. Dance is a vital art form.

How do these same artists react when placed behind a microphone, when asked to reveal in depth, and in words rather than movement, their ideas, their aspirations, their hopes and their fears? Dancers do communicate in a unique way through the medium of the human body, and choreographers and directors strive to maximise that special capacity that dancers have. Is it possible, then, to capture in words anything of what these people strive to create for the stage and for their audiences? Or is it true, as Marcia Siegel the persuasive New York-based dance writer suggests, that such people—and she is writing in particular of choreographers—go to great lengths to conceal the intellectual side of their creativity 'as if any suspicion of it would spoil the viewer's experience or somehow render the dance invalid'?[1]

The artists whose thoughts and recollections appear in A Passion for Dance were asked to sit in front of a microphone, some for several hours and some on more than one occasion, to tape an oral history interview for the significant and growing collection of dance recordings held by the National Library of Australia in Canberra.[2] Some of the interviewees are younger than others; their range of experiences is perhaps less varied than that of their older colleagues. But whatever their age and life experiences, what each of these people has to say indicates quite clearly that there is no deception, no desire to conceal. They all reveal themselves as forthright and open people. The interviews in this book also suggest that those who make dancing, in whatever manifestation, a lifelong commitment are not verbally inarticulate. They have an intellect, and when using it to convey verbally what they strive to communicate in dance, they display strength, courage, humour, warmth, determination and a host of other human emotions and characteristics. Dancers are vibrant people—to encounter them out of their more familiar, theatrical and backstage environment is a lively experience.

The people who were interviewed for A Passion for Dance engage head-on with ideas. Gideon Obarzanek, independent choreographer who is daringly distinctive in his attitude to dance, contemplates, for example, the very nature of Australian culture when he says:

What I like very much about Australia is there's a certain kind of raw vigour, a certain naivety, in a positive way. And also our New World type of culture—what could almost be argued by Europeans as this culture-less culture that becomes a culture of its own, this cultural-less-ness.

1 Marcia Siegel, 'Visible Secrets: Style Analysis and Dance Literacy' in Gay Morris (ed.), *Moving Words: Rewriting Dance* (London & New York: Routledge, 1996), p. 30.

2 Dance interviews currently in the Oral History Collection are listed in the appendix to this book.

And Stephen Baynes, one of two resident choreographers with the Australian Ballet, ponders on the relevance of the classical idiom and considers whether it is possible to manipulate the classical vocabulary so that it speaks to a contemporary audience:

I think what I'm trying to stress is that the very roots of this art form have been diminished, or they don't stand up anymore. So what we're left with is the discipline, the form itself, but none of the things that led it to be developed are able to be used in the same way anymore—in contrast to opera, for instance. If you look at Verdi they were very relevant political things that were being written about. So they can be looked at in context today ... I'm so aware of the difficult point that ballet has reached now. What can we do to this to make it as vibrant as opera seems now, but not throwing away entirely the classical idiom?

Obarzanek, on the other hand, rejects classical aesthetics. Speaking of the company he formed, which he named Chunky Move, he says:

I guess 'chunky' was a nice word because it doesn't have any held notions of professional dance or the aesthetics of dance; it's a word that really grates against it. It's nice for us because I get a feeling it frees us up. We're not held to any kind of notions of, you know, all that clean line and the ethereal beauty of dance.

These artists care, too, about where their art form sits in the wider culture, however they might define or perceive that culture. Stephen Page, Aboriginal director of Bangarra Dance Theatre, is clear about where he wants his company to position itself:

The interesting thing for me was to set a vision statement that made Bangarra very much a contemporary meeting place. It was really meant to be quite diverse and at the same time able to nurture a respect for the traditional culture. I'd love to think that this resource is the bridge between traditional and urban lifestyles. I'm interested in housing a foundation for the next generation.

And while Meryl Tankard, who worked extensively with the German choreographer Pina Bausch before returning to Australia and establishing a company of her own, wants to engage a wide cross-section of the community as an audience, she is concerned about how she can balance a variety of expectations of her and her company:

It's again this thing in Australia—and I do have to say it. I just think there's some major problem. As soon as you start to get successful, people do start to knock you. I mean, we're just starting to build up an audience. We're going to New York. We've got a European tour planned with fees. We could really, really be an international company. And I don't know if there are that many companies in Australia getting invitations from Paris and New York. But I'm always made to feel that that's not that important. You know, we can't even get a national tour.

They are also people who care passionately about their art form. 'I choreograph,' says Natalie Weir, independent Brisbane-based choreographer, 'because I adore it, it's sort of a passion with me, as is acting with my husband.' And when Maina Gielgud, the longest serving artistic director of the Australian Ballet and now ballet director of the Royal Danish Ballet, discusses the age at which dancers retire, she is clearly stating a strongly held, personal belief:

It's no good being able to continue to dance unless it's something that you yourself feel you *have* to do. That fundamentally you love—but love, I think, is not the right word—that you have such a *passion* for dance, and that can mean love or hate, that you can't really function without doing it.

Across the ten interviews, certain issues emerge as recurrent themes. None is really new, but all seem especially pertinent in Australia in the 1990s where the rhetoric of change, growth and renewal associated with the new millennium is especially strong as the country debates the issue of a republic and prepares to host the Olympic Games in the year

2000 and to celebrate the centenary of its federation in 2001. Questions concerning the past, the present, the future and the links between them are at the heart of this book. How does dance deal with its heritage? How will the art form move into the 21st century?

With regard to heritage, Australians have been slow or perhaps unwilling or unable to follow trends in Europe and America. There the reconstruction of old works from what are thought of as 'golden ages' in dance has become a serious business and part of the desire and drive to preserve the often-marginalised historical legacy of the dance world. Sadly, very few early Australian works have been reconstructed, and those few that have have not entered the repertoire of any major company where they might be seen by a cross-section of the community. Would we laugh at works reconstructed from the significant 1940s repertoires of the Borovansky Ballet and Ballet Guild? Or at Australian pieces made in the 1950s for the West Australian Ballet by Kira Bousloff and her composer–husband, James Penberthy? Equally sadly, very few, if any, of the reconstructions made overseas of critical works from the Ballets Russes eras— *Les Noces*, *L'Après-midi d'un faune*, *Le Sacre du printemps*, *Parade*, *Choreartium*, *Les Présages*—have been seen in Australia although original, or close-to-original, versions of most of them were seen in Australia when the de Basil companies performed them between 1936 and 1940. And perhaps saddest of all, there are indications that what is probably the heritage of the future may suffer the same fate. Major works in the vast output of Graeme Murphy for Sydney Dance Company, which Murphy has directed for more than 20 years, are rarely remounted in a climate where there is, Murphy suggests, an 'avarice,

appetite for the new'. Probably Australia's best-known choreographer at the present time, Murphy says 'the obsession with making things new, with being fresh, with not repeating yourself becomes really draining'. And in a similar vein, Obarzanek points out:

Australian dance works just don't last very long, you know. They go on the stage, you see them for about a year or so and they go off, and there's a new one. People don't see it as an investment of money and time in a work that you can actually use for a long period of time.

But, as the interviews in *A Passion for Dance* reveal, an interest in heritage is an individualistic phenomenon in Australia. It goes beyond the idea that heritage is about reconstruction of works from the past, however desirable such activities might be. It encompasses the notion that choreographers need, in their present works, to account for the past, and often for their uniquely Australian past. Murphy, for example, celebrates a particular Australian identity in *Nutcracker*, his culturally specific version of an old ballet classic. *Nutcracker*, made by Murphy in collaboration with Kristian Fredrikson for the Australian Ballet in 1992, is a rethinking of the traditional Christmas ballet much-loved around the world, and is a sophisticated celebration of Australia's migrant history, dance history and collective cultural memory. In discussing how he and Fredrikson came to set the piece partly in Australia, Murphy says, 'the whole thing of displaced people having to find their way, or artists coming to this country and finding new ways of fertilising the soil ... seemed so natural and so right'.

Accounting for the past may also be expressed through a search for a new dance vocabulary and a new conceptual framework that acknowledges cultural background and, at the same time, looks for a way of making that background relevant in changed social conditions. Indian–Australian dancer Padma Menon, artistic director of the Canberra-based Padma Menon Dance Theatre, with a wealth of training and experience as a traditional Kuchipudi dancer behind her, ponders on just these issues. She discusses how she wants to celebrate her Asian background, her difference, but also how she shies away from the notion of fusion of cultures: 'I just want to trigger the vocabulary that I know and push it itself ... and maybe *conceptually* push my thinking along in non-Indian ways,' she says. Page is similarly inspired to make dance that draws on his range of experiences from both traditional Aboriginal and urban situations. He says of his experiences as a student of the National Aboriginal and Islander Skills Development Association:

It's very confronting if you're brought up in an urban situation and then you've got a traditional elder there teaching you your own dances. Whereas everything else, if it was classical or tap or jazz, we were much more immune to because we had an urban upbringing—that's what we were used to, the contemporary world. So it was just an amazing moment to learn any form of traditional dance. I think when I did discover traditional dance, or the essence of it, and the groundedness behind it, it then influenced and inspired me to choreograph and to bring my experiences all together. So that's what it is, I believe, when you choreograph and create—it's just a fruit salad of your experiences, and that becomes your style.

But some artists interviewed for this book rarely consciously look back, taking their inspiration almost entirely from the influences of the present or the very recent past. Obarzanek, for example, is interested in deconstructing the popular culture he sees around him:

One of my biggest inspirations ... has been the work of some recent film directors ... pulp fiction directors. And what is meant by pulp fiction is the ability to use popular culture, to appropriate it like pulp and to shape it in your own way, to use it as an art form. So you're not a victim of popular culture, you actually begin to use it, deconstruct it and assemble it, and use it as fodder, as a material, as a communicative language.

Many are interested in film and new technologies and how they can be used to expand both the horizons of dance and an artist's personal horizons. 'With film,' says Tankard, 'you've got that opportunity to turn the wall upside down, the floor upside down, to make the wall the floor.' And Paul Mercurio, who rocketed to fame when he starred in the film *Strictly Ballroom*, is now interested in making his own dance films rather than working in a dance company as he did before *Strictly Ballroom*:

I've actually been offered a lot of stage work and I've said no to all of it, because I really can't bear the thought of doing a three- or six-month run of the same show eight shows a week. I've done that, I suppose. I like the fact that you can do something new on film and it lives, and while it's showing you can be doing something else new. So you're stretching yourself. I'm growing with each new thing and it doesn't take four years to do one or two new things.

Other recurring themes in *A Passion for Dance* are matters that are also the subject of long-term debate in other art forms. What is the relative importance of form and content? What is the nature of the artist and his or her training? How important is narrative? Some issues that emerge constantly are more specific to dance. Does the proscenium stage still offer a viable space for dance creation? Should a dance company be led by a choreographer as artistic director? Is choreography a craft that can easily be learnt in some kind of teaching institution?

Or are choreographers artists who are born, not made? In fact the question of whether choreographers are born or made is something about which most of those interviewed for *A Passion for Dance* have something to say:

'(Choreography)'s a very hard thing to teach and just getting in there and doing it, you know, by the seat of your pants is the way you find out what works best,' suggests Weir.

'I would think,' says Baynes, 'one of the most important things for any creative artist is instinct, and instinct is something you really see yourself when something hasn't perhaps worked and you begin to know why.'

But for some, like Stanton Welch, a resident choreographer with the Australian Ballet along with Baynes, there is scarcely an issue involved. When questioned about criticisms that have been constantly voiced in the press about his never having studied the craft of choreography, he says: 'I mean, really, who has? ... I mean, who has had an apprenticeship from Australia? Did Graeme Murphy? Did Sir Robert Helpmann?'

Most of the choreographers interviewed acknowledge a debt to mentors rather than to any kind of institutional study since most have achieved their successes without it. Tankard honours Bausch, Baynes those with whom he worked while dancing with the Stuttgart Ballet, Menon her Indian guru, several others the time they spent working with Murphy and Janet Vernon in the Sydney Dance Company. If questions of past and present, growth and renewal are at the heart of *A Passion for Dance*, the issue of what makes a choreographer and how his or her talents should be nurtured and used resound throughout it.

The artists whose thoughts and recollections appear in *A Passion for Dance* represent a cross-section of people who have made a contribution to dance in Australia in the 1990s. Selecting who would appear in the book was a subjective procedure. I personally made the choice from among the very many possibilities. The people I chose were artists whose work I had encountered on more than one occasion. Whether it was the work of someone who was a choreographer, a director, or both, someone who was still actively dancing or not, I had always found what they did interesting, thought-provoking and challenging in some way.

One or two of them had been interviewed previously, and in creating the book I combined parts of those earlier interviews with the more recent ones, in each case acknowledging in the text the dates and names of interviewers of earlier recordings. In preparing the interviews for publication I also edited them. In every instance it was necessary to abbreviate the interviews for reasons of space and to alter them slightly to accommodate the differences between spoken and written text. I did, however, endeavour to keep something of the individualistic speech patterns of the interviewees since generational differences were clearly apparent in vocabulary and sentence structure and needed, I thought, to be maintained as much as possible. I sometimes also took considerable liberties by rearranging the order in which questions had been asked and answers given. The full recordings, subject to any restrictions placed on them by the interviewees, are available for consultation in the National Library. Listening to them is a rewarding experience. The human voice is rich with interest.

A Passion for Dance is not meant to be a collection of mini-biographies, although often biographical information is an intrinsic part of the interview. It is meant, however, to reveal some of the thinking that goes on behind the scenes and to provide a small insight into the intentions of artists, whether we as outsiders and as potential audience members agree with those intentions or not. What I think emerges is a series of vibrant and, despite the common threads, diverse encounters with vital, creative and passionate minds.

Acknowledgements

First, last and most of all I thank the artists whose thoughts and recollections are recorded in this book. I can never be grateful enough to them for their trust and their generosity of spirit.

Many other people helped me create this book. I thank them all. In particular the National Library staff in Oral History and Sound Preservation and Technical Services were forever patient. I am indebted to them for the special attention they gave the project; without it my deadlines would never have been met.

Michelle Potter
Canberra
May 1997

Stephen Baynes
Contemporary Classicist

Interview TRC 3378

Stephen Baynes (born 1956), leading soloist with the Australian Ballet and since 1995 one of the company's two resident choreographers, was interviewed by Michelle Potter in Sydney in December 1995

As a choreographer, Stephen Baynes has unashamedly engaged full-on with one of the most emotionally charged issues to have emerged in Australian dance in recent years. In the works he has created since 1986 when he made his first piece, *Strauss Songs*, for an Australian Ballet choreographic workshop, Baynes has given the utmost prominence to the classical idiom in its most traditional manifestation. In fact with *Beyond Bach*, which he made for the Australian Ballet in 1995, he says quite frankly that he was 'waving the banner for classical ballet'. Critics in Australia and elsewhere have frequently speculated on the relevance of ballet as an art form in a contemporary and democratising society. They point constantly to its elitist image both in the sense that as an art form its execution is limited to a select few, and in the sense that historically its origins in ancient royal patronage and the hierarchical structure of an outmoded court system are alien in the 1990s.

Beyond Bach, set to some of J.S. Bach's best-known compositions and designed by West Australian artist Andrew Carter, was Baynes' second commissioned piece for the Australian Ballet following on from *Catalyst* in 1990. In creating it, Baynes did not even try to defy the major conventions of the classical technique as choreographers have often done when, while still working within the framework of the classical vocabulary, they have questioned the most basic features and structures of that vocabulary. *Beyond Bach* achieved considerable critical and popular acclaim and its success was partly due to the fact that Baynes was able to imbue the piece with a spirituality that transcended its formal elements. But it was also due to the fact that, while 'waving the banner', Baynes used the classical vocabulary to explore a whole range of concepts, including the importance of form and discipline to a creative artist, and the significance of space as a guiding principle in choreographic design. Conceptual thinking about choreography is often seen as the exclusive province of the modernist choreographer. With *Beyond Bach*, Baynes revealed otherwise. The piece was a milestone in Baynes' personal search to use the classical idiom as a valid form of expression in a contemporary world. It was also a milestone in the Australian chapter of the debate about contemporary classicism.

POTTER: What inspired you to make *Beyond Bach*?

BAYNES: Well, first and foremost, as with all my pieces up to then, and I'm sure probably for a long time to come, it was the music. I loved that music and I thought it lent itself very well to dance. But then I was also very aware that they were some of the best-known pieces of Bach—almost clichéd, I suppose—and I was very concerned that it would be just a 'dancey' classical ballet. Of course, I didn't want it to be that at all.

My first piano teacher tended to confuse Bach with God, I think, as a lot of musos do. Bach's *it*, you know; there's God, then there's Bach, or sometimes the other way round. I mean, the man was a genius, there's no doubt about it, but also what intrigued me about him was that he really was doing work in a very craftsman-like way. It was done to a formula and it was all to do with form and structure and rules. He was fighting against the grain too. In his time he was like the last great master of the polyphonic form that was already a little bit out of date in his lifetime. In fact, his own sons apparently thought he was a dag for writing that sort of stuff. He was ignored and was thrown away in the drawers for about 100 years until he was rediscovered.

I saw this analogy with classical ballet. I thought, 'It's the same thing. Everyone thinks it's dowdy just because it's on pointe and they're doing classical steps that have been around for a long time. Everyone thinks it can't say something or it can't be beautiful and, beyond being beautiful, it can't reach you in some way.' I suppose I was trying to see if it was viable, if you could basically do what you would call a 'dancey' classical ballet that would also have some sort of emotional content and that would reach an audience in some way beyond the steps. I was quite honestly waving the banner for classical ballet, and hoping desperately that audiences could look at it and not just think, 'Oh well, it's very lovely, yes, it's very pretty but it just washes over you.' I can't tell you how much I feared that that was what it was going to look like.

But one of the things that obviously seemed to me to be very important was to make it a total concept; that space that the dancers were moving in was not just decorative, it was integral to what they were doing. I wanted them to look as if they belonged in that space. They hadn't just come out of the wings from God-knows-where, stepped onto the stage and started doing what they were supposed to do, then gone off. In *Bach*, they are like spirits that just live in this environment, I think.

I talked with Andrew Carter a great deal about this. I was able to be really very specific, too, with the design. I knew that I wanted a staircase. It was important where it was in the terms of the entrances and exits, particularly the one particular movement, the cantata. I also envisaged columns. I wanted it to be a cathedral-type interior that had that wonderful sense that you get when you walk into somewhere like the cathedrals in Milan or Chartres—the light just sifts out. Certainly I wasn't aiming for a religious work or even a quasi-religious work but something of that sense of awe, I suppose, that you receive in a place of that sort. There were a lot of things within the music that led to that point of view being taken.

Also what started with *Catalyst*, which I also worked on with Andrew, was that one of the things that I felt held back ballet so much was this dreadful proscenium–backdrop–wings idea. I mean, it just contributes to the music-box look of ballet, I thought. I wanted my work to be free and evocative and for the stage space to reflect that—it should be a magical sort of space. There's no limit to what can be done with a stage to make it look like a unique environment that these people belong to, or maybe they don't belong to, they've been thrust into it. There's all sorts of drama that you can build just out of the space that people are in. I mean, you can say volumes just with that—what sort of conflicts or contexts you build up in the space the people are occupying.

So I guess what I'm saying is that a lot of elements led into *Beyond Bach*. It wasn't just finding this piece of music that I liked and putting steps to it. I tried to get this idea that there is a spirituality in the music that transcends the discipline of its composition. In spite of Bach writing this complex music, he was also able to move people in the most incredible way. I liked that. I thought that was wonderful.

I guess it gets back to the things that have been instilled in me from the beginning, that the whole challenge of anyone working creatively in art is to do so through a discipline. First of all has to come the form, and then you have to try and say what you want to say through the form. That to me is where the challenge and the skill is, to be able to apply some rules and yet interpret them in an individual way to say what you want to say. So that's where it came from.

Baynes was born and brought up in Adelaide—'in the early sixties, late fifties, a very secure sort of place to live'—and, although his early recollections include his mother's illness and her death when he was 11, he recalls his childhood as being 'very secure, a nice home, loving parents'. He was educated at Pultney Grammar School and showed a strong interest from an early age in both music and drama. His fate was sealed, however, when the Australian Ballet began to visit Adelaide in the 1960s.

POTTER: How did you first encounter ballet?

BAYNES: My really strong interest as a child apart from music was in drama. I always thought I wanted to be an actor. In fact, at different stages through my life there've been hankerings sometimes to maybe go back to that. So I was very into drama and also opera. I adored opera. From a very early age I was listening to recordings of Maria Callas and Joan Sutherland and people like that. I'm not quite sure how that came about. It was a bit of a concern to my parents, I think. Anyway, Mum used to take me to the opera which was the Elizabethan Theatre Trust Opera Company in those days. They used to come to Adelaide once a year. I also remember being taken to see Joan Sutherland when she came in 1965. That was a great thrill.

Then the Australian Ballet started to visit and at some stage I was taken along to see the ballet. I can remember from the first performance I was swept away by it. It was something quite fantastic—I think in the way it was a synthesis of music and theatre as well. There was something with the music to inspire me about it, but dancing just seemed to be a way of visualising the music. So I was suddenly swept away by dancing and I went to find out all I could about it. I remember getting books from the library. I did actually know about a studio that was just near the bus stop where I used to catch the bus home from school, in the city in Adelaide. It was run by a Russian teacher, Agnes Babicheva, and she used to have a studio up in this arcade in the city. So I used to sneak up there and watch these classes through a door or something like that and was fascinated by it all.

But I am jumping ahead a little bit because by that stage my mother had died and I remember approaching my father saying, 'Look, I really would like to start learning ballet.' And the answer was, 'No. No son of mine's going to do ballet'—although I don't think he actually said that to me, but that was the reason, I think. His reasons to me were that I was doing enough already, which was actually quite true. I mean, I was very interested in piano, I was going to drama classes I think twice a week, plus I had school. And he, probably quite normally, saw this as just another phase or something that would perhaps not be of interest for very long. Well, it was. I just kept at it.

The turning point was not very long after my mother died. Dad took my brother and I on a wonderful trip overseas. We went through India. We went to Russia, England and through a lot of Europe. Of course, we went to Moscow and Leningrad. So I dragged my father along to see both the Bolshoi and the Kirov companies when we were there. Apart from seeing the ballet itself—I don't think he'd ever been to a performance—when he saw the way that these professionals in Russia were thought of with such high regard, I think he had a slightly different view of dancing from then on. So, when we returned to Australia from that trip, then he said I could start learning dancing, and that's when I did. So I was about 14.

Baynes had his first training not with Agnes Babicheva but with respected Adelaide teacher Joanna Priest, with whom he studied full-time after leaving school. Priest's influence on the future direction of his career was immense. She insisted that her students be grounded in all the arts not just dance. 'When I look back,' Baynes recalls, 'without in any sense diminishing what she taught me, the actual teaching of the technical side of ballet was probably the smallest part of what she gave me.' Priest also encouraged her full-time students to choreograph both for themselves and for others: 'The seeds were sown quite early,' Baynes says.

POTTER: Did Priest teach compositional skills, or were you just expected to pick things up somehow?

BAYNES: Yes, I think she did actually. In fact, yes, I remember that. It probably would be looked at as perhaps a fairly unfashionable way of teaching now. I can remember going to her with a couple of pieces of music or recordings and saying, 'I'd like to do this,' and she just said, 'No, I don't think you should use that.' That would *never* happen now. People would say that's stomping on the individual's creativity. But no doubt she had her reasons. She probably thought, 'This 14-year-old boy is not up to using Schubert,' or something like that. And she would have said as much.

Yes, she was very critical. She'd say, 'Well, what were you doing here?' or 'Can you see how that shape perhaps isn't having any effect on us?' or something like that. But she

didn't criticise negatively. She just made you look at it, I suppose, with a different pair of eyes, try and see another point of view. I think that in some ways maybe it's led to my hypercritical nature. It's almost like a problem. You're criticising something almost before it comes out, which is not good. You have to get past that.

But it's also left me with an acute awareness that you mustn't forget the audience really. That's ultimately what it's all about. Whatever you want to say or whatever you're trying to say, remember you're trying to say it to someone who is going to be watching it and hopefully is going to get something out of it, not just that *you've* got something out of it. So that's one of the things I think she instilled in me. But yes, she certainly took an active part in criticising what you did and advising and things like that.

POTTER: Can choreographic skills be taught?

BAYNES: I have to say that I *don't* think you can teach a choreographer basically. Perhaps when one has identified a certain talent or some sort of skill in the area or that someone's got some originality or that there's perhaps a future there, then that's the time to perhaps guide a little bit. But I don't think you can start from the other way round—teach them the ropes and then see if the creativity is there afterwards. The originality or the impulse has to be there initially. Then most of it needs really to be learnt by trial and error.

I would think one of the most important things for any creative artist is instinct, and instinct is something you really see yourself when something hasn't perhaps worked and you begin to know why. It's the reason you make judgements about something or make decisions about something when you can't necessarily justify it. You just feel that that's what it needs to be. Either it ends up to be good or bad or wrong or right. They're the things that you learn as you go along yourself. Experience is really the only thing that you can give choreographers, I think, when they're developing.

But personally I feel I am a little negative towards the idea of actually training someone in skills per se about choreography. I just don't quite see how you can do that. Certainly I think there's not enough in people perhaps knowing enough about music and knowing enough about form in general. When I spoke earlier about having an idea of form and structure, that, as much as anything, comes from recognising it in *other* things—to see how a piece of art has a form or structure or it doesn't, or a piece of music has a form or structure or doesn't, or where it's heading. I think the sensibility and awareness you have in the other things ultimately is what will lead to a greater sensibility in what you're trying to say yourself. I mean, it's not something that you're conscious of; you grow up with different influences that just shape you and mould your ideas in a way that you're not necessarily aware of, I think, until later. As I say, you can look back and say, 'Yes, that probably influenced me in this way.' Further along the track you're aware of things that you could do or read or see or listen to or something that will perhaps assist your development, but I don't think you can be aware of that in the beginning, hoping that you're going to arrive at a point where you'll be able to regurgitate all that in your own way.

But although Priest carefully nurtured the creative talents of her students, and although the Australian Ballet's first artistic director, Peggy van Praagh, had suggested that Baynes engage in workshop choreography when he was first a member of the Australian Ballet between 1976 and 1980, Baynes wanted to dance—'like most people who start dancing, I wanted to have a brilliant career, the big dancer doing it all'. And it was while working with Priest that Baynes saw at first hand what the life a dancer might be like. Those early experiences helped shape many of his current thoughts about the nature of the classical idiom and how it sits in a contemporary world.

BAYNES: Joanna was very close to Peggy, Peggy van Praagh. In fact, when the Australian Ballet used to come to Adelaide, Peggy always stayed with Joanna in her home, which was at the front of her studio. So it was always a very exciting time when the Australian Ballet visited because they were using our studios. So for about two weeks you'd have the Australian Ballet there every morning and it was *incredibly* exciting, as you can imagine, particularly as one time—I think it was the 1972 Festival of Arts—they premiered Nureyev's production of *Don Quixote* there. So Nureyev was walking around the school—and Lucette Aldous and Robert Helpmann—and I was lucky enough to extra in those performances. So they're very special memories. It just built on the excitement of the art form. It had a lot of glamour and that was very exciting. These wonderful people, you looked up to them and thought how fabulous they were. It was inspiring. You wanted to desperately get into the company and be doing what they did.

I think that a little bit of that glamour is disappearing now. Not that I think it's a bad thing; it's just that it *is* happening. I mean, there's no doubt that there isn't this aura. Perhaps it's not seen as so important, and I think this is quite important too. I remember when I was first in the Australian Ballet—before I left and went to Europe in the early eighties—the dancers actually worked at being quite glamorous and it was something that both they wanted to do but also an unsaid thing that you sort of had to do. If you were at receptions and things like that, you were expected to dress and look pretty; and people did. Whereas now I think that sort of side of it is not seen as so important. It's something that isn't relevant so much.

Even in a company like the Royal Ballet where some of those traditions are still held on to, the reigning ballerinas, people like Darcey Bussell, are more likely to come out of the stage door in jeans and boots and hop into a four-wheel drive. It's part of the times we live in now. When you think of someone like Margot Fonteyn, who worked with the Australian Ballet quite a lot when I first joined—when we were doing *Merry Widow* a lot and touring with it—Margot was like the royal family really. You always felt like genuflecting when she came into the room. Even though she was a charming lady, she just did have this aura about her, and that was part of the mystique. But that isn't the mystique now. I think this is a very relevant point because that side of what was the attraction to people in ballet in many ways doesn't exist anymore. So there's this struggle to find a new relevance for the classical idiom.

POTTER: What is the relevance of the classical idiom then?

BAYNES: Well, I think that the people who are dancers now, the practitioners of the art, obviously have an enormous influence on the way the art is. They're very different people now and, as we said, that aura thing is no longer important or, even more importantly, relevant. It doesn't have anything to do with what you do. But the dichotomy is that classical ballet is, for all intents and purposes, a very stylised art form, very stylised. It comes from courts and royalty and it was for the ruling classes. It was a *divertissement* for them, a diversion.

Out of that we have developed a wonderful art form and a wonderful technique—a medium for expression. But the sort of things it was used for are becoming less important now—the subject matter. Really all of the surviving classics of ballet, and there's only a handful—you could name them on the fingers of one hand; in fact, probably *Swan Lake*, *Sleeping Beauty*, *Giselle* are the main three—are all concerned with mythology that says that things are going to turn out right in the end. The princess is going to get her prince and good will triumph over evil and everything will be lovely and the order will be just restored. Of course, that doesn't have any bearing in life in the late twentieth century. People don't believe that at all.

I think what I'm trying to stress is that the very roots of this art form have been diminished, or they don't stand up anymore. So what we're left with is the discipline, the form itself, but none of the things that led it to be developed are able to be used in the same way anymore—in contrast to opera, for instance. If you look at Verdi they were very relevant political things that were being written about. So they can be looked at in context today and have a lot of relevance. And the same with drama. Shakespeare's dramas were very much relevant to their time and they're to do with human passions and emotions and intrigues that are just as relevant to human nature today as they were then.

POTTER: This is very interesting in the light of the works you've choreographed because you haven't tried to move into the political arena.

BAYNES: Yes. Well, you see, I really have to say that at this stage I feel really like a beginner. I've got two works in the repertoire of the company at the moment. Whether it's entirely consciously or unconsciously, I have felt that you have to take the steps in your own way to discover your own voice or discover a form that suits you. Sometimes you don't necessarily see the way ahead, but you have to go through certain stages and it's only when looking back, I think, you can see that was leading to that was leading to that.

I do start to see that a little bit now. If I go right back to the piece I did for the company's 25th anniversary

choreographic competition in 1988, which was *Ballade*, then *Catalyst* was very much a step forward from that, and now *Bach* was another step forward from that. So I think it's a process of gradual development to find your own voice within the discipline. You have to learn about all the things that are important about giving something form. Because to me the primary thing in any piece of art is its form.

You have to have a form and a structure to it to be able to say what you want to say through that. If you just start somewhere off in the middle and you've got this thing that you want to say but you haven't developed any discipline or structure or form behind it, then it can be a one-off thing and you'll be lost after that or you'll be stabbing in the dark continually. I'm hoping that I've given myself a bit of foundation now to try to perhaps say some of these things that I feel very aware of. I'm so aware of the difficult point that ballet has reached now. What can we do to this to make it as vibrant as opera seems to be now, but not throwing away entirely the classical idiom?

Personally I find the narrative idea, this thing of story ballet, doesn't sit well with me in a way because I just think we've reached a point where that has been done, and sometimes very successfully. I think the strength of ballet is much to do with the abstract. So you have to think of a way of telling things through allegory more; that's the way I would like to find anyway. So it's a matter of finding texts or ideas or stories that you can just take one side of or treat in a more unusual way. I think that the thing is to get back to theatre being used in the way that it's actually strongest—what it's really for—and that is to excite the imagination of people, to take them away on a journey that's largely of their own making in the way that people look at art or listen to music. I think it's a personal experience.

Baynes left the Australian Ballet at the end of 1980 having reached a point where he felt unsettled both about his own career—'I was having these acting twinges again'—and about the state of the Australian Ballet, which was going through a series of political and artistic crises that eventually culminated in a major dancers' strike in 1981.

Baynes worked in Europe as a dancer with the Stuttgart Ballet for three years between 1982 and 1984. Although he did not take the opportunity of creating in the choreographic workshops that were part of the Stuttgart Ballet's activities, he did perform in the experimental works of others. The repertoire of the Stuttgart Ballet, with its works by some of the twentieth century's leading choreographers including John Cranko, William Forsythe, Jiří Kylián and Kenneth MacMillan, also provided fertile ground for Baynes' emerging interest in choreography. It was on his return from Stuttgart to the Australian Ballet in 1985, drawn home by the prospect of a revitalised Australian Ballet under the directorship of Maina Gielgud, that his career as a choreographer began to blossom.

POTTER: Your choreographic career took off after you returned to Australia from Stuttgart, didn't it?

Baynes: Yes. I think the urge was very definitely there in Stuttgart and when I came back to Australia, the first opportunity that came up to do something I did. That was 1985 or 1986, I think, as soon as I got back. That was the pas de deux for Ulrike Lytton and Paul de Masson called *Strauss Songs*. It was taken from one of Richard Strauss' *Four Last Songs*. Then I did a number of small things for just two or three dancers.

It's funny, looking back I remember enjoying those experiences so much because it really did seem to me to be creative. I'd have this piece of music that I really wanted to do something to and I'd go into the studio with just a few people. It really felt like choreography in a way that hasn't really happened, funnily enough, since this last Australian Ballet choreographic workshop that happened a few weeks ago (September 1995) when, once again, I had a piece of music that I really liked and was different for me—not like anything I've done before. I just took two dancers, Nicole Rhodes and Kip Gamblin, and went into the studio and worked on something, which everyone said was very good. This was *Dialogues I & II* and was straight after *Bach*.

I think I felt the need to do that because the things for the company have been such epics in terms of the stress of getting them on in a very limited time. With *Bach*, for instance, they'd already named me as resident choreographer, which I resisted very much before, and I was thinking, 'God, I'm resident choreographer of the company and I've only done one ballet and here's this work that's coming up and I haven't done anything as far as the main audience of the Australian Ballet is concerned for two or three years.'

I'd done things for the Dancers Company which went on regional tours every year, but that isn't in any way high-profile. So as far as everyone was concerned, *this* was the new work and what was it going to be like? It was really extraordinarily stressful, I have to say. In a lot of ways, not entirely what I would have wanted. I mean, a lot of what you do is done because you have to do it; there's no time. You've got to get something done. Rehearsal finishes in two hours and you've only got those few weeks. There's no time to dilly-dally around, so you get it out and hope that it's something like what you originally conceived or wanted.

So that's why I thought, when this workshop was announced in September after *Bach*, I really want to do it—just to confirm to myself that I really, in fact, like doing this. That's when it is fun, that's when it does feel creative. Funnily enough, everyone made more of a fuss about *Dialogues I & II*, almost, than *Bach*. It was like, 'Oh, this is a side we've never seen before; this is a different kind of work.' Of course, everything could be if you're given the opportunity to focus a little bit more.

But then the other side is you can't always expect unlimited time. There is something to be said for having constraints with time, some sort of a deadline. If you make yourself do it, you don't sort of dawdle or become too introspective. It forces you to have a clear concept of what you want to say and to get into the studio and try and see if you can get that out. And then you look at it at the end.

This is the interesting thing about the whole process, because you're looking at something that's gone a very long period of time from the original gestation of hearing a piece of music to performing the idea. Even before you get into the studio, you know, the thought process is so full and sometimes confused and hard to focus. You're not really quite sure how it's going to go. Then you actually get into the studio and you start putting down the movement and then that goes in in such a piecemeal, slow process.

It's like someone painting a painting in a way. If you can imagine a very big painting and you're shut in a little black box and you paint little squares and then the black box moves and you end up doing the whole canvas like that without ever being able to step back and get an overall look. And that overall look was a mental picture that you had before you went into the studio. You wonder if what comes out of here is going to coincide with that or if in fact you can even remember entirely what it was, because what you've done in the studio has sort of taken over, something real has taken over what was initially just imagined.

It's a fascinating process. It's frustrating and it's exciting and it's inspiring and it's depressing. It's all those sort of things. I've found in the experiences I've had, like with *Bach* and I think I remember with *Catalyst* or more particularly the experience I had in Milan earlier this year when I made *Episodes* for La Scala Ballet, the more hopeless sometimes it seems, or the more lost you start to feel, you just go back and you listen to the music again and then you know, 'No, it's fine, it'll be all right.' That's the way I feel. So long as I've got enough faith in the music and I know what I'm trying to say, I've still got this vision. So long as you've still got that vision, then even if this awful stuff is in front of you in the studio, you'll sort it out, you'll get there. It makes you more determined.

POTTER: Do you go into the studio with steps in your mind or is it a much more abstract concept?

BAYNES: Not specific steps. What I think you have to be aiming for—or what *I* aim for—is that it communicates something basically; that it does say something to an onlooker, they get something from this thing besides just looking at movement. Ideally you want it to have quite a powerful impact on people, the way Jiří (Kylián) does just about every time. You know, you sit there and think, 'Oh God, it looks so beautiful.' And it affects you in the way that is absolutely personal. It just sort of opens up your awareness, your self-consciousness.

Early on, as a sort of protective mechanism, I remember making up steps or having some idea of movement. It's just less terrifying to go into a studio and be confronted with dancers and to be able to say, 'Well, I'd like you to try this,' instead of standing there and hoping that some muse is going to come down and say, 'Well, try this,' and next thing you know, you've got this wonderful phrase of movement. But it's much more challenging not to do that. As you get more confidence, you do feel able to go in to a studio and just try something because that's what it's all about, you know, especially with individual dancers—that you like the way they move or, even more interesting, that you challenge the way they move or the way they think they can move. That's what's wonderful. This is what's fabulous about Bill (Forsythe). I've watched him work in Frankfurt and it's what he can bring out of a dancer that no-one else thought they could do or that they certainly didn't think they could do. I think that's wonderful if you can do that.

This last work (*Dialogues I & II*) with Nicole (Rhodes), I found that happened a little bit because it really was a personal time. Just for an hour and a half or two hours we'd go into a studio. I forced myself not to have literally too much of an idea of what steps I wanted until I got into the studio. But that's not to say that I wasn't extremely familiar with the music so that I knew what sort of look I was after, but it was just a process of experimentation. That's when it's such fun, you know. I mean, there's no limit to what could happen. You think something's going to look a certain way and then something else happens by accident, or all sorts of opportunities present themselves.

POTTER: Who have been your mentors in your choreographic development?

BAYNES: Apart from Joanna, sometimes it's been dancers as much as choreographers. A lot of choreographers, not necessarily of this time but in the recent past, like Cranko, Ashton, MacMillan, have all said they've been terribly influenced by individual dancers. This is something that I can understand very much. Perhaps I should only speak for myself, but when I think choreographically, a lot of what you think about, you see it being danced in a particular way. You see the movement that you are making up or envisaging, not just for its own sake but being done in a certain way. In other words, you visualise a certain style of dancing, a certain type of dancer.

Equally then, if you see dancers who make a great impression on you or you admire a lot, that influences the way you feel about how movement should be. In that respect Marcia Haydée was a great influence in the three years I went to Stuttgart. I just thought she was the most extraordinary dancer. It was so interesting to watch some of Cranko's ballets, not necessarily the ones that she's most famous for, like *Onegin* or *Shrew* or *Romeo*, but some of the other ones that most people outside of Stuttgart, or outside the Stuttgart Ballet circle of people that see that company, aren't aware of that John did for her way back—sometimes slight little pieces, in fact. You can see how he's been inspired *so* much by her movement, the way she moves. And the piece survives mainly only because Marcia's doing it.

But when it comes to actual choreographers. It's funny, when I started doing things right back to *Ballade*, people said, 'Oh, it's very like Balanchine,' which is a pretty amazing thing to say. I used to shrink at that a bit. But I didn't actually see a lot of Balanchine. What we did in the Australian Ballet was just *Serenade* and *Ballet Imperial* back in the early days when I was in the company.

So I can't honestly say that I was influenced greatly by him, and yet the more I've seen his works over the years—when I went to America and saw it—certainly his musicality and, once again, the shape, the form, the structure is something that I admire very much. But beyond that, I think Jiří Kylián is the one who's been outstanding, even though he's not what people think of as a classical choreographer—far from it—but he certainly started that way. It's the same with Bill Forsythe who's now one of the most innovative voices in contemporary ballet. Bill's first works were extremely classical. He admits without a doubt that Balanchine was his major influence and he owes a great debt to him. So you can see where these people's roots have been, where they've started from.

But Jiří, to me, has the most incredibly original voice, that seems to keep on reinventing all the time. He's never stayed still. You can trace periods of his work that have lasted a while. I mean, the works that he's doing now are *nothing* like what he was doing 10 or 15 years ago. You might say that's what you'd expect or that's what you'd hope for, but in ballet very few have been able to do that. Most choreographers have a pretty identifiable style from start to finish. I think, of all the creative things, choreography is the one that has perhaps a shelf-life, more so than some of the other arts. Perhaps it's because it's a living human art form. It only lives as it's being

done by living breathing humans who are giving their own sort of life to it. How it looks relates very much to that.

Cranko, of course, had an influence. I mean, I think the way that he was able to tell a story through ballet was very clever. I don't think you can do that now, but in his time it was good, it was right. Even something like *Pineapple Poll*, which people would probably scoff at now, just the skill in getting that narrative across is very clever without having to resort to any sort of cliché, mime or filling-in. It really is told through dance. That's a wonderful thing that really no-one has come up with since. And possibly I don't think anyone will because, as I say, I think the genre is not acceptable anymore perhaps. Mind you, things go round in circles, but I just don't see that really coming back.

Baynes says he is 'winding down as a dancer' since dancing takes away from the rehearsal and preparation time he needs as a choreographer. He also suggests that the path he took with *Beyond Bach* is just a starting point. While the waving of the banner has absorbed him until now, it seems that the urge to examine the vocabulary is growing and that Baynes will continue to fuel the debate about the relevance of the classical idiom and its ability to be an expressive medium in a contemporary world.

BAYNES: Now that *Bach*'s over—and thank God it's been fairly successful—I hope I can make some mistakes, you know, and I can do work in the way that I felt I did a month ago in the studio, in the workshop. Just do things. Maybe it's not so good but at least it's pushing myself in a little bit of a different direction because, quite honestly, everything I've done up to now—and it follows through from *Ballade* through to *Catalyst* through to *Bach*, it's very much been what I know, what I'm comfortable with. I don't feel I've really stretched myself in any way. It's sort of been very much playing safe, although it wasn't necessarily consciously that way, but I see that now. I guess in a way, even while I was doing *Bach*, I was impatient about it, thinking, 'Oh, I wish I was doing something more innovative now because everyone else is doing fab things like (Stephen Page's) *Ochres* and Meryl (Tankard)'s *Furioso* and all that sort of thing and here I am making a work to well-known pieces by Bach.' I can see a lot further to go, you know. The piece I did for the workshop, which was straight after *Bach*, was very much that these were two real people, a man and a woman, and they had problems basically. I mean, that sounds a bit clichéd—human conflict or something. But it was quite sensitive, this very remote piece of music by Schnittke just seemed to be so cold, seemed to bring up these images of a callousness that I did this little pas de deux with these two people just not connecting at all. It was quite sad in a way. They wanted to be together, were together, but weren't reaching, just were not connecting. So that was a good experience for me and I want to now step off in a different direction.

The piece that I am doing in June (*Shadow in the Facet*), I'm trying to make as much of a change of direction as I can without doing something just for the sake of it and falling on my face. In the choice of Ravel, for instance, he's a composer that's not at all like composers I've used up to now. His music doesn't help you by being strongly structured or by having something which you can anchor on to. It's mellifluous or ephemeral. Although there is drama in the sonata that I'm using (Maurice Ravel's *Sonata for Violin and Piano in G Major*), I'm feeling very much that I have to interpret it in my own way. I have to put the drama into it. I have to make my own scenario within this piece. That's very challenging and I'm quite concerned about it. I don't feel anything like as sure about where I'm going with this as I did with *Bach* and *Catalyst*. I feel like I'm really stepping into unknown territory. But then that's good. I think I'm sort of pleased about that in a way.

Stephen Baynes, introspective and self-critical, declined my first, spontaneous request for an oral history interview on the grounds that if it was to be for archival purposes, it should be treated with the utmost seriousness—I hadn't given him enough warning. Eventually, a few months later during a Sydney season by the Australian Ballet, I was able to record an interview, which reveals the depth of Baynes' thinking about the issues that concern him, and his constant search for knowledge and understanding. At the time of the interview Baynes was in the early stages of reflecting on the concept behind what later became *Shadow in the Facet*. This piece, as it was presented in its premiere season in Melbourne in June 1996, is an intimate work, perhaps best described as a chamber ballet. Its movement seems to focus inward rather than outward, and the glowing and potent spirituality of *Beyond Bach* became the mysterious and darkly dramatic 'unknown territory' of future exploration.

Choreography by Stephen Baynes

1986	*Strauss Songs*	Australian Ballet Choreographic Workshop
1988	*Ballade*	Australian Ballet 25th Anniversary Choreographic Competition
1989	*Three Years of Your Life*	Australian Ballet School Anniversary Gala
1990	*Andante*	Australian Ballet International Gala
	Catalyst	Australian Ballet
1993	*Four Reflections of a Quintet*	Dancers Company
1994	*Souvenirs*	Dancers Company
	Rococo Variations	Boston International Choreographic Competition
1995	*Episodes*	La Scala Ballet, Milan
	Beyond Bach	Australian Ballet
	Dialogues I & II	Australian Ballet Choreographic Workshop
1996	*Into Dharma*	Sydney Dance Company
	Shadow in the Facet	Australian Ballet
	Into the Darkness	West Australian Ballet

Maina Gielgud

Remarkable Years

Interview TRC 3165

Maina Gielgud, AO (born 1945), artistic director of the Australian Ballet from 1983 to 1996 and currently directing the Royal Danish Ballet in Copenhagen, was interviewed by Michelle Potter in Melbourne in November 1994, January 1995 and August 1995, and in Sydney in November 1995

Maina Gielgud has been the Australian Ballet's longest serving artistic director, having occupied the position for 14 years from 1983 to 1996. She relinquished this position with undisguised regret when, following criticisms of her management of the company, publicly voiced during much of 1994, the board of the Australian Ballet decided it was 'time for a change'—to which Gielgud retorted that she was not aware that she had a 'use-by date'—and elected not to renew her contract after 1996.

Gielgud came to Australia after a 20-year career as a dancer in Europe and the United Kingdom and took over a company that had, in the few years immediately prior to her appointment, lurched through a series of crises. There had been a rapid changeover of artistic directors from the mid-1970s onwards, five in the space of seven years. Robert Helpmann (1975), Anne Woolliams (1976–77), Peggy van Praagh (1978) in a return to the position she had occupied earlier, Marilyn Jones (1979–81) and Marilyn Rowe (1982) as caretaker ballet director, all brought their own individualistic contributions to repertoire and separate visions for the future direction of the company, which did little to nurture a sense of long-term stability. Then, the role and responsibilities of the company administrator vis-a-vis the artistic director had been a source of contention and debate over a number of years. As well, some new, expensively produced, three-act narrative ballets that had recently entered the company repertoire, in particular *The Hunchback of Notre Dame* choreographed for the company by Bruce Wells in 1981, had failed to achieve any major degree of critical acclaim. And, most significantly, in 1981 there was a major, acrimonious and divisive strike by company dancers over what was alleged were falling artistic standards but which was also connected with dancers' pay and conditions. In 1983 Gielgud inherited a company sorely in need of both a sense of stability and a new, vital sense of identity and direction.

POTTER: Why did you come to Australia—I mean, apart from the fact that you were offered a job? Why did you apply for the job?

GIELGUD: I had stopped dancing about 18 months before; I was rehearsal director of a small company in England, the London City Ballet. Since 1975 I had this germ of an idea that I'd like to be an artistic director one day. And, curiously, it was Peter Bahen, a previous administrator of the Australian Ballet, who had first planted that seed; it was in 1975 when I was guesting with the Australian Ballet. I was invited for dinner at he and his wife's house and I can remember very clearly his saying—I don't know apropos of what, or what sort of conversation we were having—'I think you would make a really good artistic director one day.' And it really planted a seed, I think probably because it made me realise that all my life, in my professional life in particular, I had been watching as many performances as I possibly could, not only to learn from other dancers but also because of a certain fascination with the whole production side of things.

When I saw the advertisement for applications in the *Dance and Dancers* magazine in London, I must say I didn't immediately think of applying because it seemed to be too big a job not having directed a company before, though I had directed my own group, Steps Notes and Squeaks. That was just a little group of seven and it was something quite peculiar and extraordinary. I mean, sort of different, idiosyncratic. But that same day, Peter Williams, who was the editor of *Dance and Dancers* at that time, and David Palmer, who was the London representative of the Australian Ballet, both of whom I knew quite well, both independently rang me and said, 'Have you seen, you are going to apply, aren't you?' And I thought, 'Well, why not? Who knows?' So I did. I got on to the short list and Sir Robert Southey came to London and interviewed me. Eventually I was flown out here in November 1982 to meet the board and see the company and so forth. Before that it was an abstract idea, but seeing the company I just fell head over heels in love with the talent. And I gave some classes, watched some performances and thought, 'This would just be fantastic because everything is there for this to become a world-class company.' And there are all the ingredients that are lacking elsewhere, not necessarily through anybody's fault, to nurture and develop very great dancers. There was the talent, quantities of it. There are year-long contracts. There's a basic repertoire that is the envy of the world, enormous versatility of styles. They have time to rehearse. They have stage time. They have two, sometimes three, orchestral rehearsals before a first night—luxury in the extreme. They have quite reasonable, by European or American standards, studios. There's a new building that is going to go up which is going to have eight studios built to measure, together with the school. They have a wonderful production department. The costumes are exquisitely made. The sets are wonderfully constructed, exquisitely painted. I mean a dream.

POTTER: Were you also aware that the company was in rather a state of disarray as a result of the strike?

GIELGUD: Yes, I knew there was a strike. That was a bit scary because what dancers in the world would strike? What an extraordinary thing! That was somewhere at the back of my mind, but I didn't want to know too much about the details of that strike because I felt—this was when I arrived to take up the reins—that we needed to go for the future and not delve too much into the past. I felt quite soon that I was inheriting both negative and positive things from the strike. Negative—I can never find the word, it is *méfiance* in French—oh, a wariness, that would be the word, in relation to the management as a whole and administration, but also the artistic side. You know, 'Is there a reason behind this?'

So I was trying to get across, 'Look, there's nothing to worry about, I'm on your side. You are hugely talented, I want you to be the best dancers in the world and the best company in the world, and it's as simple as that. You know, there's nothing else to look for.' And actually, perhaps I put down to the strike, and the aftermath of the strike, some things that weren't, some things that—I don't know where they come from, but just are there—a fear that one is going to be taken advantage of. And I think I have the sort of reputation that I want people to work just so that they're working, not for any reason. Which is quite idiotic, but I haven't been able to put that one to rest to this day. So, yes, I knew that there had been those difficulties.

(November 1994)

Quite early after her arrival, as well as working to build on and develop the company's technical and artistic expertise, Gielgud began to examine and address the perennial issue of Australia's geographical isolation and its effects, both positive and negative, on the country's artists and audiences. Her years as artistic director were marked by a number of initiatives that allowed Australian Ballet dancers to travel and study with overseas companies and that established exchange programs with some of the world's leading classical companies. She also, after a stabilising period, reinstated overseas touring as an important feature of the Australian Ballet's program. In particular, she introduced—to a much greater extent than had occurred previously, and in line with the Australia-wide push in the 1980s and subsequently to develop links with Asia and the Pacific-rim countries—touring outside the traditional venues of Europe, America and the United Kingdom.

POTTER: What do you think your innovations have been during your term as artistic director?

GIELGUD: Well, one of the first things came about through talking to Noël Pelly (administrator of the Australian Ballet, 1983–91) on a plane going somewhere about what I thought of as a dream. I said it would be wonderful if some of the dancers here, who are so talented, could get a chance of seeing what it is like overseas in the companies there, you know for all sorts of reasons—to work with some people who can't come to Australia; to see how much better off they are here, because there was, and still is, a tendency for the dancers to be really spoiled with the circumstances that they've got here, but not realise how well off they are. And Noël said, 'Oh, I don't see why not. I'm sure we could get some scholarship or other for that.' And so that started the very first Christmas and since then we've sent anything from two to seven or eight dancers overseas on study trips to work with the major companies—do class with them, watch their rehearsals, watch performances in both Europe and America, and in some cases to study with top teachers or coaches. And they've been to companies like the Royal Ballet, Paris Opera, New York City Ballet, American Ballet Theatre—only one to the Marinsky, I think—the Royal Danish Ballet, Stuttgart Ballet, Frankfurt Ballet, Hamburg and so on. Some all on the same busy tour, the same short $3^{1/2}$ weeks. But that's been a wonderful innovation and I think very helpful.

Another has been the exchange of dancers between companies—sending a dancer or a couple of dancers to another major company and receiving, usually not at the same time, but at a time that is suitable mutually, again a dancer or a couple to dance in our repertoire. And again, the companies we've got regular exchanges with are the Birmingham Royal, Royal Danish, Boston Ballet, American Ballet Theatre, the Bolshoi and the Kirov (as it was then)—and I think we're about to resume those exchanges with the Marinsky—as well as some one-offs with the Budapest Ballet, Houston Ballet and so on. And we're talking about doing that also—it has usually been done with principals, sometimes with soloists—in future with corps de ballet dancers, which could be very interesting. It would need to be for longer. It's usually from anything between two weeks and two or three months. If it were done with a corps dancer or two, I think it would need to be for six months or a year.

We've toured internationally now since 1987, almost every year. And that's been very important for the image of the company here in Australia, because there's still that feeling that it's only if you are recognised overseas that you are really, really, *really* worth it; and, of course, for our image overseas, which is more a matter of keeping up our reputation because it's very, very high. And even though we didn't tour for the first few years when I was directing the company, I personally went—or, as I said, the exchanges started right away, and the scholarships.

What else has been innovative? I think that the way we rehearse young dancers into their first important roles. It's not innovative. It is just that we have the time and space to do it as I think it should be, whereas most companies in Europe and America, apart from Russia, simply do not have either the time or the space, with the best will in the world.

POTTER: What do you mean? That they are not coached into the role?

GIELGUD: No, they'll more often than not be thrown on with an absolute minimum of rehearsals. And I think that it becomes a survival of the fittest, which is fine because you have to be very strong as a dancer. Your character needs to be very strong and to survive you need to be pretty quick and capable. But there are some immensely talented dancers who don't have the capacity to be just thrown on the stage and do a good job. It is too nerve-racking. And I think with a company such as ours it's one of the great advantages that we have. We can actually do that, that those who need to go slower than others, who need more time and more careful nurturing, can be given it.

You see, in Russia it goes to the other extreme because for a big classic, such as *Swan Lake* or *Don Quixote*, dancers will be coached for a year. And I think that's going over the top, because I think then you lose something of the spontaneity. And there are still dancers here—you know, it's always guesswork and how good is one's instinct—who one feels work better under that sort of pressure of not having too much rehearsal. So it's the matter of having the luxury of being able to work in the way one thinks is most beneficial at different times.

Bringing out guest teachers—we have about five guest teachers a year from all sorts of different schools, the best schools of dance: Danish teachers, Russian teachers, American teachers, French teachers, English teachers and probably more of other nationalities. I think that's very, very beneficial, not least in getting across to dancers that—for the detail of the basic classroom work—there are many correct ways while the base posture and placement remain the same with any really first-rate teacher. (November 1994)

The development of an Australian dance identity, whether in terms of an Australian style of movement or in terms of an individualistic repertoire, has been an issue that has concerned artistic directors in Australia since the very first efforts to establish Australian-based theatrical dance companies. Gielgud was criticised, especially towards the end of her term as artistic director, by some Australian dance commentators for being 'Eurocentric' and for not connecting with the wider Australian community. Much of her background, training and experience before coming to Australia was European, and certainly she brought with her to Australia a European sensibility along with a sense of finesse that had not often been present in the years immediately preceding her arrival. She also made no secret of her commitment to the traditions of classical ballet, whose heritage is largely European, and she expanded the repertoire of the Australian Ballet with European works. They included older European classics but also contemporary works from choreographers presently working in Europe including Maurice Béjart, Jiří Kylián, William Forsythe and Nacho Duato.

But the Eurocentric criticism was a curious one because, even from the very beginning, Gielgud also saw herself as someone who could also make a contribution to the development of an 'Australian' Australian Ballet and made every effort to put that vision into practice. Under Gielgud's patronage new works were commissioned from a wide variety of choreographers from the mid-1980s onwards with a significant increase in commissions beginning in 1990. A huge proportion, in effect all except one, of those commissions went to Australian choreographers. Gielgud's nurturing of Australian works resulted, in fact, in a number of firsts in the history of the Australian Ballet. The first evening-length ballets by Australian choreographers for the Australian Ballet were commissioned under Gielgud's directorship, the most notable being the Graeme Murphy/Kristian Fredrikson production of *Nutcracker* (1992) and Stanton Welch's *Madame Butterfly* (1995). Another first occurred in 1994 during a tour to the United States when the company presented an all-Australian triple-bill program—*Catalyst* by Stephen Baynes; *Beyond Twelve* by Graeme Murphy; and *Divergence* by Stanton Welch.

POTTER: Maina, I'd like to ask you about the 1994 tour to the United States. How was the company received?

GIELGUD: It was received fantastically and I think it was just what the company needed at this point. We performed in Seattle first of all and did *La Fille mal gardée* there, and in Washington where we did two programs, *Don Quixote*—Rudolf Nureyev's production—and, for the first time ever, a triple bill of Australian works. This was in the context of Festival Australia in Washington, DC. We had wonderful audience acclaim, at almost every performance standing ovations, including at the first night of the triple bill. Wonderful reviews in Seattle, which had never seen *La Fille mal gardée* previously. In Washington we had not only wonderful reviews from the Washington critics but the main New York press also came to *Don Quixote* and stayed to see the triple bill to which they gave wonderful reviews recognising, which not all the Australian press had, Stanton Welch's choreographic gifts in particular. So it was something that was very important. I had full confidence that the company *was* going to be successful. I wouldn't have guessed that we

would have had quite the degree of acclaim, both from public and press, that we had.

POTTER: What did they see in the Australian triple bill that really interested them?

GIELGUD: Well, new choreography basically, because it was, as I said, the first time that we'd been able to present an entirely Australian triple bill when we've been overseas. Also, the three ballets are not in the repertoire of any other company in the world. What tends to happen the world over is there are so few good ballets around that all the companies tend to have more or less the same kind of ballet, so when they go on tour it's like one international repertoire rather than one belonging to a particular company and to a particular country. The actual choreographic talent was highlighted and this was because every ballet company in the world is searching for some choreographic talent that will make inroads for classical dance for the future. I think that, the world over, there is concern that classical ballet will die for want of creators.

POTTER: Does the Australian Ballet have some kind of identity of its own?

GIELGUD: I think it has a very special identity that has a particularly Australian flavour and it's very interesting that even when we do the classics overseas, when we've done *Sleeping Beauty*, or *Don Quixote* as this time, *Giselle* as we did in America in 1990, critics again highlight the fact that, although it's authentic in style, it is still individual in flavour, and particularly Australian. And what do they pick out? The energy, the vitality, the youth, as a plus not as a minus, and the commitment of the entire company to the work at hand.

And the other special thing that the Australian Ballet has to offer, I believe, is the fact that they can adapt so wonderfully to different styles of choreography. Because I've felt that it was more interesting to use this gift that Australian dancers have, I've not attempted to stamp a particular style onto the dancers in the way they move, the way they're schooled. So, unlike some of the top companies in the world—like, for instance, the Paris Opera, the Royal Danish Ballet and the big Russian companies like the Bolshoi and the now Marinsky—one can't, or I hope one can't, identify immediately that this is an Australian 'school of dance'. Whether they are performing *Swan Lake*, a Jiří Kylián piece, an Ashton or a Balanchine, I think and I hope what you see is *Swan Lake* close to Petipa/Ivanov, a Kylián close to Nederlands Dans Theater, Ashton close to the Royal, and Balanchine close to New York City Ballet. And at the same time, and I don't believe this is a contradiction, there is something unmistakably Australian. But it's not something that is schooled into them; it's something that they have naturally, and that I'm most anxious that they don't lose. Besides that, of course, the identity on a repertoire basis, I think, is going to come more to the fore in the next few years. (November 1994)

In 1995 Gielgud appointed Stephen Baynes and Stanton Welch resident choreographers with the Australian Ballet. This was not the first time the company had had a resident choreographer. In 1976 Graeme Murphy, then a coryphée in the company, was also listed in program credits as 'choreographer', although by his own admission Murphy was given very little opportunity to choreograph during his one-year residency. Both Baynes and Welch had already been choreographing for several years, and both had important pieces in the company repertoire and in the repertoire of the Australian Ballet School's Dancers Company. In their first year as resident choreographers, both also produced new works for showing in Australia and both also worked overseas. The appointment of Baynes and Welch was, therefore, an event of major significance in the history of the Australian Ballet, a company that has always been a national touring repertory company rather than one led by a choreographer.

POTTER: Do you think your program of having two resident choreographers has been successful?

GIELGUD: I think it was a natural progression because Stanton Welch and Stephen Baynes were in the first instance discovered, if you want, and nurtured, and they produced—choreographed—some very successful works in our choreographic workshops, and everything points to the possibility of their continuing and being very successful choreographers. It was natural progression that they should be appointed resident choreographers of this company. Naturally I wanted to keep their choreographic skills going.

This is their home company. They dance in it. They have the marvellous opportunity of knowing the dancers that they are working with so well, which I think helps the development of their careers as choreographers as well as the development of the dancers' careers as dancers. And I certainly have encouraged them, and hope that in the future they will continue to be encouraged, to work overseas from time to time, both because I think it will enhance their skills and the kind of work that they produce to occasionally work with dancers who are quite different from ours, who have a different background, perhaps a different attitude, different technique, artistry and so forth. And secondly, as with the dancers, I think that, by giving them those opportunities, the Australian Ballet will have a better chance of keeping them long-term, and I think that's important for the company. But it's also, actually, important for them because I don't think they would have the same opportunities elsewhere.

I think, for the Australian Ballet, it's been fantastic to have the opportunity to have resident choreographers. It's been the dream of every classically based repertory company in the world, and for this kind of company I think it's a better situation than having a choreographer/director. After all, with the national company of any country that is classically based you need to keep the traditional ballets going—the classical ballets—as well as having new works, as well as continuing to acquire important works from overseas and from Australia that are important in this century of classical ballet. I think you need to keep all those things going and that can be difficult for someone who is a choreographer. The temptation can be great to keep doing repertoire of their own.

Also, I think it's a rare talent to be able to both choreograph and direct, as the needs for the particular jobs are not necessarily the same. I believe very strongly that a choreographer needs to work with people he or she is in tune with for the particular work that they are choreographing. They can't and shouldn't really have to think about whether some of the extremely good dancers in the company have or haven't been challenged just recently or not. They can't just put in dancers into their ballet for the purpose of challenging them. They have to have the need to work with these dancers. Whereas when you are directing a company, I think you have to try and keep a balance. A dancer's quality of work inevitably ebbs and flows and there's always a weighing of whether a particular dancer's work is ebbing because they've not been challenged just lately—and some need more challenge, some different challenge—or whether it's just a passing situation and they've actually got to work it out themselves. And whether also, of course, very importantly, whether it's ebbing to such a degree that you can't put them in front of an audience in a challenging role. But all those kinds of concerns and worries, I don't think they can be a choreographer's.   (August 1995)

The appointments of Baynes and Welch as resident choreographers were clearly major initiatives on Gielgud's part. They were also, whether by design or not, clearly politic and provided Gielgud with some much-needed credibility after a damaging period in 1994 when her position as artistic director had been subjected to public scrutiny and had become decidedly shaky. In the months preceding the appointments of Baynes and Welch a number of complaints about Gielgud had been voiced by dancers and by some members of the board of the Australian Ballet. For a variety of reasons, several dancers left the company, including two well-liked principal dancers, Lisa Pavane and Greg Horsman, who resigned over issues concerned with Gielgud's handling of the company. As a result of a meeting of directors in August 1994, to which she was not invited, Gielgud was asked to tender her resignation as artistic director of the company.

GIELGUD: Prior to the August meeting I heard privately that there was, in fact, a so-called 'dossier' prepared in response to a request by the chairman to the dancers' representative on the board to collate the *present* concerns of the dancers (if as alleged, they were serious). I was told a number of times

in the weeks leading up to the meeting, by virtually *each* director, that *they fully supported me*, and that this meeting (without the presence of the two chief executives, that is the artistic director and the administrator), would allow the board to get to the bottom of the complaints and show them up for what they were. I remember suspecting that, as a result of this meeting, I might be asked to change certain things in my artistic direction (although without any clear idea what these might be) despite the fact that I had already implemented changes to my 'management style' as a result of the suggestions of the chairman of the board after the meeting of the previous December. These changes included a more 'formal' approach and I agreed to them because I felt that the 'style' of management was irrelevant to the quality of the final product, and if I had been incorrect in assuming that a 'family' atmosphere was pleasant for the dancers, there was no problem, or difficulty, in changing it. The 'dossier' in question (which reportedly did not exist) contained, however, the complaints previously made over the years, numbered and typed out, while at the back there was a petition for the reinstatement of the son of the dancers' representative, who had received—close to a year earlier—12 months' notice.

Two days after the meeting I was told by the chairman that the directors had all agreed (or all except one, as I later found out) that I should hand in my resignation. Naturally I asked why, and was told that it was basically because there was no discipline in the company, and no respect for my authority. I was told there was absolutely no doubt about the high standard of the company's performances, that that was recognised by all directors, but, well, there had been, it seemed, instances of dancers being rude to me and I had not dealt with this properly. I replied that, in effect, in the 12 years that I have been here I could remember only two particular instances of dancers being rude to me in a way that was disrespectful to the point of action needing to be taken. Artists, by the nature of their business, get upset at times, the atmosphere can get tense and heated, and this is dealt with—at the time or later— according to the seriousness of the situation in the opinion of the ballet staff and the artistic director. There is a daily, sometimes hourly, appraisal of the discipline in the various areas and the need or otherwise for warnings or disciplinary action to be taken in relation to the functioning of the ballet company as a team, while recognising that individual artists should be allowed to behave as individuals as long as others, and the performance, are not affected. I was mystified, too, at how the directors could make such a statement about the atmosphere and discipline of the company, since only *one* ever entered the rehearsal room during class or rehearsals—the place where it all happens in a ballet company. This was despite the fact that there was always an open invitation—I love to show off my dancers in the studio as well as in performance!

Anyway, I finally asked to answer the allegations of the board, which had led to their asking for my resignation, and for the decision to be reconsidered. This was eventually agreed to. This was the end of August and we were to go overseas on a United States tour in late September. Quite apart from anything else, I felt that the timing could not have been worse; that to announce the artistic director's resignation just prior to such an important tour for the Australian Ballet would be very detrimental to the company as a whole. I also felt, and subsequently continued to feel, that there was absolutely no reason for me to resign and that if the board had their reasons for not wishing me to continue as artistic director, then *they* should do something about it, but why should *I*? I spoke on the telephone to each director in turn to let them know that I was amazed by the suggestion and especially to say that whatever was to happen in the future should absolutely not happen before the overseas tour, in the interest of the company.

The next meeting of the board, at which I was to answer the allegations, was in September. I faced the meeting having prepared a number of papers. The meeting was not minuted. I was given plenty of time to answer questions and state my case. I reiterated my amazement that these kinds of allegations could be made without personal knowledge of the workplace, and reiterated my invitation to visit it. This was not taken up at the time or in the future. I was told the 'dossier' was irrelevant to the situation, but at the end of the meeting a part of it was read out. I was told by one of the directors that it was quite incorrect for company members to call me by my first name, and that this showed the lack of respect. I was then asked to leave the room while the board reconsidered. I was then told by the chairman that there was no change in the board's opinion that I should resign. The US tour was now a couple of weeks away. I never acknowledged the fact that I was being asked to resign—and I never said anything about doing so or not doing so. Then we went overseas and the company had a tremendous success.

At the end of the tour some directors decided to have a celebration dinner and invited the administrative staff and myself. They made some very nice speeches, and I was given to understand that there was a certain change of mind in the three directors who had been with us on the tour; that they felt that perhaps after all the decision for me to resign had been made in haste, and should be looked at again.

(January 1995)

The original decision was not reversed and at a number of other meetings between September and December 1994, both formal and informal, minuted and not, Gielgud was again urged to resign. In December 1994 she was eventually offered a renewal of her contract for a further two years until the end of 1996. This was a year more than originally planned with the second year being added after Gielgud stressed that one year was not sufficient for her to achieve results in a number of areas where she had begun initiatives.

GIELGUD: The decision of the board was to offer me a contract for 1996, one year more renewal, but informing me at the same time that they would be seeking an artistic director to take that place from 1 January 1997. I felt that, however strange the situation, I would still like to accept the position for the next two years because I feel that the dancers who are here at present, like myself, are virtually—to the last one—people who want to dance, who want to work, who don't want to be bothered with all the rest. So that's why I accepted the offer.

The press release which went out from the chairman about the renewal of my contract and the search for the new artistic director was, I thought, extraordinary in that it gave no reason for my contract to finish at the end of 1996; and it only mentioned the great successes and so forth—indeed, from then on there was no more talk about lack of discipline, respect or any other *reason*, although the famous 'use-by date'/'time for a change' *was* used for a while. I can't say I was surprised that the press then picked it up and said,

'Well, if it's like this, why aren't they renewing?' There was a great deal of press about it. I would say 90 per cent of it was extremely supportive of my artistic directorship and expressed great surprise and dismay about the change proposed.

(January 1995)

Following the announcement that Gielgud's contract was not to be renewed past 1996, dance commentators around Australia began to focus, however, on what were judged to be the less positive aspects of Gielgud's directorship. Several central issues had emerged during 1994 including the maturity, or the perceived lack of it, of her dancers, Gielgud's management style, which had been the catalyst for many of the dancers' complaints about her, and her choice of repertoire.

With regard to repertoire, comments of another kind, not unrelated to the 'Eurocentric' epithet with which Gielgud had been labelled, emerged when she announced her 1996 program, her final one as artistic director. It was a mix of proven classics, additions from the international contemporary ballet repertoire and five pieces from four Australian choreographers, including four world premieres. It was an astutely conceived program for a company committed to being a repertory company but that was also beginning to nurture its responsibilities as a post-colonial ballet company. Gielgud was exceptionally proud of this program but critical of those who said it had been made in response to comments that during her directorship she had failed to nurture Australian choreography.

POTTER: One of the criticisms that has been levelled at you in recent months, years maybe, is that the company is very young and the older dancers have been leaving, for whatever reason, and that you have not been encouraging mature dancers. Could you comment on the concept of the Australian Ballet being a young company?

GIELGUD: Yes. When we go overseas, the youth of the company is looked on as a plus, and in Australia, for some curious reason, as a minus. I think that people forget, on the one hand, that classical ballet is very difficult physically and that, for the majority, it is really more pleasant for the young to be doing that kind of hard work than the old, particularly when we're talking about truly classical ballet on the one hand. But also, if you look at some of the contemporary works that are so highly acclaimed nowadays, going from Kylián to Béjart to Tetley, and most recently to William Forsythe, those ballets are *immensely* draining and require *enormous* stamina.

Take Jiří Kylián, for example. For his main company he's not prepared to even audition dancers that are over 30, and the majority of dancers in that main company would be under 30. Now that's particularly interesting because Kylián's name is bandied around as the person who is really doing something about using mature dancers in a performing, and even in a creative, situation. And he is, but to a limited extent and this for very good reason. You see, Kylián has three companies. He has a young company which is made up of dancers—young dancers who haven't as yet been professional. If all goes well, they stay in that company for two years and they then go to the main company. The third company, which is the 'mature artists' company, is a part-time company that is reorganised every year for a few months in that year and only has four dancers in it, and they are different dancers from all over the world; dancers who have been first-rate dancers in whatever field—classical, contemporary—and who are interested in working with a choreographer and having a work *especially* made for them. So you see that it's something quite, quite different from using mature dancers in existing repertoire. Anyway, that was a long way round, but I think it is worthy of mention.

I believe personally that, depending on the facility, physical facility, and maturity of personality and of temperament, a dancer or a student can turn professional, say, between the ages of 16 and 18, although not only the famous 'baby ballerinas'—Tamara Toumanova, Tatiana Riabouchinska and Irina Baronova—but also Alicia Markova, Margot Fonteyn, Svetlana Beriosova and Beryl Grey all danced leading roles from the age of 14 or 15. Around 40 could be considered an average age for a ballerina to retire, but we all know about Margot Fonteyn who went on, I think it was, into her early sixties. It could be verified. Some others have gone on even later, like Maya Plisetskaya and Alicia Alonso. Whether there was merit in their continuing quite that long is an open question and I think, again, it depends on the repertoire that they've done. In some cases it's been quite extraordinary to see them, and in others one could wish that they had left us with the memories. So it's possible for a woman to go on—I would say, normally, only principals would probably even contemplate it—to 55, 57. With men it's more difficult because it's hard to imagine a dancer who doesn't jump and it's hard to imagine a dancer who doesn't partner, lift, and so on. And here I'm talking about pretty much existing repertoire, or repertoire that might be created with a classical, basic vocabulary. So a man is really not likely to start before the age of 16 in any circumstances, and is unlikely to be able to do or to give a worthwhile contribution after 48, probably at the very maximum.

Now, between those ages—women and men—you've got a whole variety of possibilities because it is one thing to be able to continue to dance, but it's no good being able to continue to dance unless it's something that you yourself feel you *have* to do. That fundamentally you love—but love, I think, is not the right word—that you have such a *passion* for dance, and that can mean love or hate, that you can't really function without doing it. And usually those dancers who've continued, I would say, past the age of 37, would be those who can't do without it. In Australia, if one looks back, and long before my time, dancers have tended—and I'm talking of all ranks—to retire a little bit earlier than 30 on the whole, and even principals in their early thirties. It's been very rare that Australian dancers have continued. On the other hand, it's quite phenomenal that it is so usual for Australian principal dancers to put their pointe shoes back on after periods of months, or sometimes years, and most successfully and well perform sometimes very difficult roles again for a season as guest artists. That, I must say, is peculiar to Australia and it's quite wonderful.

Dancers overseas tend to retire a bit later and it, of course, does rather depend on the situation of the company. The kind of contracts that the dancers have, for instance in the

Scandinavian countries and also in the Paris Opera, includes pension schemes. So, often in those countries you have a completely opposite problem to the one here in that you have dancers who don't really want to dance but who are quite content to stay on in the ballet company where they were trained, where they started performing, until they get their pensions. And if they're not really interested anymore in the dancing, this causes *enormous* problems, problems to directors, to choreographers who work with the company, because what it means, if you don't really want to dance, you're not going to work terribly hard at it. If you don't work terribly hard at it, your standard is going to suffer.

But, if at some point you were good enough to become a soloist or, heaven help us, even a principal, and you've got to that stage so you don't care anymore and you've lost your standard, if there are certain rules governing the casting, it means that the audience is going to have to suffer seeing these senior dancers well past their particular prime, and that the young dancers, who may be of far greater quality, would be blocked. And this is a problem peculiar to those companies. The advantage, on the other hand, is that you have mature artists who are capable of fulfilling the character roles and the demi-character roles, which play an important part in most of the big full-length classical ballets, and you have these at hand on full-time contracts. Again, this is a bonus when they are artists who are of such quality that they are performing all the time, and I think it's a wonderful thing for those artists because it is also a recognition of what they have offered and can continue to offer to a ballet company and to its audience. And it may be that they are not used for one program, two programs, three programs. They are paid a salary throughout, and I think that that's correct if they've given those years of quality and service. What one could wish is for something in between for the ideal ballet company, which one hopes is in all respects—I think it is in many—to be the Australian Ballet at some point in the future.

I hoped very much when I came to Australia that I was going to be able to encourage dancers to stay on longer in the profession, because I thought it was a great pity that they should retire from dancing around the age of, I suppose, 27 or 28, or perhaps in their early thirties if they are principals. It's quite interesting because, looking at companies now overseas, it seems to me that dancers all over the world are now retiring earlier than they used to. I have a theory about that, but it's not one that I can often talk about because it's easily misunderstood. It seems to me that nowadays there are many dancers in the profession who'd *never* have been dancers in the past. I believe this comes about because, although dancers are not well paid compared to other professions, particularly if one thinks about the kind of work— the quality and the quantity of work—that is expected of them, they are extremely highly paid compared to what the situation was certainly 30 years ago. You see, 30 years ago and before, a dancer who had some physical facility and technical facility, but not a great passion, could not have continued in the profession, or many of them couldn't have and wouldn't have, because the life was too hard. So I think that there was a sort of natural selection, if you want, in that only those who *had* to dance would go through what you had to to become, and then to stay, a professional dancer. Nowadays there is the possibility, because there is some money, to do other things but dance. You can have, if you can make the time, money for all kinds of hobbies. You can— I mean it really comes to this as well—you can eat well. In the past, unless you came from a wealthy family, you had to watch every mouthful that you ate. Not for reasons of diet but for reasons of money. In the past in a rehearsal period you didn't get any salary. Now, you can see why that's a very dangerous thing to talk about because it could appear that I'm against dancers being well paid, and that's not the case at all. But it has its reverse side.

POTTER: What then about the criticism that your management style has been over-friendly. What is your management style?

GIELGUD: Yes, this is very, very interesting because no-one seems to be quite able to make up their minds whether I'm over-friendly or whether there's too much discipline or not enough discipline, too formal or too informal.

When I came 12 years ago, one of the things I perceived very quickly was that there seemed to be a fear of the boss and that it seemed very difficult for dancers to come and talk to me about their career, ambitions, problems, and so on. Without, I think, stopping to define it from one day to the other, it gradually evolved that I tried to make it easy for them to do so. From the very first day I've always had the door open and tried to encourage, verbally, the dancers to come and see me if there were questions, problems, concerns, whatever.

I tried also to criticise dancers in a friendly way in the first place, and in an informal way. You see, I feel that it's a most important part of my job as artistic director to be educating. It's part of nurturing young dancers who come into the company. So take, for instance, a young dancer in their first year or two in the company who was not doing class every day—tricky area, because in their contract they're paid to do only four classes per week, which is the bare minimum to keep your standard. But you see that is a new departure because in the old days you never got paid for class, that was just something that you *had* to do. You were paid for your rehearsal time, eventually, and you were paid for your performance. But of course, with unions and so forth, there it is in the contract, it's four classes a week. But any dancer who's going to get anywhere has to do six classes a week. But you can't impose, you can't say you *must* do six classes a week, bring them into the office in a formal way because it's not legal. But with a talented dancer if they don't get that habit right from the beginning, you can kiss goodbye to their career right there and then. So that, too, is one of the reasons why those kinds of things were done in an informal way. We saw them the next day after they missed class, saw them in the corridor, took them aside and said, 'You know, you weren't in class yesterday, were you unwell? You know it's really important for a dancer ...' And so on. And the sermons—but as a *teacher*, as opposed to a director. And a multitude of things like that. The unwritten laws of being what I call a 'real dancer' as opposed to a dancer who just does what they're supposed to do in their contract and rehearsal schedule. The career is so short that there isn't time to waste. It's no good saying that they'll discover when the casting doesn't include them. They don't. Young people don't usually put that kind of two and two together. It's much easier to say, 'I've been overlooked.' But even more seriously, often those dancers *will* get cast because at present they have the qualities to get interesting roles—and then, of course, what has happened is that when young talented dancers have got opportunities this has made me even more afraid that, if they don't behave as 'real dancers' do, their career is going to be very short. They're not going to fulfil the expectations. So then if there were details of their work that were not happening, again I would be nagging them even more, as I've said, about those areas. And then, of course, that easily gets turned into a perception of 'favouritism' when in fact what one is doing is nagging them because, yes indeed, the talent is there, they are getting opportunities, but at the same time they are expected to work and behave even better than their peers who may not be seen to have the talent necessary to be given the same opportunities.

That in turn leads to peer group pressure which is a terrible thing in this country, in this company certainly. Quite often exceptionally talented dancers will try and bring themselves down to the common denominator, will want to show that they *don't* work harder, *don't* put in more energy or thought than their peers who are not getting as much opportunity and so forth. Very complicated. The peer group pressure—it seems to have much more value to be like everybody else than to be individual. And fighting that perception, which is necessary for anyone who is going to make it and stay in the top positions, is just such an uphill struggle. Again it's a question of trying from when they first come into the company—if the potential is there—to educate them that it's okay to be different.

POTTER: Maina, the next thing I want to ask you about is repertoire, because it seems to me there was a certain degree of criticism about the Australian Ballet's repertoire focusing on full-length ballets at the expense of the more experimental sort of works. Do you think there *is* room for experiment within the Australian Ballet and what are the problems of triple bills as opposed to full-length works?

GIELGUD: Well, first of all, you have the present worldwide problem that the full-length ballets are really the only ones that are guaranteed to fill your houses. You put on *Swan Lake*, *Sleeping Beauty* and *Don Quixote* and the very few more that we can count on that are quality ballets. And I would now include some of the Cranko ballets such as *Romeo and Juliet* and *Onegin*, although they won't fill your houses to quite the same capacity, *La Fille mal gardée* of Ashton and, for us, *Manon*—that we have just acquired now—and some of the MacMillan works in other companies. After that, it's very, very difficult to get an audience to come and see works that they don't know. At the same time, ballet has got to keep going further. Choreographers must be given an opportunity to create. Dancers must be created on.

I believe that it's not the place of a national company to experiment at random. For me there are various steps that need to be taken, and some of them by a national company, before one can sensibly ask a choreographer to create a new work. I believe one needs to see that choreographer's work elsewhere and know it sufficiently to believe that the choreographer is of value. I don't think that one should ask an audience to pay the high price of tickets nowadays without some kind of assurance that the work is going to be at least interesting. And I think that one can do that if one has some knowledge of the choreographer's work prior to that—if one looks very carefully at what the music is, what the theme is, what the choreographer intends to do with it, who the set and costume designer is, and so on.

So one can do that with choreographers who have worked with other companies that one believes in. Or, even more interestingly, one can do it with choreographers that one has discovered through workshops in the first instance. Workshops in the studio, first of all, that have been done just for an invited audience who are quite intimate with the company. If one sees talent in one of those workshop situations, then perhaps there is a possibility of choreographing a piece for the junior company, for the Dancers Company, which means not a great deal of expenditure on that ballet. When we do so we use existing cloths, existing costumes out of productions that are not in use anymore. And again, if that proves successful, then look at doing a work for the main company.

But now we have got this wealth of talent, how do we go about developing that? In the normal course of events in repertoire in any given year, we would be able to put in one, if we are lucky two, new one-act ballets in that year. And we have also done, for several years now, one new creation or two or three small works for the Dancers Company. But that is really very little. You can't give young choreographers the opportunity to do a full-length work before they have done their one-act works and proved that they are worthy. And some choreographers may be wonderful for their entire careers doing one-act works, but they will never be the kind of choreographer who can do a full-length work.

So there we come up against the difficulty of triple bills. Historically, during the Diaghilev time, it was triple bills that sold and the full-length ballets nobody was interested in. Why? We don't know, really. I mean when Diaghilev put on *Sleeping Beauty*, it was an absolute disaster; nobody came. The present situation seems illogical because, after all, in a triple bill you can get to see a lot of different types of works; sometimes a dramatic work, an abstract work,

a very contemporary work. You get to see, usually, more of the principals and more dancing—more individuals dancing a greater quantity. You get to see the young up-and-comings as well as the principals in the same program. And, of course, it's the opportunity to put in a new work. It's now become traditional—this generation of directors certainly has not invented it—to organise a triple bill in such a way there's at least one popular work and you are introducing perhaps a new work and one that is more difficult so as to gradually educate your audience.

Here we tend to do, in any one season—in Melbourne, for instance, where we have five programs—either two or three full-length works and, in proportion, two or three triple bills. The last couple of years, because of the recession, I have been persuaded to make it three full-lengths and two triple bills. I think it was two years running, whereas normally we would rotate that. And I agreed to do that because I think, on the one hand, you have to be realistic about finance, but within artistic reason. But at the same time I rang very loud bells in relation to our marketing operation and administration, warning that this must not become a habit, but also warning that we were going to run out of full-length ballets very shortly because if we kept to the tradition in this country that has been going from before I came, with the subscription system and everything, you can't repeat even one of the most successful full-length ballets more than every four years. For instance, if you are doing *Swan Lake* in 1990, you will not do it until 1994 or 1995 at the very earliest.

The Australian Ballet has actually commissioned many more works than is generally realised. And 99.9 per cent of those are Australian works by Australian choreographers, and many of them are Australian designers for the sets and costumes as well. Less, at this point, of Australian composers. And I'm not quite sure why this is, because I believe that there's some wonderful music out there. That's, of course, a question for the choreographers because I think it is very important that they should work with music that they are comfortable with. I personally think it's dangerous to entrust a young choreographer with a work and expect him to be working with a commissioned score and perhaps, although we've just done it in one instance, with an inexperienced designer—inexperienced in the theatre. I think it's more sensible to have a young choreographer working with experienced

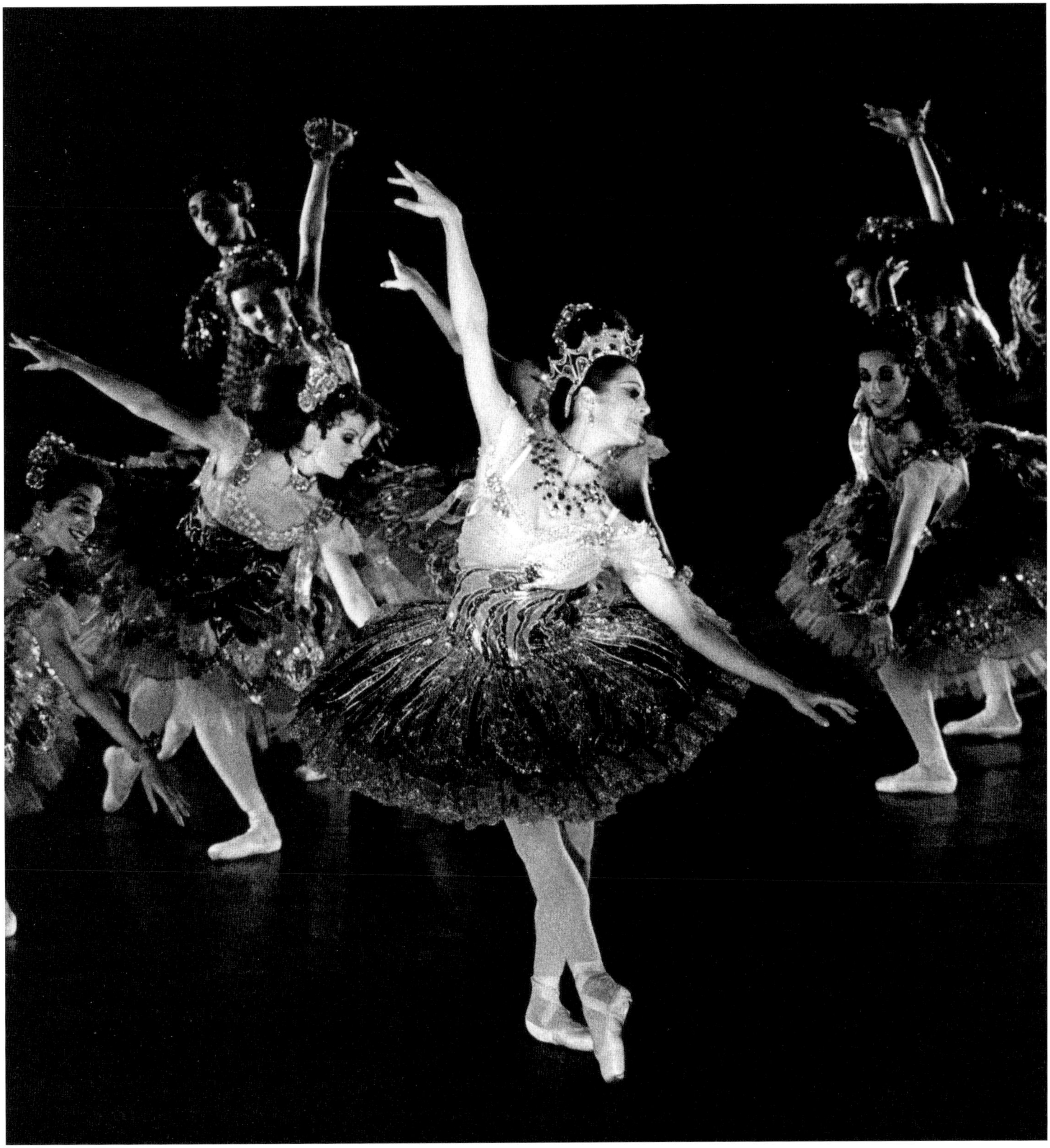

designers and with an existing score, as I said, that he or she feels comfortable with. And, on the other hand, with an established choreographer use an inexperienced designer and/or perhaps commission a score. I think you're more likely to come up with interesting work that way.

So, back to your question. I don't believe that we do full-lengths at the expense of other works. I would like us—it would be my ambition for us, as a general rule—to be looking at two full-length and three triple bills, although not always, because at times there can be all sorts of reasons to do a third full-length, not least if you are in a position to believe you will have a work of value in commissioning a new one.

POTTER: How do you think the Australian Ballet repertoire has changed since 1983? What has been your aim in developing repertoire?

GIELGUD: I think what I've done is bring in quality works from overseas—one-act works. Whereas in the few years prior to my coming, there was a great leaning towards popularity perhaps at the expense of quality. And, for instance, in the case of *The Merry Widow* I think we've got both, which is why I revive it every now and then. But there were others that were really more popular than quality. So I've endeavoured to bring in works of quality to help educate the audience's taste and works of quality to develop and nurture the dancers' technique, artistry, acting abilities and even, as in the case of *The Competition*—Béjart's *Competition*, acquire different kinds of skills of the theatre that they wouldn't in a normal ballet. And, of course, as I said, in the last five years we've discovered huge choreographic talent. Prior to that we did workshops, we commissioned works always, but not to the same degree as we can do now.   (November 1994)

POTTER: Do you aim to please anybody with your repertoire, your annual program?

GIELGUD: I think 'please' would be the wrong choice of words. It's a balancing act in terms of the audience. I suppose first up, if one was trying to prioritise, one would say 'involve' and involve of course means interest. I think one tries to shake up sometimes, surprise, entertain of course in the theatre, amuse, move. Sometimes all of those things at once. I certainly do try and cater for different kinds of audiences. Some people love to see the classics. Why not give them to them? They have a value for the audience and the dancers.

And you need the other side of the coin. You need creativity. You need the excitement of new challenges. You need the risk taking. You need to bring in the young people and perhaps you are more likely to do that with contemporary ballets, although I don't think that that's always true. So certainly, catering for all of that, and interesting and involving as wide a range of audience as possible, yes, that's always been in my mind.

POTTER: Would you like to talk about your 1996 program for the Australian Ballet?

GIELGUD: Yes, it really is a bonanza year. I wouldn't call it a culmination. It *is* a finale, but it wasn't meant to be a finale, just the beginning of a peak decade with all the elements from the time that I've been here in place and to some degree matured. Now there seems to be a feeling that the Australian part of the repertoire with three works by the resident choreographers and two by outside choreographers is a response to criticisms of not having enough new and commissioned Australian works in the repertoire. But, of course, it's nothing like that. I couldn't have appointed resident choreographers before I did, I don't feel. I don't think that sort of talent was around, and I certainly couldn't have commissioned five new works in one year because I would not have had the confidence in that many choreographers to do so.

The rest of the year's repertoire, well, it's pretty terrific to have perhaps the two greatest living choreographers, certainly amongst those who use classical repertoire as the base, Jiří Kylián and William Forsythe, not only doing ballets new to the Australian Ballet, but coming themselves to stage those ballets. There's been a regular input of Kylián ballets into the repertoire which culminated in a visit by Jiří to stage a whole Kylián evening two years ago. During this visit we talked about what the next ballet would be and he mentioned *Stepping Stones*, a ballet that is important to him and that he feels our company would do particularly well. With William Forsythe, I have been trying to acquire a work of his for us, I would say, since 1985 or 1986 when I went to Frankfurt and had talks with him about what would suit the Australian Ballet. It's literally taken until now until we've found the right period of time scheduling-wise for him to spare not only an assistant but him to come himself for two weeks prior to the premiere and for us to do *In the Middle, Somewhat Elevated*. So it's been a long, hard road but it's been well worth it. Most of the worthwhile ballets, I suppose, have been a process of hard work and nagging people to get them, mainly because Australia is so far away. There's always great enthusiasm about putting on ballets for the company because our reputation is so high, but it is a matter of scheduling and, of course, I'm always anxious to do so at a time when the choreographer can come because it's not the same thing, no matter how good the ballet, if you can't get the choreographer. (November 1995)

During the search for a new artistic director, and after his appointment in December 1995, Gielgud fulfilled her contract with the commitment to the job at hand that had marked her directorship since 1983, believing that her final year with the Australian Ballet would be one of 'the best years of the company's and of (her) life'. She did, however, reapply for her job when it was advertised, met with the consultants who made the final recommendation, but was not interviewed by the selection committee.

POTTER: Is there an optimum time for an artistic director to be artistic director of a particular company?

GIELGUD: In all honesty, to my mind the answer is no. How can there be an optimum time? What does that mean? It could be two years for one person in one situation. It could be 30 years for another person in another situation and all sorts of permutations of that. It depends on the person. It depends on the circumstances. Clearly, being the artistic director of a company such as this is not a permanent position. It's not straightforward at all. Is there an optimum period as in looking at it from the outside? I think that that relates to the quality of the company, the goods that it's producing, and whether it appears that it is continuing or being creative in the best sense of the word, fulfilling its role in this country and overseas and so on.

As far as I personally, as the artistic director, am concerned, I don't think that I would wish to leave as long as I have the possibility of continuing to develop things. Now, there can be all sorts of reasons why that doesn't continue to be the case, whether they be financial or whether they be because of lack of support from the board. Whether there is a sudden drying-up of talent. I suppose those are the three elements. And I suppose even with those three elements right and in place and positive, I suppose there could come a time when I think, 'Well, I don't want to do this anymore. *I've* dried up.' But I don't feel like that, yet, anyway.

POTTER: In your career before you came to the Australian Ballet you had worked with a number of legendary artistic directors. Have you modelled yourself on any of those, or is your model Maina Gielgud's model?

GIELGUD: Look, I never thought about modelling myself on anybody or being Maina Gielgud's model or whatever. It seems to me I just tried to look at the situation of the Australian Ballet at different moments in time over the 13 years and tried to do the best in terms of that company and the dancers that that company had, or has at the moment. Certainly, I've tried to use the experience I had of working under different artistic directors and, when applicable to the present situation, tried to use what I felt were the assets, the best things that an artistic director had to offer and tried to avoid what I felt to have been the negatives when I was in that situation. And I think that's all that one can really do, because one can never really put oneself in the shoes of the dancers and, of course, there *are* times when it's not the dancers' reaction that counts.

The priority at all times has to be the artistic performance that you put on stage and the best way of producing that. And there's always—which is very exciting, and I think which is different from a business—that inevitable occurrence that at 7.30 the curtain goes up. So a dancer has that feeling 24 hours a day, I think, and as director you also do because the way you proceed is still always coloured by that. There is only *x* amount of time and what matters is how you are going to do the best you can and produce the best possible results of performance within the timeframe.

I think that if I had directed, and if in the future I do, another company in another country, perhaps I would do so differently, again according to the material at hand.

POTTER: I want to ask you what your aspirations for the future are, because you must feel that there is some kind of turning point in your career approaching.

GIELGUD: Yes, I'd like to be able to make more inroads, I suppose, in the ballet world at large, in relation to classical ballets and the style of classical ballets because I feel that, perhaps, that's one area—or one of the areas, let's be arrogant—where I have a lot to offer in an area that's been neglected desperately worldwide. Maybe there'll be an opportunity, whether it's by directing, whether it's by coaching, to keep those different styles defined in classical ballet elsewhere in the world. Because it really is frightening, and I think it's one of the things that is doing classical ballet a lot of harm because it's all melding into one pot and it all looks the same. Then I think the audience starts to get bored too.

So I don't know what shape that would take, but I would like that because I think I can be of use to classical ballet, and I'd like to be because of the good fortune that I had, of the people that I've worked with. To be able to pass that on, I think that would be interesting and it would be useful, and I would like to be useful.

Teaching fascinates me, I suppose for the same reason that I think I can be of use to classical ballet. I don't know that I would want to teach for a contemporary company even if they did have classical classes. I'm not sure. It's to be seen, I probably won't be able to pick and choose.

POTTER: Did you reapply?

GIELGUD: I did.

POTTER: Do you feel regretful about the way things have gone?

GIELGUD: Oh, yes. I would have liked to stay.   (August 1995)

The Maina Gielgud tapes represent Gielgud's right of reply to the criticisms that were levelled against her, especially in the last few years of her directorship. But they are as well a statement of her commitment to strongly held ideals and values that lost favour in a particular political climate. In their primary, oral form, the recordings also highlight the problematic relationship between the oral interview and its written, edited manifestation. Gielgud has, on the one hand, an exceptionally agile mind that is revealed in the manner in which she rapidly makes connections, anticipates, and cross-references her thoughts, but, on the other hand, her sometimes measured tone and her pauses at critical moments indicate the care that she attaches to choosing the most appropriate words for the particular occasion. There is little that is rash about her response to questions. But the oral version of these interviews also reveals Gielgud's wit, warmth, sophistication and, above all, a rich and engaging sense of humour that can never emerge in the written text.

Commissioned Works for the Australian Ballet from Australian Choreographers, 1983–96

1984	*Meander*, Graeme Murphy	1991	*Of Blessed Memory*, Stanton Welch
1985	*The Sentimental Bloke*, Robert Ray	1992	*Nutcracker*, Graeme Murphy
1986	*Canzona*, Jacqui Carroll		*Sand Siren*, Gideon Obarzanek
	La Favorita (pas de deux), Petal Miller-Ashmole		*Symphonic Poem*, Timothy Gordon
1987	*Gallery*, Graeme Murphy	1994	*Divergence*, Stanton Welch
	Sonata for Seven, Timothy Gordon	1995	*Beyond Bach*, Stephen Baynes
1988	*Ballade*, Stephen Baynes		*Corroboree*, Stanton Welch
	Moments Past (pas de deux), Alan Cross		*Madame Butterfly*, Stanton Welch
	Snugglepot and Cuddlepie, Petal Miller-Ashmole	1996	*Alchemy*, Stephen Page
1990	*Catalyst*, Stephen Baynes		*The Deep End*, Meryl Tankard
	My Name is Edward Kelly, Timothy Gordon		*Red Earth*, Stanton Welch
	Three of Us, Stanton Welch		*Shadow in the Facet*, Stephen Baynes

Commissioned Works for the Dancers Company from Australian Choreographers, 1983–96

1983	*Three Sisters*, Robert Ray	1993	*Before the Rain*, Stanton Welch
1986	*Summer Nights*, Mark Annear		*Four Reflections of a Quintet*, Stephen Baynes
1987	*Jarabina*, Timothy Gordon		*Sweetheart*, Gideon Obarzanek
1988	*Sacred Dances*, Rosetta Cook	1994	*Souvenirs*, Stephen Baynes
1989	*The Romantics*, Robert Ray	1995	*Many Colours Blue*, Stanton Welch
1990	*A Time to Dance*, Stanton Welch		*Seascape*, Margaret Wilson
1991	*Sketches*, Alida Chase	1996	*The Brother of Sleep*, Natalie Weir
1992	*Canon*, Stanton Welch		*Motion Pool*, Adrian Burnett
	A Gershwin Pas de Deux, Mark Annear		
	Passion, Stanton Welch		

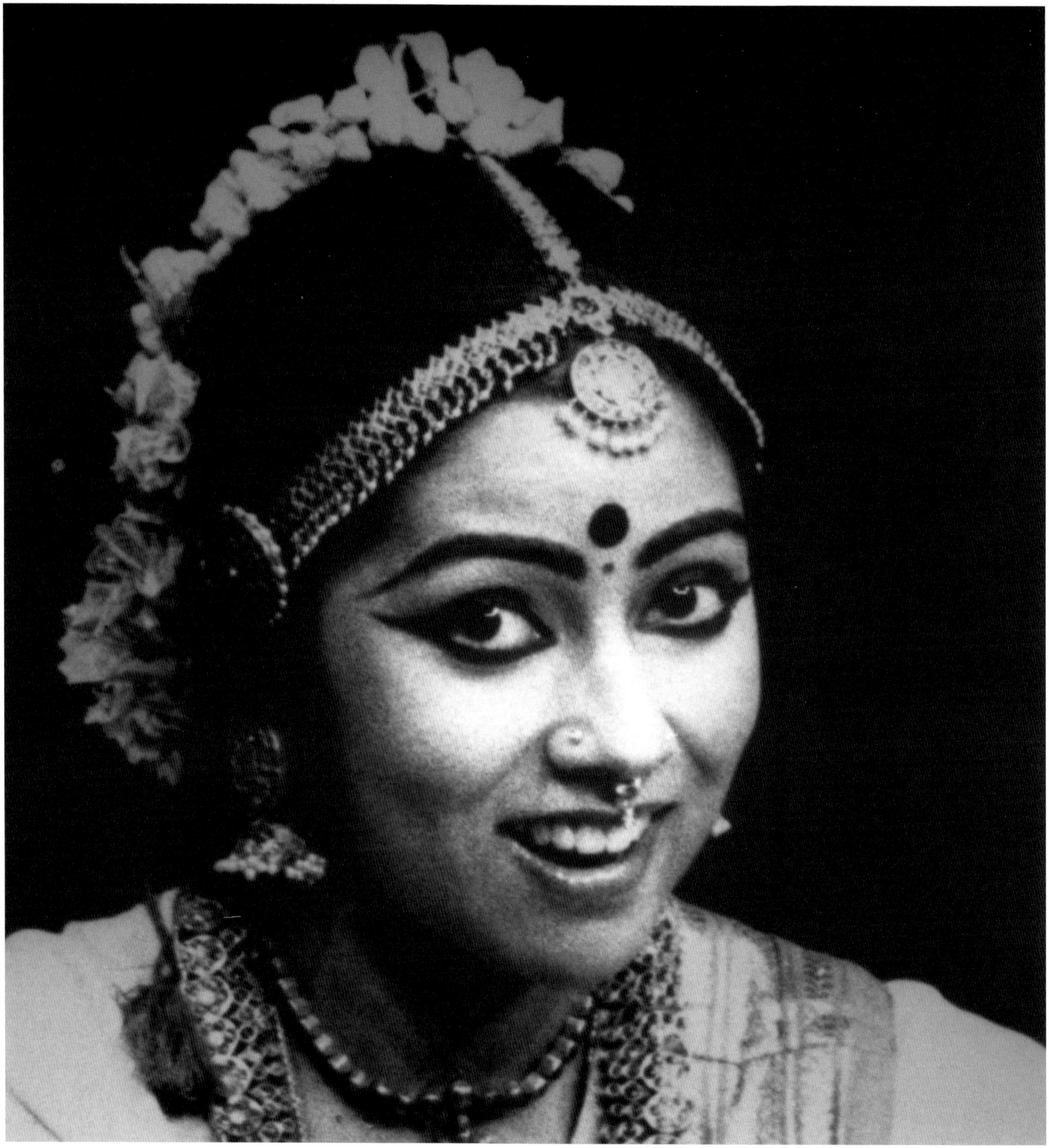

Padma Menon — Dance Reborn

Interviews TRC 2734/3; TRC 3419

Padma Menon (born 1966), Canberra-based dancer, choreographer, teacher and director of Padma Menon Dance Theatre, was interviewed in Canberra for the Multicultural Music and Dance Project by Jennifer Gall in November 1991, and again in Canberra by Michelle Potter in May 1996

Indian-born Padma Menon, who as a Hindu says that in every rebirth she has she still wants to be reborn as a dancer, is one of a growing number of Australian artists trained in a non-Western dance style whose aim is to make that style relevant and challenging in changed social, cultural and geographical conditions. Initially Menon's dance training was in the Bharatha Natyam style but at the age of nine she heard about Dr Vempati Chinna Satyam, rejuvenator of the ancient priestly dance style of Kuchipudi. She began training as a Kuchipudi dancer under this master teacher, her guru, and while still very young joined and toured extensively with his Kuchipudi Art Academy Company. Menon came to Australia in 1987 and moved to Canberra in 1988 where she began performing as a solo Kuchipudi dancer. Later she established a dance school and then a company. Now Menon says her ambition, which she aims to realise through both her teaching and the works she choreographs, is 'to create a context for Kuchipudi in Australia; to make the style live and grow'.

Menon's early childhood was spent in Hyderabad and her dance studies were encouraged by a family she describes as 'progressive'. They fostered a love for the arts and they gave every support to her ambition to be a dancer. But they also gave equal priority to her academic education. They fully expected that Menon would attain academic qualifications and she studied for and graduated with a Bachelor of Arts from Madras University at the same time as she was dancing professionally. She has continued with higher academic studies in Australia and believes that her academic background provides another context to her life—'it helps me retain my humility, to curb the drive towards egocentricism that all artists have'. But there is no doubt that the driving force behind her career in dance has been her guru. She sees her work as a continuation of his and says that he gave her not only a love for the Kuchipudi dance style but also 'respect for art that is something that is beyond value'.

MENON: I was born in 1966 in Trichur which is in Kerala, a State along the western coast of India. My mother was rooted to the State because it was where her family had lived for several generations. She actually went back to that State every time she had a child because she felt that the child had to be born in Kerala. My mother comes from a very old family which had aristocratic origins. They were related to the old kings of the region and a lot of them were ministers to the kings. Many of her family were patrons of the arts. My father on the other hand came from a half-Brahmin, priestly caste. They didn't have quite the same interest in the arts as my mother's family. I attribute my love for the arts to my mother. I think I took after her family a lot in that.

We lived all our life away from my native State. So although I was born in Kerala, I don't consider it my birthplace because I spent my childhood somewhere else. I grew up in Hyderabad, which is in Andhra Pradesh where Kuchipudi originated, and that's where my interest in Kuchipudi started. I moved to Madras because the greatest teacher of

Kuchipudi was based in Madras. My family has moved back to Kerala now because we have an ancestral house there.

I started dancing when I was seven, which was back in 1973. It's actually a bit late in India. You usually start when you're three or four but my mother believed that I needed to have some element of choice in the matter and she thought I would be too young when I was four or five to make that decision. Even at seven I can remember distinctly the conversation we had about my taking up dancing. Her first question was, 'Are you interested?' I didn't know anything about it, apart from watching it and knowing that my mother was very interested, and I said I would like to try. That's when she put me in a dance school in Hyderabad. I gave my first performance when I was nine and, looking back at it now, I think I was very young. I became something of a child prodigy.

I joined a company when I was about 15 and I was performing lead roles. It put tremendous pressure on me and it also made me devalue everything I had achieved at that stage. I was too young to realise where I had reached and what I needed to stay there. When I was 16 I nearly gave up dancing because of arrogance, I suppose, because everything happened so easily. Then came a turning point in my life when I realised that that was the easy part—getting there. From then on would be the hard part—to stay there and find qualities that would let me dance for the right reasons.

GALL: Can you talk about Kuchipudi, its origins and how it was modernised?

MENON: Kuchipudi started as a dance–drama tradition many years back. It actually started because people at the time believed that the element of *bhakti*, or devotion, was dying out in the dance practices of the day. Kuchipudi was a way of reviving that particular sentiment. It was practised by groups of men, Brahmin priests, who were attached to a temple who then travelled from one village to another. During the day they performed several rituals and at night they had a performance running all through the night depicting various stories. In about the fifteenth century or thereabouts there was a revival led by a man called Siddhendra Yogi, who was a poet and a writer. He went to the village of Kuchipudi in Andhra Pradesh and ordained six or seven Brahmin families to practise the art. So it was part of their sacred duty as priests to keep this tradition alive. He also wrote several dramatic pieces for Kuchipudi, which are still today the core of the Kuchipudi repertoire. My guru comes from one of those families. He is about the seventh or eight generation of practising artists from that family.

In the 1950s my guru actually moved from Kuchipudi to Madras, which is the cultural centre in India, and established a school of Kuchipudi. That was a very, very difficult thing to do because Madras was the stronghold of another dance style, Bharatha Natyam. Bharatha Natyam had been long established and it didn't have the problems that Kuchipudi had as an all-male, priestly tradition. Kuchipudi got fairly stagnated in the little village and when my guru brought it to Madras, it met with absolute opposition. People wrote it off. They said it was a folk tradition, that it wasn't classical but vulgar. But what they couldn't contain was the audience reaction to Kuchipudi. Audiences just loved it. It didn't matter what the critics said or what the other dancers said, the audiences just loved it. It grew. Even when I started Kuchipudi in 1975, it wasn't very well known. But today it's fashionable. Every Bharatha Natyam dancer now wants to learn Kuchipudi so they can have a couple of pieces in their Bharatha Natyam repertoire.

What my guru did in the way of modernising it was to make it a solo dance style. He choreographed several pieces and he introduced women to the style. He also gave it a solo repertoire structure. In an Indian dance recital you have a specific structure. You begin with an invocatory piece, you have a pure dance piece, then you have a fairly long piece that is the test of your ability basically; it's a very demanding piece. Then in the second half, you go on to the more expressive pieces and finally you have a concluding piece. Kuchipudi didn't have that structure because it was a dance–drama tradition. He began to choreograph pieces to fit in with this particular solo structure. He also used some of the sections of dance–drama as solo dance styles, which retained the expressive nature of Kuchipudi.

GALL: Could you talk about your guru, what you think of him?

MENON: Kuchipudi owes its revival and resurgence to my guru. He was a man of great vision. As someone who came from a traditional background, he was a very modern man. He was able to see what was good about other styles and to use it to make Kuchipudi survive, much against the opinion of several traditional teachers of the time. The most important

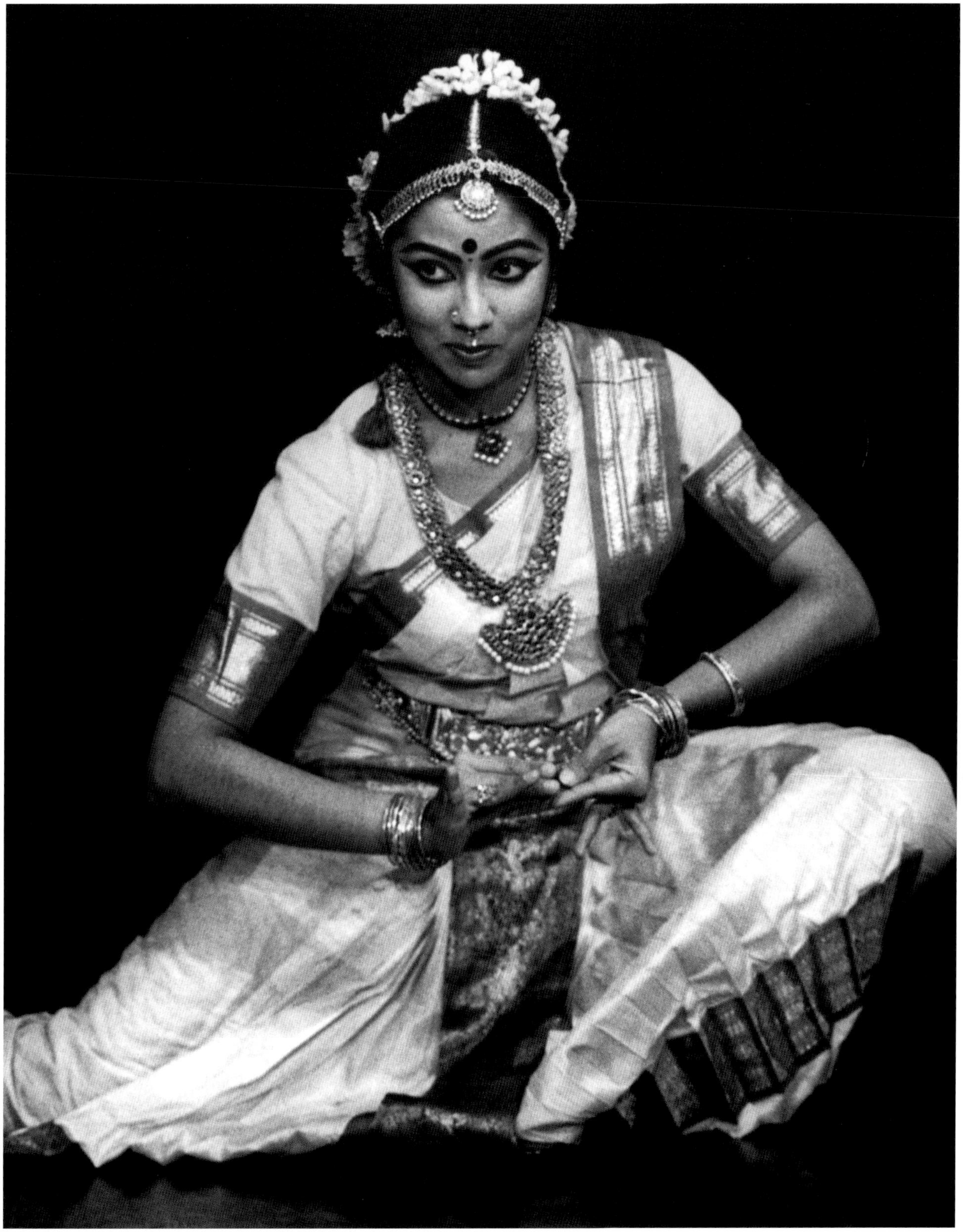

thing he's imparted to me is his attitude to dance as an art form. I've grown up with him telling me how much of a divine art it is and how much respect it needs, the degree of commitment and discipline it needs, and also how fortunate I am to be able to perform it. He's also imparted the great love for helping the style to live. I see my work as part of his own struggle to make Kuchipudi live and to grow. He's given me that kind of love and respect for Kuchipudi, and also respect for art as something that is beyond value.

GALL: Can you describe his classes and his teaching techniques?

MENON: The Indian gurus don't have very sophisticated theories of teaching techniques. He was just an inspired teacher and his inspiration was so obvious that none of us needed anything else. To be taught by him, who was so inspired, was enough. We all partook of that inspiration. But, thinking back on it, there were some things that I find problematic. The concept of the Indian guru can sometimes be overwhelming; the fact that it can cramp or even kill your own individuality. That's why a lot of Indian dancers are not very good choreographers at all. They still keep churning out the same sort of pieces that their guru has taught them. That is a problem, that strong bonding you have with your guru. The other problem I find is the fact that you don't question enough. Your theoretical knowledge is limited unless you make your own effort to find out everything behind the dance form. I think that's true here, too, in the mainstream dance tradition. You don't think very much about what you do; and you don't find out enough about what you do. I think with a guru sometimes you can become his clay. He models his vision using you, and it's wonderful to be able to do that. But I think I'm very fortunate in the fact that I've been able to move away from that at a time when I'm still young enough to develop in my own way.

GALL: What is the main repertoire? Are they mythological stories that are drawn on for Kuchipudi?

MENON: Yes. The major productions tend to be stories and legends from the myths. But when you do a solo repertoire, you can also have what is very peculiar to Kuchipudi, and what a lot of the other dance styles in India have drawn on, that is character portrayals where you fully explore a particular character. For instance, in a character called Satyabhama you explore the arrogant, headstrong woman who dictates what the man should do. You can also have exploration of particular emotions where a heroine portrays a particular emotion and you have different, linked incidents which explore or illustrate that particular emotion. So there are all these different kinds of themes you come across in the Kuchipudi repertoire.

GALL: What are the technical points that distinguish Kuchipudi from other traditions?

MENON: First of all, it's a totally different mental and philosophical approach and I think that's where Kuchipudi is, sadly, losing out in India. With a lot of dancers from other traditions learning Kuchipudi, the essence is being lost. Kuchipudi calls for a letting-go, for a freedom of expression and interpretation. It's a very extroverted style. And that for an Indian dance style is very peculiar. It is also a style that follows what in Sanskrit we call the *lokadharmi* way of expression, that is as close to real life as possible. So you have a funny kind of combination of imitating real life and yet enlarging it because you're on stage. In most of the other Indian dance styles expressions are always stylised.

The technical aspect in Kuchipudi is actually less important than the expressive aspect. The speeds in Kuchipudi are also faster than a lot of other styles and many other styles are borrowing that from Kuchipudi because audiences now want to see something that's racy and fast. But mainly what I would stress is the approach to Kuchipudi is very different. You're looking at a dance–drama tradition rather than a dance tradition.

GALL: Can we go back to your student days? What were the highlights of studying with your guru?

MENON: For me the highlights are being part of my teacher's choreography because he actually used to choreograph pieces using a couple of the dancers. He would choreograph a whole production just using three or four dancers and then *we* would teach the others. Being part of that creative process is a very special experience. I have since then worked with other choreographers in Australia and in India as well. But there was a difference in the way that things came to him, in the way that he suddenly would come up with a movement. It wasn't technical, it was something beyond all that.

GALL: How do men regard you as a dancer and a woman dancing in what was a man's tradition?

MENON: It's not unusual anymore to see a woman doing Kuchipudi. Women have given to Kuchipudi an entirely different dimension. With men dancing the roles of women there was a greater element of the *bhakti*, the devotional element. The man would transcend himself in terms of gender; in every way he had to forget about himself. Women have made it a far more sensuous style than it originally was. Kuchipudi, because it was a male style, tended to exaggerate the sensuousness because men had to convince the audience that they were women. In a woman's hand it becomes something entirely different. The other problem is, when men were doing it, they could do a lot of things that women were not allowed to do on stage. That's why you have some of the very strong women characters in Kuchipudi. But I think that Kuchipudi has lost some of its original quality because fewer men are doing it; now you have women to play the female roles and men to play the male roles. You don't have the crossing of genders that was wonderful in the beginning. Still to me one of the most powerful experiences is to see a male performer perform Kuchipudi.

GALL: Can you describe the differences between performing in India and in Australia?

MENON: It's completely different. In India you're performing to an audience who are aware of the myths and narrative that underlie the things that you do. But what I stress is that they're still not aware of the technical vocabulary, so it's not that they understand every single movement and every single gesture that you do. But they sort of understand the general content of the myths and narratives. The Indian audience looks for very, very different things in a performance. When you're talking about professionalism in India, it's almost a personal quality. It's a reflection of your own quality of dancing and standard of dancing rather than other things that seem to be part of that concept in the West. I'm referring to things like lighting, sound, the stage, and things like that. Now an Indian audience tends to ignore that. That is something that I'm having to adjust to in the West. Here it doesn't matter how brilliantly the dancer performed, if there was a little bit of crackling in the sound system I think critics discount the whole performance. That wouldn't happen in India. I think Indians are a bit more tolerant of human and mechanical errors.

The other difference is that the audiences here, at least the audiences that I get, tend to be more questioning, more critical. And I suppose that's inevitable because they're coming to see something that's out of their own context and their own experience. But what I also find, and it sometimes makes me a little bit angry I suppose, is the expectation of an audience to comprehend completely what is happening on stage. And putting that expectation on to the dancer—this whole concept of accessibility. I sometimes wonder how much is a contemporary performance accessible to an audience, how much in fact is a ballet performance accessible to an audience. I think it's a bit unfair to expect something like an Indian dance performance to explain itself. Part of the experience is the mystery of the movement, and the ritual. I don't think any ritual is fully comprehended by anyone, including people who perform the ritual, and that's part of the magic of the ritual. I believe that it is the responsibility of the audience that if they want to know more, they have to take the trouble to find out. There is a limit to how much you can explain things.

Dancing in India is an exhilarating experience because I think Indians tend to be more emotional in their response. When we do some of our dance productions in India, people actually stand up and begin to chant the names of the gods that are being portrayed. There is that kind of spontaneous response. Somehow you almost forget you're a human being. For them you just become a god or the character you're doing. In Australia they don't know how they're meant to respond. A lot of people come and tell me that clapping seems irreligious. I derive a lot of strength, enormous energy from the audience. It's wonderful to look into the audience, which I do, and see someone expressing quite clearly what they feel.

GALL: Why do you teach?

MENON: I teach because that is the only way that Kuchipudi is going to live. Also because teaching, especially in a country like Australia, is the most amazing experience I've ever had. Seeing Kuchipudi being used by so many different people, not Indians, just people coming from totally different contexts, totally different patterns of thought, experience, and seeing what Kuchipudi develops into in their hands is such a wonderful experience for me. That is the way that any dance form is going to live—if it can transcend its context and its boundary, if other people can use it. That is my main driving force in life: to see where I can develop it. I find that Kuchipudi is far more accessible than a lot of the other Indian dance styles. It seems to give audiences a specific, special kind of experience and I want to explore how relevant it can be to the Australian experience. And the only way I can do it is if Australians are doing it. I am far too rooted in my own context and my own background and it's going to grow in the hands of my students. I think the future of Kuchipudi, at least part of the future, is going to lie with them. I try very hard not to impose myself on them so they can bring something of their own to the style.

GALL: Do you see yourself as a guru?

MENON: Yes and no. I have to see myself as a guru to infuse the element of spirituality and discipline that is part of the whole process of learning Kuchipudi. Because I have that training and that inspiration from my own guru, in some ways I have to see myself as the source of that knowledge and that inspiration to my own students. But I don't know whether I'm quite comfortable with the connotation that a guru has in a Western context. It's a trap to fall into. As an Indian and as a teacher you fall into the stereotype of this guru, this person who dictates your moral and spiritual life. I don't think I want to take it that far. I would like to be a motivation, a guide. But I don't think I want to be someone who knows everything that's right and wrong in your personal life. I want my students to be independent, to be their own people. To use what I've taught them in their own way. At this stage, I only want to give them ways and means. (November 1991)

Menon's company, Padma Menon Dance Theatre, has flourished since it gave its first performance, as Kailash Dance Company, in 1993. Its performers have included Anglo-Australians as well as Indian–Australians and the company has, courageously, already toured twice to India in addition to taking its contemporary repertoire to various venues in Australia. Some of Menon's most recent works include *Relations* (1995), in which she considered the tensions between generations caught in a migrant situation, and *Ramayana—A Mother Speaks* (1995), in which she examined an ancient, epic text within the framework of modern discourses on feminism. Then in *Rasa* (1996), Menon worked with Meryl Tankard and the dancers of the Meryl Tankard Australian Dance Theatre in a collaboration that looked at extending the boundaries of dance vocabulary. Like most directors and choreographers creating in the 1990s, Menon is constantly concerned with the boundaries both of her art form in a general sense and of her Kuchipudi dance style in particular.

POTTER: What was your inspiration for starting a company?

MENON: It was basically a structure into which the more skilled dancers of the school, those who could tackle professional work, would find an avenue to work as a dancer. It's very difficult for dancers coming out of this kind of training to find work easily with companies, so really I had to start something.

It was also for me really a space to create works that expressed where *I* was—in a different place and in a different time from where I had actually started in India. I felt that somehow the things I was doing needed to become more meaningful, and that was only possible if somehow I could make it part of this landscape and this time. So it was really a space for that to happen as well.

But it's changed dramatically even from 1993 to now. The company's human resources have just changed so much; the kind of work that I'm interested in doing now is very, very different from the kind of work I was doing in '93. But I think the desire has always been there even in India as well as after coming here; the desire to somehow make everything that I was learning more relevant to me. I'm still trying to find that.

POTTER: How have your works changed? What have the shifts been over the three or four years that you've been directing the company?

MENON: I think initially I started off by thinking that there was a way in which you take Indian culture per se, or Indian mythology, or whatever the art form was concerned with, and try and make the whole package relevant. So initially the works were still based on the narrative and mythological structures of Indian dance itself. Take *Siva*, for example. A traditional production about Siva in India would look at a fairly literal depiction of the god complete with plastic snakes and tiger skin costumes. I always had a problem with that because I've always thought the notion of Siva is such an abstract concept that to make it literal always seemed a bit ridiculous to me. And I thought I would like to do a production where that complexity was retained but as a concept rather than as an anthropomorphic depiction. And *Siva* for me was really and still remains a work that's very close to my heart. I think it was successful. It was still Indian and Hindu in the sense that it was talking about a very, very deeply rooted Indian concept. However, treating it differently perhaps gave it a place within the thinking of a different culture.

But moving on from there, in *Relations* I wondered what would happen if I did away with the mythological structure and took up a secular narrative, still rooted in concerns that are migrant or Indian. Then it was very problematic because you find that the whole movement vocabulary is geared towards particular stories, particular narratives. The whole attitude of the form is geared to that sense of distance between the audience and the performer, the sense of the performer being transformed into a person who is more than ordinary. Everything is so based on that, that when you start looking at an ordinary household, ordinary people, or people who sometimes were less than ordinary, you just find that you have this tension with the form. And that is a challenge. I don't want ever to throw away that vocabulary because I think it's a very, very rich movement and performance vocabulary.

With *Ramayana* I tried to do that again, but what I did was take a mythological narrative and tried to relate it to the secular concerns of the day. I'm not sure how successful *Ramayana* was. I think on some levels it was, and on some levels it was fighting too many things at the same time. I would like to remount *Ramayana*, but I would need to identify specific areas to work on. I think *Ramayana* tried to work on too many things. It was trying to work on a narrative, a discourse, a movement vocabulary, music, costuming all at once. I think it was far too ambitious in what it tried to do. That's something I'm taking on board with the works I'm doing this year; perhaps working on specific things. You can't try and change everything all at once.

POTTER: Your training has been purely in an Indian-style vocabulary. Do you feel there is a difficulty in that you haven't had training in some Western-style vocabulary?

MENON: I would love to have had exposure to a non-Indian movement vocabulary, a non-Indian way of thinking about dance. Indian dance has specific ways of thinking about dance itself. In Western dance, from what I've seen and worked with, from my limited exposure, for example working with Meryl (Tankard), watching and talking to other choreographers and dancers and collaborating with them, you think of dance very much as body in space. In Indian dance the body is completely subsumed, you never talk about dance in physical terms, you talk about it in other ways, as conveying an emotion, conveying a narrative, as part of a larger devotional structure. There's very little self-conscious discussion about how you're moving the body. Although there's a huge amount of focus on technique, it's still always that technique is an instrument to do something else, not technique per se. I want to bring that Western dimension into discussions of Indian dance.

I want to be fairly specific in where I'm coming from and where I'm going. And in many ways I feel it's a good thing I haven't learnt another vocabulary because there isn't a superficiality. I'm not attempting fusion. I just want to trigger the vocabulary that I know and push it itself, because that's where I see that you make that particular form relevant. I think I may be tempted to kind of discard certain things, or simply pull together things from another form if I had learned something so different. So, because I've learnt different Indian dance styles—I think each Indian dance style has its own performance philosophy, movement philosophy—I feel I still have a fairly broad base to draw upon. I can draw upon Kuchipudi for particular elements, Bharatha Natyam, Mohini Attam for certain elements, or Kathak. So I feel I've still got those different theatrical modes to draw upon and maybe *conceptually* push my thinking along in non-Indian ways.

POTTER: Would you like to say something about *Rasa*, the collaboration you did with Meryl Tankard?

MENON: Meryl talked about doing something together when she was first here in Canberra. She left soon after and we never got a chance to do it. But I think, for me, that opportunity to work with her came at the right point of time in my own development. I enjoyed it immensely. I find Meryl's work unique. It's very emotional and yet it's not sentimental. She's someone who's able to evoke a very strong emotional response in me through using the body and combinations of dancers and choreographic structures. That's something that I'm really interested in doing.

The other thing is I find she's always terribly unselfconscious about processes. She doesn't have this long discussion about intellectually setting up a framework of what are we going to do, what are we going to achieve. It was very, very simple. It was very natural. We were in the studio. I took classes for the dancers. We talked about certain musical triggers, some sort of basic narrative structures. But Meryl and I didn't sit together and actually say this is what we want to achieve out of this; we want this to be fusion and we want Indian dance to be taken somewhere. We weren't meaning to create history or anything of the kind. It was just an interest of two individuals to work together.

I think there were lots of things that emerged. I think the dancers absorbed so much when I took classes for them and it was not possible for all of that to emerge for *Rasa*. But I believe that what they learnt in terms of just a different way of looking at performance, looking at why you use the body—not just in the ways that you would imagine for Western dance, but there are other reasons why you have to create shapes with the body—will come out at different points in time for them. I think *Rasa* was a product of a process at the end of a particular amount of time. It wasn't a process in which Meryl borrowed from Indian dance because they all took on ownership of what they had learnt and transformed it. She encouraged me to do the same. She actually worked with *me*, giving me concepts which were outside of my own thinking. It was very, very frightening sometimes because I'm so used to being in charge, but there I had to let go. Even things like looking up and moving the body at the same time. It's just something that I've never, ever done and in a completely simple thing like that I lost control. The minute I tilted my head up, I didn't know what my feet were doing and I lost contact with the ground. And I had to spend hours in the studio with her working through things like that. And maybe bending the body more than I would, or just letting go of the shoulders. I found it immensely enriching and I tried to use some of that in *In Praise*, the solo season of traditional works I just did. I wanted to take on some of that—being aware of spaces around the body. I think because Indian dance is so two-dimensional there are some spaces around you that you don't even think about.

POTTER: Can you explain to me how *you* go about creating a work? When you go into the studio what is your process?

MENON: It's very different with each work. With *Relations*, for example, I built it very much around the dancers I had. I had a framework of what I wanted to do with the form but I tried to use the personal histories of the dancers, because I knew that it was a theme that needed a great amount of honesty, because it was about ordinary living. It wasn't about Rama or Sita where you could just act. You really needed to feel. So I thought the way might be to actually trigger some personal histories, to evoke the kind of emotions that they have been through and therefore to then get them to move. How would you show certain things if you were in this particular situation, or a parallel situation? A lot of it was stories. Out of that would evolve particular movement patterns. That's why perhaps *Relations* was quite successful because in a way the dancers felt ownership of the vocabulary.

In *Ramayana*, the process was complicated because the dancers had to have an intimate knowledge of the original two texts I was working off. Plus, they had to be aware of the more modern discourses that I was situating the two texts in, like all the nationalist discourses in India, or the feminist discourses about those texts. I think that was a problem because it was hard enough for them to understand the original texts, and then to take the distance to then push it into a twentieth-century context.

POTTER: What about the specific vocabulary? Do you ask for input from the dancers in terms of vocabulary?

MENON: In *Relations*, certainly, if I found that a movement was not sitting comfortably on a dancer, then I would actually say how would you say the same thing? Is there another way? And then maybe work on developing that. In *Ramayana* I was more specific because there were certain things I was trying with movement. For example, in the mourning scene I was using the ritual gestures of mourning in Indian dance, so in a way I was more reluctant to abandon them. I think that's where the problems were happening because I suppose I should have been saying, 'Okay, well, this is not working, so let's abandon it.' But then, for me, that would have taken away my objective with what I was trying to do with the form. I wanted to retain the gestures and tried harder to make it work because there were reasons why those movements were there. They were mourning movements. I wanted to liberate them, make them more free.

POTTER: You've mentioned the word 'fusion' and you've said you're not interested in fusion. Could you just elaborate on that? Why aren't you interested in fusion?

MENON: I think that in the sixties and seventies when the West discovered the East so to speak, dancers like Uday Shankar— I mean, he's a beautiful dancer—went overseas and did those East–West works, and set a kind of framework, a model, for any kind of cross-cultural work. But I believe we've progressed from there. I'm looking at, for example, a choreographer like Chandralekha, who is now said to be leading the whole contemporary Indian dance movement. I don't find anything

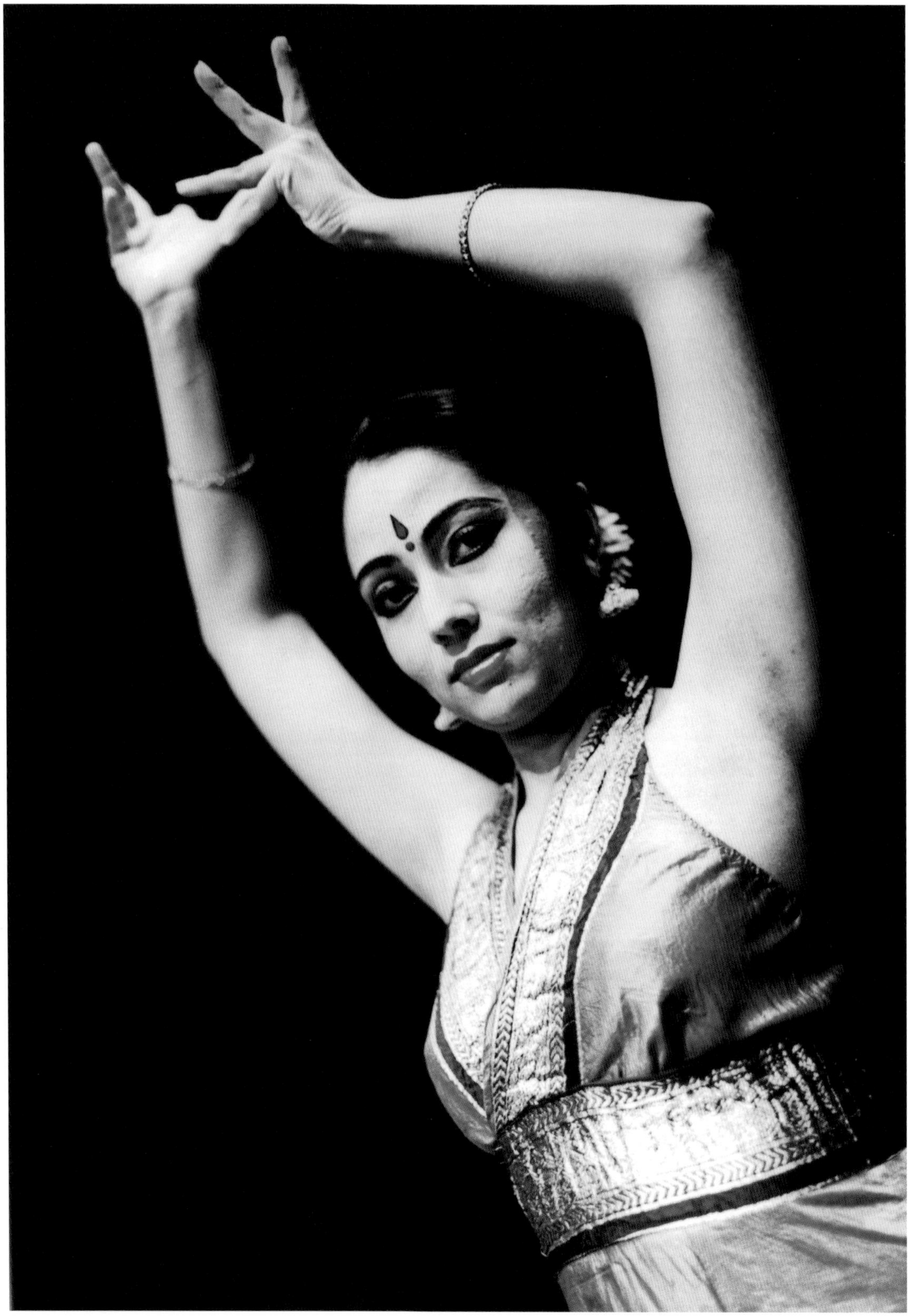

that is non-Indian in her work and that, for me, is the most exciting thing. She is someone I look up to as somebody who has conceptually tried to understand different performance modes but is still very passionate about her own background, her own training, and is trying to push that. In very successful ways, I think.

I think if we continue thinking about such things as fusion, it seems to be an easy way out. For me, you're denying the dynamic within forms themselves to push you towards change. It's like saying if you just had a few Western movements in there, or just put in Western music and did Indian movements, that's enough to make it different. And maybe it was the only way it could have been done earlier, but I believe that now people are living in more of an international society. Maybe you can challenge them not to take that distance that you do in fusion work when you think of two separate forms and when you think, 'Well, I relate to this one but not to this.' Maybe you can engage the audiences more if you yourself don't think about it like that.

POTTER: I want to ask you about taking the company to India. What kind of reaction did you get in India?

MENON: We went in '94 and I took the dancers who were trained here. The reaction was very positive. They danced differently from dancers who were trained in India and I don't think it was quality but just again an attitude. There was a sense that they were more open and it was very interesting because I wouldn't have picked on that if I hadn't seen them performing there. There was certainly a sense of women who were born and brought up here. More open, more free, more direct. I think some Indian critics had difficulties in even touching on that, so they preferred to dwell on me. They had seen me there before and I was someone they were familiar with, even though they admitted that I had changed my style as well. But at least I had a history and they could focus on me. But certainly when they spoke to me about the dancers, they all thought they were strong technically but there was a difference in the emotional depiction. They didn't reject it; they didn't say it was inappropriate or disrespectful. But they certainly sensed a difference. For me that was a good thing. They have to feel they are people from here. That for me is the really exciting thing.

POTTER: Have you found, over the few years that your company has been in existence, that the attitude of Australians to your work has changed?

MENON: It's always going to be a balance because the work is evolving. In a way I'm not giving the audiences a comfortable niche. They can't ever come back knowing that this is what they're going to get. If I stuck to a particular mode of work, I may be giving them that comfort, which is both good and bad. But because in my own mind I'm unable to do that, the audiences constantly have to keep evaluating where they stand with regard to my work.

For me as an artist it's important that I keep changing. I don't think everybody has to do that. I wouldn't think that that's the only way to be. I think there are some artists who are very, very good at what they do and they keep doing and they always keep bettering that particular style. I'm changing in fundamental ways. The important thing is that I'm not discarding what makes me different and I don't want to discard that. I think somehow audiences sense that. I think there's more of a problem if you reject what you are.

(May 1996)

As a performer Menon says it is important to her that she feels she has 'something special, something larger than life' to communicate to her audience and that this is not possible if she thinks of herself as 'an ordinary person' or 'part of mundane life'. Yet she sees the need to balance the demands of performance with a wider philosophy. Her thoughts on what is the essence of dance centre on key Hindu concepts and are marked by a blend of humility, passion and determination to see the Kuchipudi style live and grow, to see the rebirth of an ancient style of dance wearing a new garb for a new country.

GALL: How does the spiritual side of dance cope with the ego, particularly in your form of dance which has a strong religious theme running through what you're doing? How do you balance that?

MENON: Hindu philosophy has the drive towards selflessness. The ultimate liberation, or *moksha* as they call it, is when you realise you are one with everything around you. The same soul that emanates from you also emanates from everything else around you. To me, I interpret that as a drive towards a consciousness of your union with what's around you, and that's not possible if you have the stumbling block of yourself to overcome. The way I translate it into dance is, when you've got to play a character or to portray an emotion, you have to become that character or that emotion and the role that your self plays is only in the interpretation of that particular character. But when you have thought about the character enough, you then just have to stop being yourself because the only way you can contain the audience in the illusion of dance is to be convinced yourself, paradoxically, of the reality of that illusion. If you are convinced of that character, you can then convince the audience of that character. Otherwise they'll just be seeing Padma Menon on stage and then that defeats the purpose. I've seen lots of dancers never being able to transcend themselves. Some people go to dance because they want to see a particular dancer but, for me, what is primary is the narrative, the character and the emotion, and to get the audience to feel the same emotion.

GALL: Does dance have the power to transcend culture?

MENON: I feel dance has the potential to transcend all cultures. Whatever it is, I feel that in its myths and legends it is ultimately depicting certain root emotions, root narratives, that exist in all different cultures. Once we can get past the stumbling block of names and places, if you look at what it's depicting, it's just basic human emotions. In many ways I think that a lot of the people who come to see things like Indian dance often come with a preconceived notion that it's going to be too difficult to understand. Part of the beauty for me of Kuchipudi, or any other Indian dance, is the mystery. I don't think there is any Indian audience who understands very much more than an Australian audience does, and that is part of the whole mystery. It creates so many different meanings for you. Once you understand the root emotion, then all the other related emotions are different for each person. And that's the way it should be. (November 1991)

POTTER: What are your aspirations for your company?

MENON: I'd like for it to collaborate with really exciting Australian choreographers and other performers. I'd like it to be really adventurous but somehow still relevant to the Australian audiences. To keep the audiences, to get new audiences. To make Indian dance be treated seriously as an art form. Not like Tandoori chicken! And I don't mean let's all take ourselves too seriously, but just as an art form so that other choreographers and dancers will be interested and it will be something that Australian dancers and choreographers can draw upon. That's why I admire Meryl for taking that step of collaboration. It's a very brave step to take and I think she was perhaps ahead of her time in taking that on. Just so it becomes another vocabulary, another source, so that people would find it natural to use without being too self-conscious of whether it's religious, whether it's mythological. You know, this is a dance style and that's really how I hope it will be seen. And yet it's still different. I don't want to ever lose sight of that. But I think it's naturally different anyway. There's always a dynamic within cultures to change, but retain something unique. (May 1996)

Perhaps what is most striking about Padma Menon as an interviewee is the extent to which she has thought about her art form as something that combines body and mind. As well as having a strongly developed kinetic intelligence, she is highly educated in an academic sense and has a mind that never stands still. A concern that she expressed about having her interviews published was that what she had recorded was out of date. Her thinking had moved on—'so many new issues and quests'. She was anxious to stress that what is published represents simply a moment in her career.

Choreography by Padma Menon

1992	*Parijatham* (includes choreography by Vempati Chinna Satyam)	Independent work
1993	*Siva—The Cosmic Dancer* (includes choreography by Vempati Chinna Satyam)	Independent work
1994	*Chandalika* (includes choreography by Vempati Chinna Satyam)	Kailash Dance Company
1995	*Relations*	Kailash Dance Company
	Ramayana—A Mother Speaks	Kailash Dance Company
1996	*Rasa* (with Meryl Tankard)	Meryl Tankard Australian Dance Theatre, Adelaide Festival
	Agni	Padma Menon Dance Theatre

Numerous shorter works and solo seasons for festivals in India between 1984 and 1989 and in Canberra from 1990, including *Haara—A Garland of Pearls* (1993) and *In Praise* (1996)

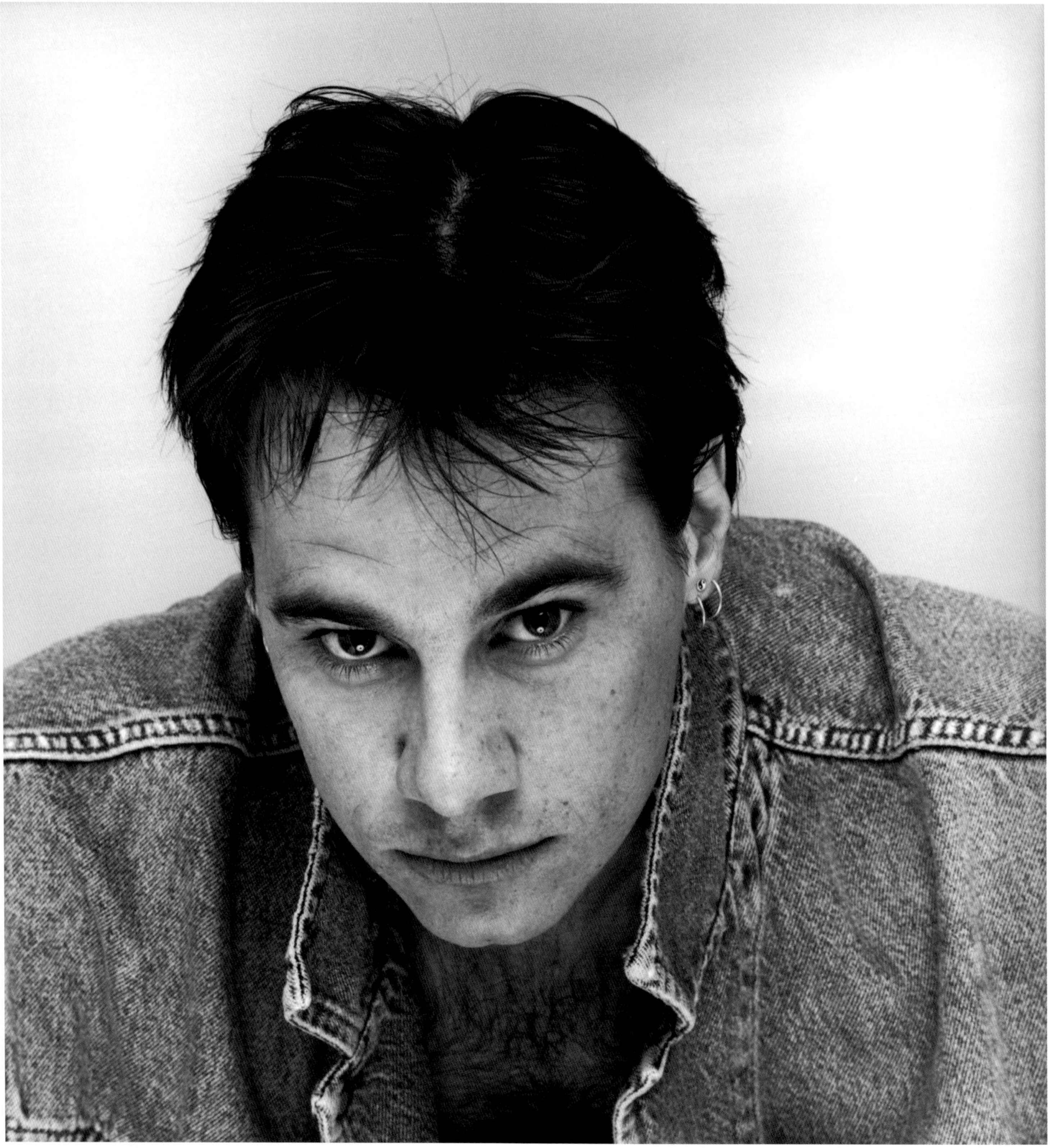

Paul Mercurio

Wild Card

Interview TRC 3395

Paul Mercurio (born 1963), independent dancer, actor and director, was interviewed in Sydney by Michelle Potter in January 1996

Paul Mercurio rocketed to stardom, although he would prefer to call it notoriety, when in 1992 the film *Strictly Ballroom* became a major box-office success in Australia and around the world. Mercurio played the leading role of Scott Hastings, champion ballroom dancer who defied the rules of the governing body, the Federation, to dance his own steps. Mercurio had no previous ballroom dancing training before taking on his role in *Strictly Ballroom*, and none either in the flamenco dance technique that he also needed to perform in the film. He had, however, danced since 1982 with Sydney Dance Company. He had also choreographed a number of pieces for Sydney Dance Company and was by no means unknown to Australian dance audiences before the release of the movie.

Before *Strictly Ballroom* Mercurio had also begun to think about developing his own dance company. It was while on tour to the United States with Sydney Dance Company in 1989—'in a hotel room in Seattle, my daughter had been born and she was 10 days old and I was on tour and away from the family'—that he came up with the name Australian Choreographic Ensemble (ACE), which he eventually gave the company when he established it 1992. His aim with ACE was to bring dance to a new audience not normally exposed to contemporary movement. ACE performed three seasons of pieces by new Australian choreographers, touring these works to various States. Mercurio has also developed, with ACE, an interest in making dance films.

Strictly Ballroom did, however, change Paul Mercurio's life. He was marketed as a star and, while he has no doubts that after *Strictly Ballroom* he was offered unprecedented opportunities, he also suggests that his new status as 'the next Mel Gibson' robbed him of some of his choreographic potential.

POTTER: Paul, I would like to begin by asking you about *Strictly Ballroom*. I'm really interested to know what the circumstances were that led up to your being given the role of Scott Hastings.

MERCURIO: Okay, that's an easy one. I know how to answer this question! The way it happened was Baz Luhrmann, the director, originally approached me to *contribute*—please witness the word 'contribute'—some choreography to the project. John O'Connell was the choreographer of *Strictly Ballroom*, and they were interested in me contributing some contemporary style choreography for Scott, kind of his own steps. So Baz came along and had a bit of a chat and spoke about the film, spoke about his interest. I obviously said I was interested. He came along to a performance of *Cafe*, which I had co-choreographed with Kim Walker for Sydney Dance Company in 1989. He watched that performance and, as I said, we spoke about it and then pretty much left it alone. I think it was about a year later from that initial discussion—my dates might be incorrect—he rang me up and said, 'Paul, I've finally got the money to make the film and, in fact, I would like you to come along and do an audition for the lead role.' And in retrospect Baz has said to me that he'd come along and started to watch me not as a choreographer but actually as a dancer and a performer.

I went along and did an audition. I didn't learn my lines and I was a very typical dancer—dancers are very blinkered in dance; they don't kind of do much else really. So I came fairly unprepared for the audition, but there was no problem.

I learnt my lines fairly quickly and impro-ed and danced and did all that kind of stuff. John O'Connell choreographed some ballroom steps and that was fine and Baz seemed to be impressed. He said to me, 'You know, even if you don't get this role, you should think about a career in film or whatever because there was a natural ability.'

So that was that. Then six months after that audition he rang me up and said, 'Paul, everything's going ahead. I actually would like you to play the role, but come in and do another screen test.' So I did that and the producers were not sure. The producers were concerned that I would look too old to play Scott Hastings—I think in the script he was 18. So they changed the age in the script to 21, gave me a haircut, I shaved, dressed me up in a tuxedo and we did a couple more testings and he gave me the role.

POTTER: This was your first film role, wasn't it?

MERCURIO: Absolutely—well, actually I'm lying if I say absolutely first film role, but that's what I tell everyone. Back in Perth when I was a ballet and drama student I did appear in, I think, two short films—two very experimental kind of films. I don't think they saw the light of day; I think they were just people wanting to have a play and try and make a movie. Again, I was probably 14 or 15 at that stage. So, you know, I do think of *Strictly Ballroom* as not the first time I was in front of a camera, but certainly the first time I was acting in a really professional and kind of true level.

POTTER: How did you cope with that very different—well, I assume it's a very different—style of working from working in a dance company?

MERCURIO: I never looked at it as being too different and, in fact, I remember about a week into the shoot—we'd rehearsed for a month beforehand—I suddenly stopped and went, 'Oh, wow, I'm acting.' It dawned on me what I was doing—you know, making a movie and being an actor and all that kind of thing. Making a film is much like making a ballet. Obviously they're very different mediums, but they still require an incredible amount of concentration and discipline. There's a certain amount of boredom and pain involved and there's also a certain amount of joy and excitement and creativity that goes on.

As I said, they're very different forms and the benefits you get from each form are delivered in a different kind of timeframe and on different levels. But I don't look on it as being too different. Obviously *Strictly* was great because I was playing the role of a dancer, which I know incredibly well. So, in a sense, half of the film for me was something that was very real, although I hate ballroom dancing—it's not my cup of tea!—so that was a different sort of environment. But the politics of the dance world is the same as the politics of any dance world, any company anywhere. So 50 per cent of it was pretty much what I'd done every day for the last 20 years. The acting side, the discipline of standing in front of the camera, of learning the lines, of rehearsing, of dealing with other actors, that was new and very challenging. I suppose I like a challenge and I like to take a risk, so again I just found it a very positive experience, as opposed to a daunting one.

POTTER: How difficult was it taking on a totally different technique? You said you hated ballroom dancing. And there was quite a lot of flamenco work in it too.

MERCURIO: Thankfully. Obviously I liked the flamenco much more. I've always danced from passion and emotion. You know, for me dance is abstract. I don't understand dance. When I go and see a ballet I think, 'What the hell does that mean?' The only way you can really appeal to anyone is not on an intellectual level, as far as I'm concerned—and this is my bent. Post-modernism is based at an intellectual level and that's not my cup of tea either. For me, dance—and performance in dance—is an emotional journey. Flamenco is all about passion and emotion and *anger* and *fire* and *lust* and all those things, and that's how you get when you dance it and think about it and watch it. Ballroom, however, is all about winning, and it's a blood sport. I don't doubt that people dance it with conviction and passion, but it's not an art form, it's a sport. I mean, they classify it as a dance sport and it really is about winning, and it's who can smile the best and who has the best breasts and who goes and pays for lessons with what judge. You know, it's very political.

And it always frustrated me because, as I was learning some of the ballroom steps, my teacher, he would always be like, 'No, Paul. Paul, head's meant to be up here. Don't look at the girl, don't do this, don't do that' and I was forever wanting to dance it, emotionalise it. I found it very frustrating. But much to my annoyance I must admit that I did enjoy some parts of it. Like any technique, when you start to understand it and excel at it, or even feel comfortable with it, that's a nice feeling. But I just wanted to dance it from the heart, and that's what Scott wanted too, so I suppose I was perfectly cast in that sense. But I watch ballroom in the same way that I watch Olympic ice-skating—it's not from the heart, it's about can you do your triple twist; it misses the point. But then I'm an artist and dance sport—and ice-skating sport—is not necessarily done for art, it's done for other reasons: winning, competitions, trophies.

POTTER: Did you find the flamenco technique difficult? Even though you said you enjoyed the emotional aspect, what about the actual technique?

MERCURIO: I found the ballroom technique difficult; I found the flamenco technique difficult. It's a different way of counting, it's a different way of feeling, it's a different way of understanding the steps. You know, change is a difficult thing to comprehend and when you don't want to change, it's even worse. Especially with the ballroom I didn't want to like it and I didn't want to do it, and so I found it more difficult to grasp because I was fighting it. Flamenco I loved, but again it's a very different form of dance and, although I had the natural aptitude for the emotional content or the emotional fire that is required, which helped me pull through some of the more difficult technical aspects, again it's a change of training. Dance is about body memory and it takes quite a while to unlearn, untrain the body from what you're used to and to make the new technique a habit. It takes time, it's a muscle thing, it's a muscle memory thing, not just an emotional or an intellectual thing.

POTTER: Did you identify with Scott?

MERCURIO: Well, when Baz approached me to play Scott, and indeed when I started playing Scott, I had been dancing with the Sydney Dance Company for quite a few years—eight years, I think—and I was getting a little bit tired of being with the company inasmuch as *I* really wanted to dance my own steps, I wanted to create my own ballets. The Dance Company, Graeme Murphy, Janet Vernon, had been fairly supportive, and I think as possibly supportive as parents can be—I was living in their house—and they gave me opportunities to choreograph. But I wanted more. I wanted to really explore my steps and my ideas, and I suppose they gave me as much opportunity as they felt they could. And like any child you think, 'Oh, Mum and Dad don't give me the keys to the car enough.' You know, very much on that basis.

We started shooting *Strictly* in '91 but, ever since 1989, I'd really been planning to start my company. I'd been developing the idea of becoming a choreographer, a director of a company, of dancing my own steps, of finding that freedom, and also of creating a company that allowed other people that freedom. So in that sense I identified very much with Scott, who wanted to dance his own steps. I was a little bit further along in terms of evolution. I wasn't a victim of the political circumstances of the ballroom world or of the Sydney Dance Company or whatever. I was in the process of developing my ideas and my dreams, understanding where my steps came from and trying to fulfil the desires and the needs and the wants of my own self but also, I hoped, the Australian dance community. I think there was a lot of identification but, as I said, I was just a little bit further moved on than Scott.

POTTER: Did *Strictly Ballroom* change your life?

MERCURIO: Yes. I think all the changes have been very beneficial, but there's a downside and negative issues involved. Before *Strictly* came out I actually left the Dance Company and started my own ballet company and that, obviously, was quite a change. Sometimes I feel a little bit the conflict between doing the PR schedule of *Strictly* and trying to have my own company affected in a negative way my ability to be a director and a choreographer. It took me away from the company more than was healthy for it perhaps. So, in some ways I feel that's unfinished business— I never really fulfilled my ability or my dreams perhaps. No, I take that back. I *did* fulfil the dreams but not to the potential that I knew I could.

But *Strictly* threw me into international stardom and all that kind of crap that goes on. All of a sudden I was the next Mel Gibson and a sex symbol and all that silliness, which is just really a sales device. I think I understand, and understood then, that the whole deal really was I was a salesman and if they wanted to say the salesman was a sex symbol or the next Mel Gibson, that was just part of the parcel, even if I didn't necessarily agree or like it that much. You know, an actor is not just someone who turns up on set and acts out dialogue or a role; an actor is also someone that goes and

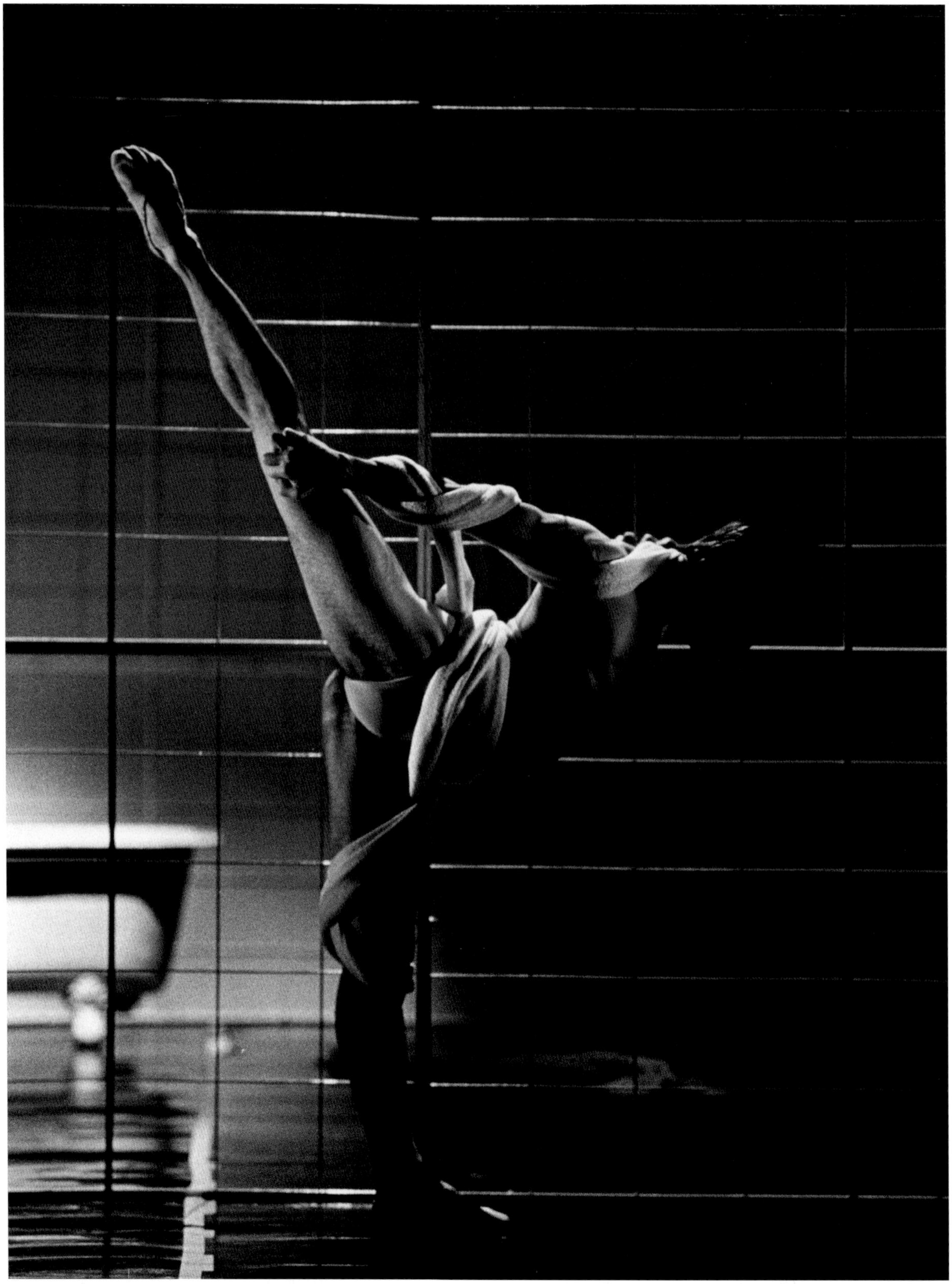

promotes a movie and develops and does all of those things. I think being thrown into the international kind of light was wonderful because it's brought me and afforded me a lot of opportunities to continue acting, to do various roles. It was all very unexpected and my wife and I had to run to keep up and really comprehend what was going on. Not that I thought *Strictly wouldn't* be successful, but you can't expect what happens when something is successful within the film world. It's a very different kettle of fish, it's a very different life experience.

POTTER: What's the position of your company, ACE? Does it still exist?

MERCURIO: Yes. It exists. I've just been doing budgets this morning. I'm going to make a short dance film, a 10-minute dance film. I got some money from the New South Wales Ministry for the Arts, so I'm in the process of starting to actually put into motion making this short film. ACE works when it can work, pretty much. There was always a conflict between Paul Mercurio the actor and the star—and all this crap which kind of annoys me to some extent—and Paul Mercurio the choreographer/dancer. There's two personalities. And then, of course, there's Paul Mercurio the bloke at home. There's all these kind of images that people want fulfilled. Yes, so I'm about to do a work, late March I hope to shoot it. It's a work I choreographed about three or four years ago—again, that was experimental and I want to go back to and finish it in a sense. And I'm using the profile that Paul Mercurio the star has to pull in a great group of people and make a little dance movie so that Paul Mercurio the dancer/choreographer can continue to spread the word of dance throughout the community. The lucky thing is that someone with international notoriety can sell that to Channel 4 and whatever; it's a nice kind of lever, I suppose.

It's a piece called *Emotional Disconnection* that I did for stage. It had roller-blading and tapping and singing and what not; I'll get rid of the roller-blading and tapping. You know, it works very well as a stage piece—it works *very* well actually; it's a nice little piece—but I can see how by putting it on film and taking it into locations and using some of the medium and the miracles, not special techniques or anything, but just the fact of taking two people and sticking them in a different environment can add a little bit more appeal. When it's on stage you can identify to a point, but film tends to pinpoint more. For instance, if two people are dancing at home in the kitchen, it suggests a whole lot of domestic ideas and relationship values, but sitting on a bare stage, it's got to be more abstract, because you can't suggest those ideas of a kitchen or domesticity or whatever with setting, unless you've got a lot of money. So I'm taking a stage piece and making it a film piece.

POTTER: Are you interested in the idea that film is a much more permanent medium than dance on stage?

MERCURIO: I *love* the idea that it's permanent. I spent my time doing 13-week seasons, eight shows a week of the same show and then taking it on tour and then taking it elsewhere. I was thoroughly burnt out after doing some ballets, and I hated the fact that we'd do them year in, year out. As an artist it was murder, suicide. I like in film that you do a work and it's there. You know, shooting *Strictly* or any movie, you might do a scene 10 times and you get sick of doing it 10 times, but you only do it 10 times in the one day; you don't do it month in, month out for three or four years.

I've actually been offered a lot of stage work and I've said no to all of it, because I really can't bear the thought of doing a three- or six-month run of the same show eight shows a week. I've done that, I suppose. I like the fact that you can do something new on film and it lives, and while it's showing you can be doing something else new. So you're stretching yourself. I'm growing with each new thing and it doesn't take four years to do one or two new things.

The whole thing is that I can't dance forever. You know, part of the pain of being a dancer is something that none of us understands. At the end of the career we want to keep going but we can't. I was lucky that, in the time where I was wanting to make a transition, *Strictly* came along and it's afforded me a fantastic opportunity to continue talking to people on a much broader basis. I can still contribute ideas and things that I think are important. I can still use the device of dance, but also I don't doubt that there is the day when I won't dance anymore. People are always saying, 'Oh, we want to see you back on stage' and sometimes I think they're confused with saying, 'I want to see Scott Hastings again. I want to see *Strictly* again. I want to see *Some Rooms* or *After Venice* again.' And there's also the other side of it. People get disappointed because I'm not the youth I used to be, I'm not playing the role they liked me in. There's all those kind of pressures as well. You know, after *Strictly* came out, it was hard being a dancer because people were coming along to see Scott and I was Paul, and I was doing very contemporary work. It wasn't necessarily what they wanted. We drew a good audience in, and educated people to something that they weren't expecting to see but there was also that pressure of not disappointing people. That's kind of a hard one at times.

POTTER: This seems an appropriate time to ask you about Sydney Dance Company because you brought up some of probably your best-known roles in *After Venice* and *Some Rooms*. What did you learn from Sydney Dance?

MERCURIO: Oh, I grew up, I learnt to be a dancer. I suppose I had the opportunity to develop my ideas as a choreographer. I had a great time, saw the world, met my wife, had some great friends. I think I was very lucky that when I was with the Dance Company, it was a very strong company and we did some *amazing* works and we did some amazing tours and we made an impact. That, I suppose, is always important. But I can also see that things go in cycles, or ebb and flow. I suppose I'm now talking in hindsight rather than what I learnt on the day. Those impacts will last forever but perhaps only in my mind or perhaps in an audience's mind for back then. You're so full of trying to do something for someone and when you do it it's terrific, but you can't hang on to it, it just keeps moving on. I suppose I've seen that and learnt that and understood the fact of going on and seen too many people that haven't been able to go on and perhaps wrecked themselves or their lives. Not specifically in Sydney Dance Company, but just performers in general. What else did I learn? Teamwork, some sort of discipline, I suppose. I've always been kind of undisciplined really, a bit of a wild card, very committed and very disciplined in my own way, but it doesn't necessarily fit into what the idea of discipline is, I suppose.

POTTER: Audiences who saw Sydney Dance in that particular period do remember you for particular roles. Do you have roles that you thought you were particularly suited to and performed particularly well?

MERCURIO: Well, I think I performed them all well!

I was overseas. I left the company and bummed around for eight months overseas backpacking, you know, hitchhiking and looking at companies. Graeme (Murphy) rang me and said he wanted me to come back and play the lead in *Shéhérazade*, which he was redoing. I said, 'Okay, great, that would be terrific because I haven't got a job here and I need some money. I've decided I want to come back and live in Australia and I'd be happy to come back to the Dance Company.' Of course, I came back and he didn't give me the lead role. He made me sit on a box—a perspex box—for the whole ballet, which was half an hour long. I was never angry about it. I mean, I was a bit miffed that that was what happened. He didn't say, 'I'm sorry' or this or that, but at the same time I sat on that box like no-one else did—I was brilliant at it. I had pride in the fact that I was communicating and being part of a team that was communicating an idea.

That's part of the teamwork and that's part of what's important, I think. It is all teamwork and all this film star business gets me riled sometimes. Just because I'm the lead and I'm on the poster, I couldn't make it without everyone else—from the caterer to the laundry to everybody—you just can't make it. And you can't make a ballet, you can't make an idea, you can't express anything to an audience without a total canvas. Being part of that canvas is such an important role. And I think I try to approach most things like that. I can't say I always did because sometimes my ego would get in the way, or my anger or my boredom or my lack of discipline or whatever, but that was something I always tried to work at.

I suppose the favourite ballet for me, apart from the ones I choreograph myself, was *King Roger* and mainly because I had long hair and a goatee and I played an old man—not an *old* man, but I played a wise, matured man. I wasn't playing Tadzio in *After Venice*, some young boy that a woman or a man lusted after or whatever. I was playing this mature Arab kind of bloke that advised the king. That, I suppose, was the most fulfilling role I ever played because it gave me an opportunity to act. It wasn't the lead role, but in a sense I made it a very important kind of role. It was just really fulfilling, you know, at that stage of my life as well, I suppose.

Mercurio was born in Swan Hill, Victoria in 1963, the second child of four. While his boxer–actor father continued to live in the eastern States, Mercurio grew up in Perth with his mother and siblings. He began dancing at the age of nine, inspired in part by watching musicals at the Saturday matinee movies. His theatrical interests were nurtured at the John Curtin High School in Perth, which had a small performing arts component as part of its curriculum, although not all of his subsequent training experiences were satisfying. It was in the West, too, that Mercurio got his first choreographic experiences.

POTTER: Can I ask you about your early childhood experiences and your early dance training?

MERCURIO: I had a pretty happy childhood. I was pretty easygoing and all that kind of thing. My sister was actually doing ballet and I decided I wanted to start. There were a whole number of reasons, but I just remember watching an Elvis Presley movie—and I can't remember which one it was—but he was in black and singing and dancing and it was all groovy and flower-power hippies, people kissing and getting spaghetti dumped on their heads. I don't know, whatever it was about that movie and all musicals, Danny Kaye and *Sweet Chariot* and Dean Martin and Jerry Lewis and Gene Kelly, you know, all those people, they were inspiring in those days, and still are now. So I started dancing and my two younger brothers also danced. We all did ballet, tap, jazz, song and dance, you know, the theatre kind of stuff. And then I quit because I was sick of going into a room with a couple of little old grey-haired ladies and having to tell the theory behind what a *tendu* was. That wasn't dance to me, you know, 'Hey, I got a pass with honours because I knew what a *tendu* was.' Dance was about dancing, it wasn't about anything else.

Then I went to a special high school in Perth, because I was living in a rather difficult neighbourhood, Mum being on social security and all that kind of thing. To get out of that neighbourhood, we all went to a special school which had a theatre arts course. So I did drama, theatre, learnt a bit about directing and lighting and sound, and I started dancing again. I got a scholarship with the West Australian Ballet company, a part-time scholarship, and I got out of sport because I'd go and do ballet instead, which was kind of good. Generally the school was fine. They used to stir me and call me 'twinkle toes' and that kind of thing, but it never bothered me too much. Sometimes I was threatened to be beaten up, and every now and then I was, but it never put me off or whatever. I did physics and chemistry and maths and I loved it, but I didn't understand it. You know, I loved the idea of it, and the concept, but whenever I tried to do those kind of chemical equations they never added up. So I think I was always involved in the emotional impact of the experiment but the technical thing just didn't work. So eventually I could see that I was failing in school and I was excelling in dance, so I left school and went to dance and here I am today.

POTTER: Did you get your first opportunities to choreograph in Sydney Dance Company?

MERCURIO: No. When I was a scholarship student with the West Australian Ballet, Steven Heathcote—who's a principal with the Australian Ballet, and a bloody good bloke and my best friend—and I studied together. We used to go into the WA Ballet company and do classes in the evening, and everyone would leave and Steve and I would stay and put on music and dance. I'd choreograph a bit and he would, and we'd muck around. The WA Ballet company was being directed then by Garth Welch and I kind of made sure Garth caught me choreographing a couple of times. They were actually about to do a dancers workshop, you know, where the dancers choreographed. I was 16 or whatever and Garth caught me, as I kind of hoped he would, and said, 'If you'd like to choreograph something, do.' So I did. I choreographed a five-minute piece called *Just Another Poor Boy*. It was sung by Chris de Burgh and it was about the story of Jesus being just another poor boy on the road to life who got crucified for his beliefs. It was performed at the workshop. My mum says when she came to see the opening of that she knew then that she'd lose me to dance. So it was a very important moment for myself and my mum. But that was the first time.

I left Western Australia then and went to the Australian Ballet School and, while I was there, I used to get some of the dancers and choreograph bits and pieces, and again contemporary not classical. I didn't really fit into the Australian Ballet School; I wasn't rebellious as such, I just had other ideas and they couldn't stick me in that classical ballet box. So I think to some extent they were relieved when I decided to leave. I finished the year, not that I turned up a lot. I mean, I'd turn up generally but I could see no point in learning the history of ballet. It wasn't going to make me a better dancer. I didn't understand why no-one taught me how to put on make-up and yet that's such a huge part of what you do. Why don't they train you in theatre? As a dancer, you should be trained in theatre, voice work. Things just are missing and at that age obviously I didn't know what was missing, but I just didn't fit in because I had other ideas.

POTTER: I want to ask you about the pieces you choreographed later for Sydney Dance Company. I'm especially interested in two that you did in collaboration with another choreographer, *In the Company of Wo/Men* and *Cafe*. How does that work? How do you balance your ideas and someone else's?

MERCURIO: That's tough. Kim Walker and myself did *Cafe*. I don't want to tread on anyone's toes, but I think Kim would agree that *Cafe* was kind of my idea inasmuch as I used to live or hang out in a cafe called Reggio's in Darlinghurst. When I first went to Sydney, that was really where I lived. I used to go down there and write poetry and there were prostitutes and drug addicts and street people and I used to hang out with them. We were all a bit lost, you know. It was family and you could go there and play pinball and drink coffee and talk. Or you could read a book, or write, or be left alone. I'd still go home, and it was a lonely place at home, because that's the period of life that was going on. Kim used to come down. He certainly didn't go there quite as much as I did, but sometimes we'd wag class and go surfing and then go to Reggio's for a coffee and then go to the rehearsals and things like that.

But I always wanted to make a ballet about it, about the cafe. I think Graeme was taking a year off. I'd just done *Waiting*, which was the first professional work I'd done for the company. We'd done a couple of experimental kind of dance workshop seasons and things like that and out of that Graeme asked if I'd like to do a work. I'm glad he did because I would have left the company if he hadn't. I was kind of getting that 'I want to do my own steps, bugger the Federation' feeling. *Waiting* had a very good reception and was performed at the Opera House with two New York choreographers and the work by Graeme. It held its own, so I was very pleased and proud of that. Graeme then offered the opportunity for Kim and I to do a work together and put it on at a small venue in Sydney. Kim and I pretty much sat down and said, 'Well, what do you want to do?' and I said, 'Well, Kim, I've always wanted to do a work about Reggio's.' And he said, 'Great idea.' He knew it, I knew it, so we went about doing it. All the characters in the cafe were people that we knew, actually except for one, one character. The good thing about *Cafe* is that Kim and I would go, 'Right, I really want to do this piece about the smack addict, his girlfriend and the guy that cares about the girl and helps.' Kim would go, 'Okay, I really want to do the pinball piece.' So, off we'd go and there was never a problem. It was good, we really shared the vision and I was very pleased with the work; it went well.

In the Company of Wo/Men was a bit different because the idea was more Graeme's, and I suppose in all honesty—and I've never said this to Graeme, and so I suppose it's going to be on tape forever—it wasn't as shared as *Cafe*. Graeme had his vision and I had to kind of fit in with that a bit more than I liked, which made it difficult. In fact, there was a section where Graeme said, 'You go and choreograph this' and I didn't want to—it wasn't something I saw, felt, needed, wanted, all that kind of thing. So with Graeme it was more of a struggle, and I suppose that's understandable because Graeme's older and he's more set in his ways, more famous, much more prolific in experience than I was, and I suppose it's hard for him to give over the reins as completely as Kim and I did with each other because we were, in a sense, equals. So *Company of Wo/Men* wasn't as successful in terms of my own fulfilment, nor as a work—and I think that's part of the reason. But still a very valid and valuable experience.

POTTER: When you go into a studio to choreograph a new piece, what do you do?

MERCURIO: Well, it depends, because I've done it a couple of different ways. In the early days I used to storyboard it; like when I first started doing things for Sydney Dance Company such as the *Risks* workshop, when I did *Still Life*. It was very informal. There were a few pieces of music I loved and I was forever thinking, 'I love this music, what can I do to it?'

Eventually I came up with an idea and then I drew little pictures and drew the whole ballet out. If it's a five-minute piece, it's all right, but when it's a long piece you're in big trouble. So I'd come prepared into a studio and go, 'Right, this is what I've seen. There's this lift that goes into that.' It's kind of already drawn on paper and in my head and it's pretty much a matter of seeing, once I've got the bodies, if it works.

I've always kind of prepared anyway. I mean, you listen to the music and you hear the beat and the rhythms and you know what you want to say, and so you go in saying, 'Right, today's about two guys having an argument here and here. I want to bring this kind of sensitivity and I want to try and take the audience on that kind of a journey, so let's try moving like this.' And you kind of put it together. I've also choreographed without music and then put music to it later, and that's hard. I think choreography's supposed to go with music, unless of course the music is silence and then that's a very different thing. I mean, I've done pieces that are completely silent. The silence is music in itself and you use that as an accent.

So, you know, you can do it any way you want and that's very much circumstance and how you want to work. Sometimes the music, if you're getting it composed, is not ready when you want to start. So you choreograph and you say to the composer, 'Well, 21 bars in, counting sixes, on the sixth six and the twelfth six and the thirteenth, fourteenth and twentieth sixth I need these beats.' Then the composer comes back a week later with all the beats on the fifth, ninth and twelfth, which is completely not what you choreographed, and you've got to make the best of it. You know, there's all those kinds of situations that go on. But again I prefer to work with hearing music that moves me, putting an idea to it and creating a ballet, or having an idea that moves me and finding the music that supports it and then create a ballet; they're the two ways that I prefer to work.

POTTER: Where do you get your vocabulary, your movement vocabulary from?

MERCURIO: Buggered if I know. It's the one thing that my notoriety (I prefer to call it notoriety) robbed me of—the opportunity to really find out what my vocabulary could be, and to what extent and to really develop it. I don't think I have ever really got to a point where I was really strongly developing my style and my vocabulary, heck. And, you know, I allowed it to happen. Movies are more lucrative, and that's just the way it went. No doubt with some of the plans I have coming up I shall be tested very, very thoroughly—excruciatingly—in terms of broadening my vocabulary and creating it and making sure there is one there. But, you know, you just close your eyes and you feel and it comes out; that's the idea, really, for me.

If Mercurio is reflective about his own career, and the effects of circumstance upon it, he is also reflective, passionately so, about the future of dancers in general. As for his own future, Mercurio, like Scott Hastings, is forever dreaming, in the most positive way possible, about doing his own steps.

POTTER: You've made some comments during the interview about dance training and the future of dancers. Do you just want to elaborate a little bit?

MERCURIO: I suppose the thing that gets me is that dancers—probably dancers and gymnasts—start their training very young, and they start to destroy their bodies very young. They're surrounded by people that tell them how to destroy their bodies, but don't tell them how to continue living, or how to construct a life after they've destroyed their bodies. It's just so unfair and so common that, once you're destroyed, people just don't give a shit, you know. I've seen too many people that have to struggle and really go through a lot of struggle to find out who they are, where they are and what they're going to do next.

And there is a big kick now for dancer transition programs and stuff like that, but there's never going to be enough money or support. Where it needs to start is at the very basic training levels—how to do make-up, how to act, how to balance a cheque book and how to take care of your life after dance. I'm 32 and I've been in the industry 24 years and if I'd been in any other industry for 24 years, I'd be 54 or whatever and I'd be on a retirement package and this and that. But as a dancer, you know, too many careers are over by mid-twenties and there's no-one there that really cares. Or there are people now that are starting to care, but for too long people have just been left. It requires a lot of change but I think it requires it at the schooling, the education level.

What's the point of going through school years and not knowing how to put in a tax form? I know we're not talking dance but we're talking life. I mean, what's the point of going through all those years at school and not learning how to take care of your own personal finances, and some things that are very basic in the dance world—things like make-up or preventative medicine for injuries? Diet—as long as the girls are thin and eating chocolate bars, it's all right—but they never really teach people how to eat properly or how to balance the body through vitamins or carbohydrates. You know, all those things are really about promoting long-term health, which can only be of benefit financially to any company with less injuries occurring and that kind of thing. But they're just not taught.

POTTER: What's Paul Mercurio's aspiration for the future?

MERCURIO: Oh, a positive one. The thing is, I've had such a large upheaval in the last few years with *Strictly Ballroom*—just with the whole way my life has all of a sudden changed. You know, it wasn't until late in my dance career that I decided I'd become a choreographer—no, I always wanted to be a choreographer from early on. But I decided to become a director of my company because that was the way I could continue choreographing and doing things that I thought were important, rather than doing someone else's ballet whose concept or whatever wasn't what I felt or thought. Not to say it wasn't important, it's just the way I perceived it.

You know, when *Strictly* came along, I was thinking about getting into film and things like that. My father is in film and television and it was something I always thought about doing, but I had the old dance blinkers on. So theatre and film was something I always thought about but never actively pursued. *Strictly* pretty much threw that all up in the air. And it's very hard, when you've got a '9 to 5' job in the dance world, you know what you're doing year by year. The thing with film is you never know what you're doing, and even when someone says, 'I'm definitely doing this film and you're in it,' that's not definite until you've actually finished making it.

So I must admit to being in a bit of upheaval, not really knowing. There's no definite security, there's just dreams, hopes, aspirations, and so I say hopefully the most important thing for me is just to stay positive. I believe in creating your own reality. You need to do that in association with other people that are like-minded, and hopefully if you stay positive and, you know, like attracts like and you'll attract the right projects and the right people, and that's what I'm going to do for the rest of my life. One hopes that it will work out and I'm sure there will be tough times and I'm sure there will be very positive and wonderful times. I suppose that's about the most definite I can get. What I'm going to do day by day I have to find out when I wake up.

I've got dreams. I mean, follow your dreams, that's the main thing. And I've also learnt in the past couple of years no-one's going to do it. I've had some nice ideas and I've thought, jeez, wouldn't it be good if someone did that. I've realised that that someone has got to be me. So I've got a team of people that I work with, and that's why I'm about to make my own dance film and that's why I've written my own feature film. Hopefully I'll continue on doing that and developing great projects, and eventually I'll produce and direct great movies and act in them. And by the time I hit 50, I'll have my own little brew pub somewhere on the coast where I can just enjoy my grandchildren or something, I don't know, write books. But embrace change with positivity. That's all I can say.

Paul Mercurio arrived for this interview, slightly late, on his beloved Suzuki motorcycle, mobile phone in hand, and anxious about the imminent arrival of his third child. We talked first about how to describe his current multi-faceted occupational activities and he opted for 'general all-round nice bloke'. He was. And the oral version of the interview resounds with a kind of leisurely, but direct, openness. When answering my question about what roles he felt he performed well, he replied: 'I performed them all well!' But there was nothing arrogant about this answer, just a larrikin, tongue-in-cheek sense of humour.

Choreography by Paul Mercurio

1980	*Just Another Poor Boy*	West Australian Ballet Choreographic Workshop
1983	*Still Life*	*Risks* Workshop, Sydney Dance Company
1986	*There's Always Time, Always Space*	Time Theatre
1987	*Duo for Two Boys*	*Risks* Workshop, Sydney Dance Company
	Two Men and One Woman	*Risks* Workshop, Sydney Dance Company
1989	*Dancing with I*	Sydney Dance Company
	Waiting	Sydney Dance Company
	Cafe (with Kim Walker)	Sydney Dance Company
1990	*In the Company of Wo/Men* (with Graeme Murphy)	Sydney Dance Company
1991	*Emotional Disconnection*	Dance Collection
	A Moment of Choice	National Capital Dancers
	Looking for Rhythm	Nepean Dance
1992	*Edgeing*	Sydney Dance Company
	Envy	*Seven Deadly Sins*, ABC-TV
	Contact	Australian Choreographic Ensemble
1993	*Imprint* (with Stephen Page, Jan Pinkerton and Carolyn Hammer)	Australian Choreographic Ensemble
1996	*dancing with the clown*	Sydney Dance Company
	Master Plan	Sydney Dance Company
	Spilt Milk (short film)	Feel Good Films

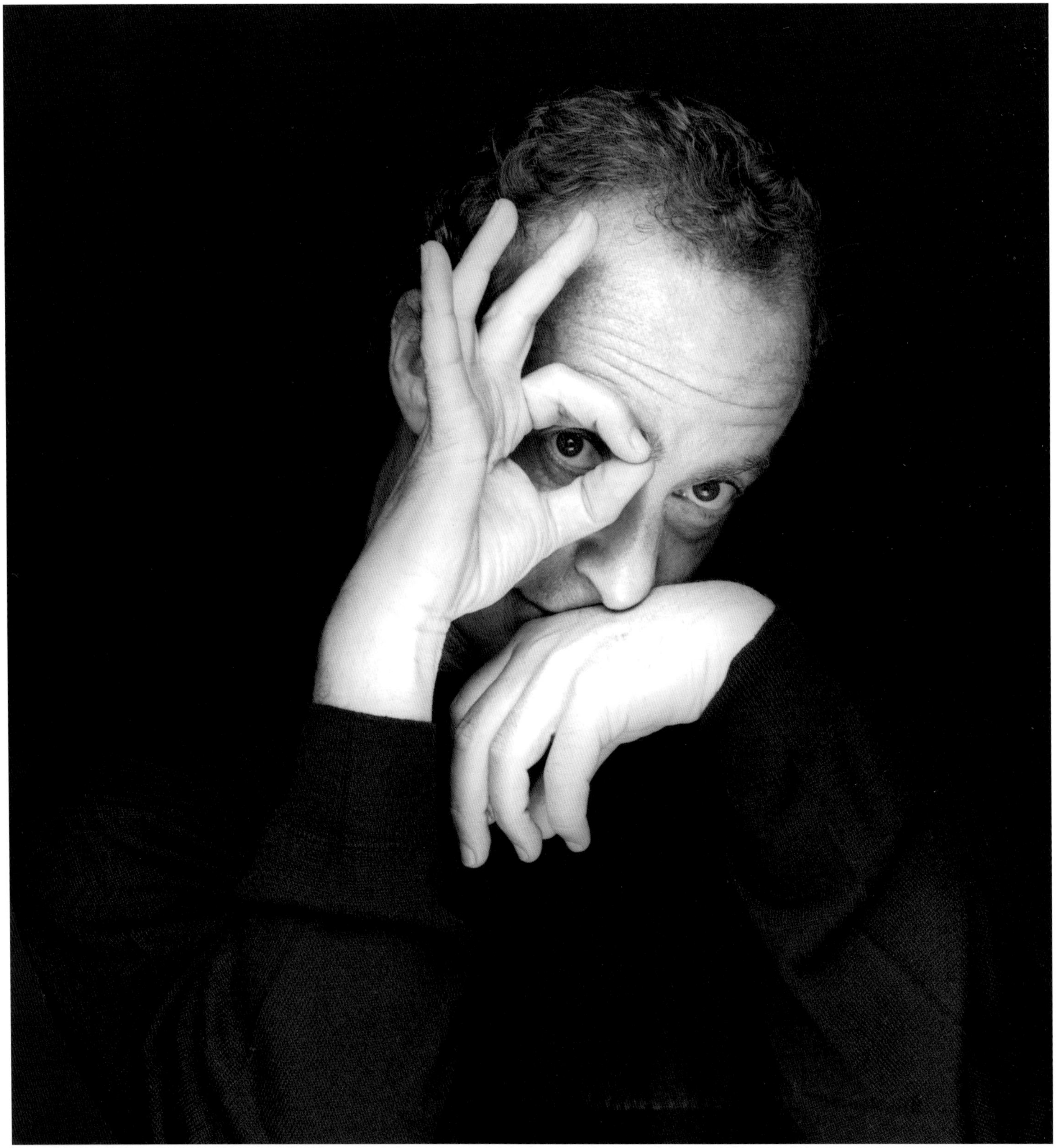

Graeme Murphy

Humanity Revealed

Interviews deB 1222–1223, TRC 2680 and TRC 3478

Graeme Murphy, AM (born 1950), artistic director of Sydney Dance Company, was interviewed in Sydney by Hazel de Berg in April 1981, by Shirley McKechnie in May 1990 and by Michelle Potter in August 1996

With a prodigious body of work to his credit, and with a public profile that extends beyond the boundaries of a narrow dance community, Graeme Murphy is arguably Australia's best-known choreographer. His work, created over more than 20 years, spans both narrative and abstract modes. It is sometimes large-scale and commercially popular, and other times rewardingly intimate. But it has always emerged from Murphy's highly developed theatrical and collaborative sensibility, and constantly and diversely draws its inspiration from notions of what it is to be human.

In 1996 Murphy celebrated 20 years as artistic director of Sydney Dance Company. He was appointed director of what was then called the Dance Company (NSW) at the end of 1976, changed the company's name to Sydney Dance Company in 1979, brought it in 1983 through a serious financial crisis that had it on the brink of receivership, and went on to develop it as a major, choreographer-led contemporary dance company. With his associate artistic director, Janet Vernon, Murphy has nurtured the work of other Australian choreographers, including dancers from within his own company. He has also sought out leading international choreographers to create and remount works for Sydney Dance Company. More recently, he has developed entrepreneurial initiatives that have brought contemporary companies from overseas to perform in Australia, endeavours which he sees as part of a process of audience enrichment—'of giving people choices'.

As a creator, his own work has not been made exclusively for Sydney Dance Company. He has been commissioned by a diverse collection of companies and individuals, from the Australian Ballet to the world-champion ice-skating duo of Jayne Torvill and Christopher Dean. He also has major credits both in Australia and overseas as a choreographer for and director of opera companies.

Murphy was born in Melbourne in 1950 but spent much of his childhood in Tasmania. His parents were both schoolteachers and were transferred frequently to various small towns in that State, including Meander, after which Murphy named a piece he made for the Australian Ballet in 1984, and Mathinna, which featured in *Astonish Me: Graeme Murphy Choreographer*, a television documentary made in 1989. Murphy speaks fondly about his childhood, and especially about his sister and her influence on his creativity—'life was a huge adventure because of Diane'. He began his dance training in Tasmania with Kenneth Gillespie, travelling long distances to Launceston each week for his classes. After successfully auditioning for the Australian Ballet School at the very young age of 14, he spent 2½ years at the School before joining the Australian Ballet in 1968. Murphy left the company after being inspired by the wealth of dance outside Australia, first discovered on a tour to America with the Australian Ballet in 1970–71.

MURPHY: Betty and Gerald, my parents, had an older child, my sister Diane. I can remember quite distinctly that my sister was like no other person I'd met. She had the most extraordinarily fertile imagination and her whole existence as a child was to create fantasies. I remember that I must have been the oldest kid in town that still believed in Santa Claus, and that was basically because Diane went to enormous ends to create the illusion. At a time when I was ready to reject Santa Claus, she would do something incredible that would continue this belief—Santa Claus disappearing up the chimney in a flash of red and white. She had the most wonderful sense of adventure and the ability to make the most common event into adventure. I'm sure that's had an enormous influence on the fact that I love the bizarre. I love things that have little to do with reality. I love pushing situations in dance that go beyond reality. And yet, eventually, by pushing something far enough, I find it will come back to reality with a new sort of truth. I like to extend things beyond, and I'm sure my sister, who was quite, quite mad and quite unique in her way of thinking, had an enormous influence on my creative ability. And though she herself was never interested in dance—she would paint and she is a very accomplished writer—I think of her often as I'm enduring the creative process. And I must say I smile quite often when I do think of her. (April 1981)

MCKECHNIE: Apart from imaginative adventures with Diane, what other things were important to you as a child?

MURPHY: When I think of the adventures of childhood, I think of Mathinna. It was beautifully evoked in a TV documentary. It captures something of the essence of that little town, and that town itself was an adventure. One had a feeling of danger because of the old, sunken mine-shafts. You threw a pebble in and you waited for what seemed like an eternity before it splashed in the bottom. There were tiddlies in creeks and things like that. I think possibly Diane was bolder than I was, being older, and I think she encouraged my sense of adventuring. Sometimes I still have to force myself to be brave. I often think of her in those things. Sometimes she would be pushing me ahead of her as we wandered through the bush or as we were attacked by plovers. If you went into the paddocks while you were looking for mushrooms, one would swoop down. We always imagined that their spurs were very dangerous. No-one ever got hit but you carried a stick just in case. I have beautiful memories of the bush. My parents had a very close relationship with nature and the bush too. So many things were a huge adventure. (May 1990)

MURPHY: I began my dance training in Tasmania. I think I was 11 or 12. I know I had wanted to dance for a long time, although I wasn't really aware of what dancing actually was. I think I imagined it to be a refined circus act, or perhaps the Follies, which I'd seen and which inspired me incredibly when they did their once-yearly trip to Tasmania. I was living in very much remote Tasmania, a very small town called Mathinna, when I was first permitted to dance. But I can remember having nagged for quite some years prior to that, with not too much success. It was very hard to convince one's parents that dancing was a profession, especially when they were schoolteachers and to them the noblest profession was the teaching profession.

It was a 100-mile trek to go to these classes with Kenneth Gillespie in Launceston, which my parents were fantastic about. I mean, I'm sure they didn't want to really go 100 miles every weekend for my one-hour class, but they were fantastic about it. My sister was at high school, my brother was just a baby and I think that my parents thought, well, in my sister they had someone with great scholastic potential, and then perhaps in my brother they had someone they could guide into the directions that they wanted to, so they were prepared to take a bit of a risk on me. And they did, and I'm most grateful for that risk because, without that risk, I would never have had the potential to get into the Australian Ballet School. I really barely had the basics when I auditioned. I'd indicated, I think, that my—well, it was a near obsession at that stage—was for the dance. I'd indicated it very clearly by getting very bad grades at high school, and by occupying myself basically with the things that I felt were important, which turned out to be my music and recorder lessons and singing in the choir, very badly, and all the activities that I cared about. I think this softened the blow when I finally said, 'Look, I want to audition for the Australian Ballet School.' And they said, 'All right, we'll let you. But if you don't get in, I mean, that's really going to be it. We don't want you to pursue it because if you haven't got the talent to get in ...' I rebelled at this instantly, knowing that the competition for the Australian Ballet School was very tough and that they took 20 each year out of the whole of Australia. I felt my training wouldn't get me in. It was Maggie Scott's (director of the Australian Ballet School, 1964–92) foresight that overlooked the fact that I was green.

Then my father, as if to throw an extra obstacle in my path, said, 'Well, you're not going unless you get a scholarship. We can't afford it.' And I thought, 'Can't afford it! Everyone is made of money, and that's what it's for.' But I'm so glad that he stood out for that because I applied for a scholarship and I worked for a scholarship. And about halfway, or one-third of the way, through my first term a scholarship was forthcoming—the Lady Nathan Scholarship. I think this just reasserted my parents' belief that I would be all right, and they stopped worrying.

So, at the age of 14, I'd successfully auditioned for the Australian Ballet School and I think I was the youngest boy at that stage—or perhaps the youngest person—ever to be taken in, which has its disadvantages, of course. It was quite a social shock to jump from Tasmania to Melbourne and to be thrown into the dance world—and a very exciting one, one that frightened me at the time. But I think the dance obsession overtook it all and it became quite easy. In the second year I was finding myself improving fairly rapidly and aware of improvement, which was exciting. (April 1981)

MCKECHNIE: At the Australian Ballet School, were there any particular issues that were important to you at the time?

MURPHY: I guess the ones that are important to all adolescents—the sexual experiences. But politically? Socially? The social and political aspect of country life was a huge one. My father's position in the town as headmaster was far more than one thing. It wasn't to do with education. It was to do with community events. It was to do with getting the water and getting the road sealed. He was very progressive and an active person in the community. I think a sense of commitment to more than just the immediate necessities became quite a natural thing for me. I don't know, one becomes very self-centred in the early days of one's dance training, and so, I think, a lot of things become the continuing saga of making oneself a more beautiful object in space. And so my energies went very strongly into that. But the influence of music and art and those broader issues were really important to me. I remember listening to music on the radio, on some little primitive transistor radio, in Melbourne when I was first at the School and looking for the unusual music and not being content with what was drab and predictable.

MCKECHNIE: How aware were you of the social changes that were taking place in the sixties?

MURPHY: I was fairly affected by the fact that conscription included me for the Vietnam War. That was a great terror in my life. The terror was not of Vietnam, or of dying, or of being shot, it was of having my career nipped. This was in the early days of being in the Australian Ballet. I remember Ian Spink was going to conscientious objector classes and I was inquiring about things like that because I was terrified that it would be the end of me as a dancer.

In a very minor way, as I'm one of the most drug-free persons you've ever met, I remember the early days of my first joint, which were very sixties things, and trying a cigarette in the back of the Holden, one of those wonderful round Holdens—bright emerald green. Wonderful, wonderful memories. But it was a time of experimentation; it wasn't just the experimentation of the late teens, it was of the times.

We were fashion wise. I remember Paul Saliba setting trends, outrageous trends. But you could be outrageous in those times. The more outrageous, the more fashionable you actually were. A look could be anything and it was the beginning of what I think of as an amalgamation—the quick change of fashion that hasn't stopped since. The sixties made incredibly strong statements, in terms of technology, in terms of clothing, in terms of looks, in terms of optimism. We were little hippie children who believed we could make the world a better place with love and peace and flowers. It's funny because I think the nineties are not very much different. (May 1990)

MURPHY: It was a good time at the Australian Ballet; it was a time of great strength. Peggy van Praagh was a wonderful person to work with. She was a harsh taskmaster and she demanded heaps of the dancers. Sometimes I thought she was quite unkind but, in a way, the way she pushed you was very wise. She would say things like, 'That really isn't good enough' and 'I can't accept that' and threaten to take the

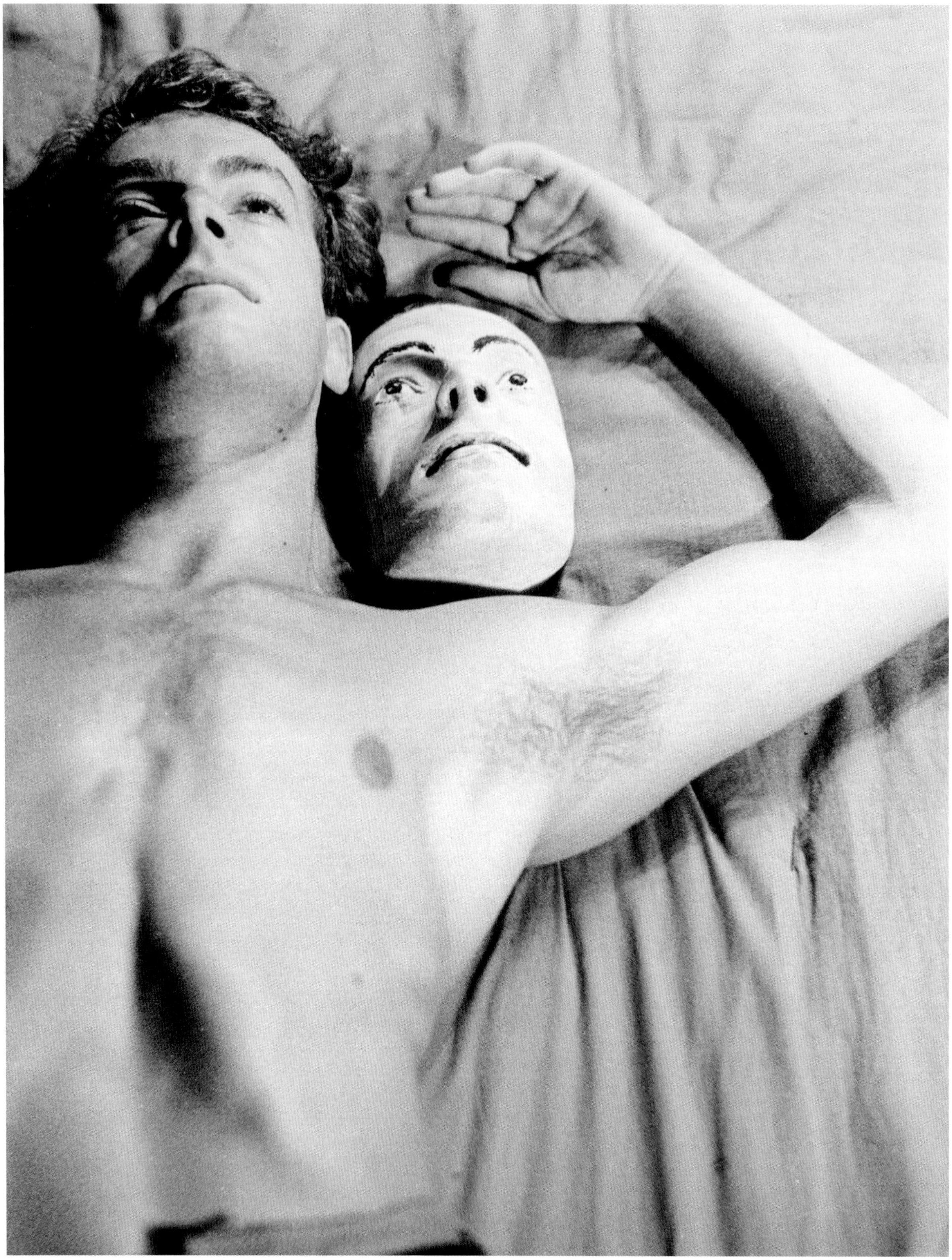

role from you. We all guarded our roles very jealously at that point. There was a fabulous element in the company at that stage. We were very competitive, yet the best of friends.

The American tour (1970–71) was a fantastic high point. It was the first time we, as a group of worldly young men, fully aged 20 or so, got out into the world and saw America for the first time. It brought home to me the fact that there was dance outside Australia and there was another sort of dance that I really knew nothing about. I was able to sneak out to some performances; we had so little time but I managed to see a few performances in New York. I think it was then that I decided that the Australian Ballet wasn't perhaps the beginning and the end of dance and that, I think, is when I swore that I would return. In fact, at the end of that very year I resigned from the company and made plans, with the help of an Australia Council scholarship, to go back to the States and study. (April 1981)

Murphy began to choreograph while he was at the Australian Ballet School and his emerging talent was nurtured during his early years with the Australian Ballet. He also drew inspiration from his connections with French choreographer Félix Blaska in whose Grenoble-based company he and Janet Vernon danced in the early 1970s. Blaska provided Murphy with the kind of creative working atmosphere he felt he had not encountered before—the experience of working in a choreographer-led company. Murphy returned to perform with the Australian Ballet and to be its first resident choreographer in 1976, but not before he and Vernon, having returned from Europe, had spent 1975 freelancing in Australia. It was during 1975 that Murphy's choreographic career began to blossom. His earliest works include *Ecco le diavole*, made as part of an Australian Ballet choreographic workshop in 1971, *Three Conversations* and *Sequenza VII* for the Queensland Ballet in 1975, and *Glimpses*, the winning entry in a 1976 choreographic competition, Ballet '76.

MURPHY: Part of the notation training at the Australian Ballet School was actually having to make up a little *enchaînement*. My notation was very bad; I wasn't one of the diligent. Most of the girls in the class could do very complex things, but I didn't put a great deal of energy or effort into it. I found that creating the *enchaînement* was more interesting than the notating of it. I think there were a few opportunities, tiny little projects that gave me a real clue as to how to link movement and why. I always wanted to do spectacular and different things. I was a bit extreme. But that's the earliest choreographic output, apart from school concerts in Tasmania, that I can remember. Initially it was just part of a school exercise. One did it in a studio and it was finished. (May 1990)

MURPHY: I think it was in my second, or late in my first, year at the Australian Ballet School that Maggie Scott arranged the very first choreographic workshop that I'd ever been involved in, and that had an enormous effect on me. I think that sowed a seed that, some years later when I was in the Australian Ballet, started this whole thing which made me an obsessed choreographer, a person who is forced to create. (April 1981)

MURPHY: Then when I was in the company, Peggy introduced her choreographic workshops. We just did them, after hours, with anyone who was willing to stay back. I worked on *Ecco* after hours. It was interesting because the cast of five was all women and I think that stemmed from the fact that I wasn't a good partner. I think I was probably quite scared of having to tackle partnering and yet the women did some extraordinary things, including lifting, which was very unusual for that period. People were quite uproariously hysterical about the piece. It made people laugh, maybe because it was unexpected in the situation. There was a lot of classical fare coming out of that first choreographic workshop and I don't know why I wasn't in that vein. The basic discipline was fairly classical, but the concept, the feeling, didn't feel like a conventional classical work. And the next work I did was *Off* for Félix Blaska in a similar workshop situation.

MCKECHNIE: You wanted to join Blaska's company after seeing it. Did you already see a possibility of yourself doing a work?

MURPHY: It was very much a one-man company. It was Blaska's company. It bore his name. It bore his stamp.

This was a rare opportunity, this workshop. I think it was something the dancers organised because there were a number of budding choreographers. But having said that, Blaska, by his very example, encouraged us. Just looking at his work made me want to do things. The other aspect, which I think is quite important, is that Blaska used his individuals very much for their qualities. It was a company that created whole new programs. There might have been only one new program every two years and then we toured it. But the works were created on the dancers.

MCKECHNIE: Did he do most of it?

MURPHY: All of it. And he had the most fabulous musicians and live music. We worked with the Labèque sisters constantly. They played for us. Berio too. I met Berio during that period because he created works for Blaska. Blaska, for me, was the first time I'd seen an ensemble company where people were contributing artists in a real way. Prior to that I'd seen the big companies, the big classical companies. I'd never been in a situation where you felt you had a voice. (May 1990)

MURPHY: I think working with Blaska sowed the seeds for the type of company that I have now—one where the dancers have thoughts, have their minds open, have the ability and the right to say, 'I think this, or I think that,' and not one where the dancers are subservient pieces of clay to be modelled by a dominant hand who doesn't want to know what they think. I think the strength and the beauty of Sydney Dance Company is that it's one which runs on a shared respect between dancers, one which also delights in the fact that within the company we are all individuals. We are people that have rights and have thoughts and have different personalities and aren't cloned. We are never required to look the same and to make a perfect row of 18 dancers. We just couldn't do it and we wouldn't want to. (April 1981)

After taking on the directorship of the Dance Company (NSW) in 1976, Murphy's choreographic 'obsession' was able to flourish and thrive. Perhaps the first milestone was his first full-length piece, *Poppy*, which considered aspects of the life and loves of Jean Cocteau and which Murphy has often revived since first making it in 1978. But his manner of discussing any of the pieces he considers to be major ones, including *After Venice*, his meditation on the physical and the metaphysical made in 1984 to Olivier Messiaen's *Turangalila Symphony*, and the abstract work *Kraanerg*, made in 1988 to a score by Iannis Xenakis, reveal him wrestling with the diverse concepts and ideas that are at the heart of his output: making work that is theatrical, the innovative use of narrative in dance, collaborating, developing and nurturing artists, structuring a work so that the ideas are apparent, and building audiences for dance. *Kraanerg* was also a major piece for him because he says it put 'an almighty full-stop to 15 years with the company', and allowed him the space to take a year's sabbatical leave in 1989.

MURPHY: *Poppy*, based on the life and art of Jean Cocteau, was the first full-length Australian ballet with original music, original decor and concept. It was a very exciting project for us and the absolute turning point in Sydney Dance Company's life from the point of view of me being director. The situation prior to *Poppy* was one of a contemporary company—some people would have said a modern company—as some of the dancers were more modern-trained than perhaps widely trained in a number of styles as we are now. This company had done short works basically, and repertory works, and a lot of works by choreographers based overseas. The format of triple bills was very common. The full-length work came as an enormous shock to all of us, but it was something I was determined to try. I felt that Australians, as an audience, would perhaps respond to the theatricality of a piece like *Poppy* and to the fact that it was a continuing event. Unlike a meal of entrees, it was a meal that was balanced and that grew over the period of the work.

The subject matter, of course, gave enormous scope to the imagination. It was a theatrical event that employed dancers in many ways. It employed puppets. We even had laser lighting and we pushed ourselves in whole new directions. We were ill-equipped to do so; we didn't have the finance to back it up or the theatrical knowledge of staging. At that stage we were primitive in terms of where we were going but, somehow, *Poppy* worked and it captured the imagination of the public and, although I think it caused an enormous deficit in the early days, I think it's a work that has paved the way and paid for itself a hundred times in terms of audience growth that has continued from that date to this.

Poppy was an enormous and complex subject. My biggest problem was what to discard. One could have put so many people into that ballet; so many characters could have emerged. People would always come up and say, 'Oh, why didn't you depict this aspect of him, or why not that?' The whole problem was that Cocteau was so diverse in his art. The lovely thing was that he grouped everything under poetry in a sense. I mean, whether it was a tapestry or the inside painting of a church, it became a poem for him. What I hoped was that the ballet *Poppy* was like a Cocteau-esque poem, that it was created in the style of Cocteau, and that the tableaux were Cocteau-esque. The decor was sparse and like a Cocteau design—a brief sketch that Cocteau might have done.

Poppy, of course, enabled us to say, 'All right, we've been brave once. We'll do it again. We got out by the skin of our teeth and we'll fight on.' It gave rise to other full-length works which broke new ground and which I think have expanded the appeal and thrust of dance in this country.   (April 1981)

MCKECHNIE: I'd like to ask you about what, I know, is one of your most important works, in your view, and that is *After Venice*.

MURPHY: For me, *After Venice* was a work of major importance in my output. I don't think people generally understand to what extent it breaks new ground as a storytelling device of contemporary dance. I never intended it to be a retelling of the Thomas Mann novel. I was looking for what was behind every character as opposed to depicting the characters. Fortunately it was a work that was so well known through the film and through the novel that you could actually make those characters, give them the physicality of those characters. Then you were free of their history, and free to delve into their inner souls. I was free to create whatever feelings I wanted to create about them.

I painted Tadzio as a bad seed. He might have been the bad seed that took the plague out of Venice and back to Poland. This boy was able to take everyone and seduce everybody, even when he became a cohort with Death as they went around reaping their plague victims. The AIDS analogy was something I was aware of. I was actually more frightened than I need be at the premiere—you must remember this was very early days. I remember I was talking to Alfred Williams, who performed the role of Death, in the dressing room before we went on for the first performance and saying, 'I'm not sure how people will react. I'm not sure how they will read the AIDS analogy thing. I'm quite worried that it might be scandalous.'

MCKECHNIE: Do you think people made that connection?

MURPHY: They made it five years later mostly. It was there from the beginning, the plague and the AIDS thing were always there. The steam room scene. I thought it was terribly apparent. But in the first reviews only one or two picked it up.

MCKECHNIE: Was the character of Aschenbach, and your choice of Garth (Welch) in that role, related to this other obsession you have with time passing, with ageing?

MURPHY: Yes. The other thing is, consciously or subconsciously, we as an Australian public have seen Garth pass from a beautiful boyhood to a fine manhood and retain exquisite artistry through that transition. No-one was happier when Garth was a member of our company than myself. Or perhaps Garth—Garth was pretty happy. The dancers could just look at someone whose depth of artistry was just staggering to them. I think it made them feel better about their futures. That artistry doesn't die—like the soul doesn't die when the body does. That parallel, that metaphor, was what the work was about. Garth made the role grow with every performance. When we did revivals of *Venice*, it was like you saw this person with more wisdom, more beauty, more technique even. It was quite wonderful. I loved the work for that reason. I also loved it because, when we created it, Paul (Mercurio), who danced the role of Tadzio, was a boyish creature and now he is a man with a wife and children. I saw him translate and work so hard to make the role work in later years. It took a lot of us through many transitions. To me, it was one of the first times I had been able to explore and invent a psychology for characters that were wildly mysterious. I loved it. I felt like I had created a sequel to the novel. *After Venice*—is there life after *Death in Venice*, I think I was saying? And I think I discovered there was.

MCKECHNIE: I wonder now, could you talk about the way in which you structured the piece, the way in which you found movement? Did you begin with character, or did you begin somewhere else?

MURPHY: I remember, even prior to beginning the work, I had the image of an old man on the beach, perhaps with a trumpet record player, you know one of the old-fashioned ones? I was actually going to play the Mahler, the Adagietto from his *Fifth Symphony*, because it's associated very strongly with the Visconti film of the work and with that particular image of Aschenbach on the beach. I wanted to establish that security, that people were going to get comfort from what they knew from the film or the novel. Then I was going to have this whole series of stage-flats that just fell like a deck of cards, and then have the Messiaen begin. In a sense I did it; it just didn't come out in that form. Kristian (Fredrikson) and I developed a wonderful set, a moving landscape that represented the walls of Venice. It also represented the decay of Venice—millions of things, coffins, everything. So that image was there and I started working from that point of view.

I gave the dancers pieces of music, which I felt were right for their characters, to explore their relationships in terms of Tadzio. Tadzio was always the protagonist against which people worked. He was the constant. Then I discovered I wasn't happy with the way I jumped from piece to piece to piece. I wasn't happy with the way the device was working, in terms of the total structure. I was happy with the individual modules, so I started moving them round, right up to the last dress rehearsal. I think at the last dress rehearsal I made a final decision, which I lived with and which I'm happy with now. The sections of music were complete in themselves, so I didn't feel too guilty. I don't know if the fact that the music wasn't in the order written had some influence on Messiaen, who later refused to allow me to use the music. But the sections were complete and the music wasn't one of his profound religious statements—it was about love. I didn't feel bad about that aspect but I am really very sad when I think that the work has now been laid to rest. (May 1990)

POTTER: Can you explain what happened with regard to the music?

MURPHY: I'll try to. It got very complicated. We were so emotionally involved with the piece, it's really hard to be totally accurate. But initially when we created the work, we sent off the normal letters that you do asking permission for the work, the recording, to be used. We didn't ever receive any reply. And I think there's some law which says that in the event that you hear nothing you *can* go ahead, because by this stage we were well under way and the work was happening. So we paid the recording rights, but we'd never actually heard back from Messiaen following our request for permission. We used the work long term. We did huge numbers of performances. It was a very popular work for the company and a work that we all loved doing.

It was the European tour in '88—it was the bicentennial year, I remember—that we actually toured it extensively through Europe and we also performed it in New York. But in Europe we were performing in Spain in a number of outdoor arenas, really wonderful places; we did some fabulous performances, performed for Spanish royalty at the palace. And when you perform in Europe there are other copyright laws. The presenters have to get all the information about all the music rights because they actually pay the royalty out of the box office. So the information about the *After Venice* music went off to France to the Messiaen agent and just towards the end of our Spanish tour we got a very strict letter saying that we weren't to perform it anymore. Well, we had commitments; we'd signed contracts with presenters. We sent Mary Stielow, our tour manager, off to Paris to protest, saying we're contractually obliged, and to try and get permission to speak to Messiaen himself. I actually tried to make contact with him when I was in Paris also, but his wife, who survives him now, was very protective of him at that stage—I think his health wasn't too good at that point. The agent said, 'Look, don't even bother. He's actually said no to any of his music being performed except in concert.' A lot of his music was actually written for the glory of God. This was one of the pieces that was secular, so I thought that maybe we had a leg to stand on, since it wasn't one of his big church choral pieces. Mary had no luck with the agent whatsoever except that we got a stay of execution and were allowed to complete our contracted tour in Europe that year. Thereafter we were forbidden to use it again.

Every so often we got a need for an *After Venice* hit and we'd try again through another source. We sent videos, but we don't know whether they were ever looked at. He was one of the composers who was most sought-after in the concert hall. A lot of dancers have wanted to use his music, especially the piece he wrote in the prisoner-of-war camp, *Quartet for the End of Time*, but have found that they're not allowed to use it. So it's a lesson for young players not to assume that all music, just because you can buy it at your local record shop, is available for use. And I do think there's something wrong there. You can understand that you want your music used with integrity, but it's not as if you can control how it's being listened to. If you're going to put it on the open market, if you're going to let it be recorded, it's in the public domain. When we first performed it in Australia and in America, it was obviously out of the jurisdiction of that European policing. But once we actually hit Europe with it, the Messiaen estate was clamped in on it. And I don't think that will change with his death. It'll probably get fiercer now that he's gone. They'll probably be even more protective and more vigilant. It was a real drama and it upset me. (August 1996)

MCKECHNIE: You seem to be attached to *After Venice*.

MURPHY: I think because I don't believe to this day that it's been appreciated to the level that it could be. Some of the choreography, against my choreography today, is fairly simple, fairly clean. There's a complexity there, but it's not so textured in terms of movement. But in terms of meaning, it's probably one of the deepest statements I've made about people.

MCKECHNIE: Let's look at another major work.

MURPHY: *Kraanerg*. If I hadn't done *Kraanerg*, I couldn't have taken a year off. It put a full stop, but it put the next sentence in view. It was a work that, musically, was monstrously unpopular. We maybe had 20 or 30 walk-outs a night in the Opera Theatre (Sydney Opera House). We had good houses but we had an incredible reaction, because again the eyes are usually much more tolerant than the ears. The music was a monumental piece that you had to move into like a great cathedral. Unless you were actually in it, you couldn't appreciate it. The music was harsh and extraordinarily relentless, merciless. If you were prepared to go inside it you could cope, but if you were going to stay outside and watch it from there, you had no hope.

It was a mixture of live music and tape. In the auditorium you had a huge surround of back speakers, a front bank of orchestra. They were switching constantly. It was quite overpowering. You couldn't escape, so if you resisted it was horrible. Most people who couldn't do that left. It was, I think, 65, 70 minutes; no interval. People who could, usually got over that by the first 15 minutes and then they wore the structure. It is a work that I'd like to bring back every three years because I think it's a work that actually pushed our public ahead. The ones that accepted it jumped up and caught up with us. But the ones that left, we may have lost forever; there were things like abusing the box-office girl and demanding money back.

It was wonderful for me because it gave me a whole new movement vocabulary. I knew I couldn't compete with the music; I couldn't wash the audience along with it. So I worked against the music; I worked through it, never in any real parallel with it. It was so important to me, creatively, that piece.

MCKECHNIE: What sort of ideas were you coming from to create the actual movement for it?

MURPHY: I think that was the other thing that was really hard. I was experimenting with the movement in a pure sense. I think I divided the music somewhat into sections. Often there wasn't a true beginning and an end to a movement. Sometimes I found pieces of the score that I felt were complete and often I would put them aside. Sometimes I wouldn't put the music on while I was choreographing. We would do large hunks of choreography in silence. The dancers found that quite hard. They had nothing really to link to, but one movement would suggest the next movement and I would go with that. I think I had an idea of the weight of the music, or the style. I thought of the music in terms of numbers. This piece of music needs the weight of more dancers, and needs a structure that is looser and freer. Then I would do it. Then afterwards, by merely adjusting a step here, the speed of something there, adding or subtracting a tiny section, I would find the balance that way. The work was giving birth to itself constantly. It is an architectural work. The set was by an architect. The music was by an architect. I approached it very much in that way—pieces, small bricks, that build together to make a work.

Kraanerg was like my notebook. Writing that notebook enabled me to take a year off. If I hadn't done *Kraanerg*,

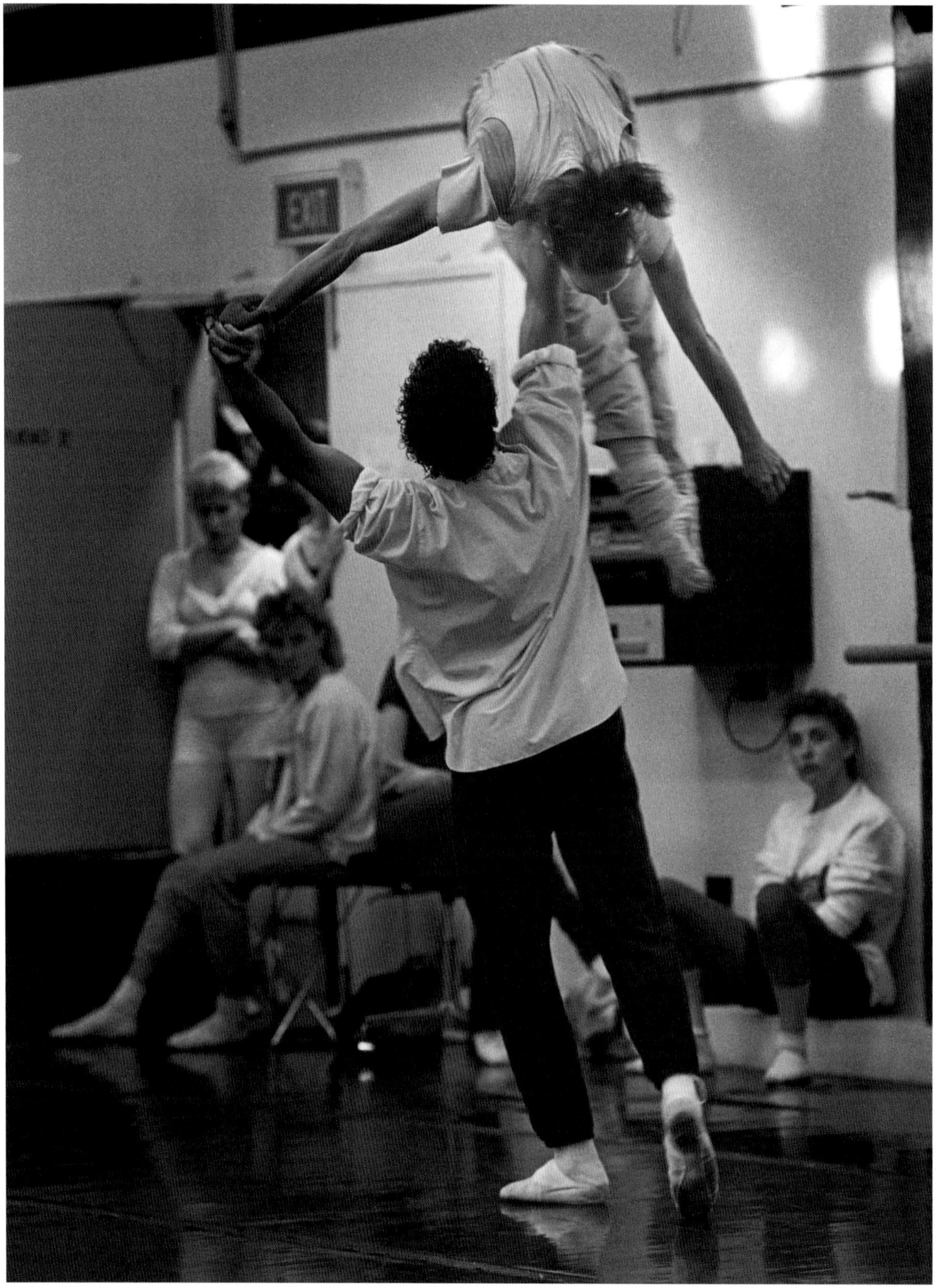
EXIT

I would have felt I didn't have enough material to pick up and continue on. It gave me the right to have a year off.

MCKECHNIE: What did it mean to you being away for those 12 months?

MURPHY: It was important to me because I'd achieved a certain notoriety—if not fame—in Sydney particularly. A bit generally in Australia too. I began to question my individual worth as a person, in terms of relationships, in terms of who I was. The insecurity is quite a ridiculous thing, but I wanted to test it. So I went away to somewhere where nobody knew me. I didn't even know the language. I went to Sicily for six months.

It was fantastic after the initial fear and terror and loneliness. I found myself alone in a villa on the outside of town with just the waves crashing and the dogs barking down the street and the odd Italian hoon going up and down on the motorbike. After the fear of why have I come to die on my own in this strange country, because a couple of frightening things happened in the dead of night, I just started to make a new life in a new community, in a tiny little town. It was like being back in Mathinna again in Tasmania—to meet people and to win their friendship. No-one had a concept of what I did or who I was. I was just some eccentric Australian who arrived on their beachfront in early spring and left in late autumn.

MCKECHNIE: Did you have another view of Australia from there? Did you acquire a different way of viewing your own country in that situation?

MURPHY: I think you have to become very articulate because people ask you so many questions. The Sicilians are incredibly frank and incredibly curious people. They will ask you point blank: Are you married? How old are you? Why aren't you married? That was the inevitable chronological order. They just want to know.

MCKECHNIE: Did you learn to speak the language?

MURPHY: At the end of six months I was doing pretty well. I really had to—it was a small town, so the chances of speaking English were fairly negligible. I did learn to articulate how I felt about Australia, which was very good. I didn't work consciously on any project, or any movement thing. But I did have a new physicality—I worked, I swam, I ran, I went mountain climbing, I went down one of the most wonderful canyons in the world, the biggest canyon in Europe. It was only minutes away. A very healthy lifestyle, beautiful food. I concentrated on making my body a better thing, and my mind. I read very little. I didn't listen to as much music as I would normally in the course of a year. There was a certain cleansing.

MCKECHNIE: What happened in the other six months?

MURPHY: I spent some time with my parents. I made a documentary. I came to Sydney and got my body back into some kind of shape to do a gala. (May 1990)

In 1992 Murphy made *Nutcracker* for the Australian Ballet. It was a new, iconoclastic version of the much-performed, nineteenth-century Christmas ballet. Murphy retained the Tchaikovsky score, but with Kristian Fredrikson, who also designed the work, he reworked the story so that it crossed generations, continents and cultures. Set partly in Australia in the 1950s, it moved backwards and forwards in time and location examining Australia's migrant history and the foundations on which Australian theatrical dance grew and flourished. It received major critical acclaim for the way in which it revealed multiple layers of Australian cultural history.

Nutcracker renewed Murphy's associations with the Australian Ballet, for whom he had created a number of shorter works during the 1970s and 1980s. Murphy had also applied, unsuccessfully, for the job of artistic director of the Australian Ballet in 1982. He says he did it then because it was 'a good thing to do politically'; he felt that the marketplace for the job was, wrongly, thought to be overseas rather than in Australia. He was also considered for the same position in 1995.

POTTER: Can you talk a bit about *Nutcracker*? How did it come about?

MURPHY: Maina (Gielgud) had asked me years ago to think about doing a *Nutcracker* and I'd rejected the idea on the basis that the story was silly, the piece was clichéd, and I'd never really seen one I'd liked. The clinch for me was the music, of course, which I adore. So Kristian came over and we played the tape and, I think, somewhere in the course of that listening I was going, 'I can't do a *Nutcracker* set in postcard snowland, white Christmases and all that stuff. It doesn't mean anything. Maybe if you could do a *Nutcracker* set in arid Melbourne suburbia ...' And that was really the beginning of it. Then the detail started filling in about Russian émigrés coming here, the Borovansky thing, the whole thing of displaced people having to find their way, of artists coming to this country and finding new ways of fertilising the soil. It seemed so natural and so right. And I'm very visual with music. I never just hear it, I always see it. *Nutcracker* was just wonderful in that it all fell into place except, of course, the bête noire of that piece, the travelogue scene, which I actually would love to have arranged. I'd love to get someone to link the pieces so that it didn't have that 'four-minute *divertissement*' feeling. The sudden stops in all that were very hard for me. All the other pieces are substantial and they give you time to get to the guts of something. The only one I really love out of the travelogue section is the Tai Chi scene, and I started in silence with that anyway.

Nutcracker was an easy nightmare. It was hard because we were working under enormous pressure, but I'm very bad at preparation. I rarely write things down. But because Kristian was there demanding, and the Australian Ballet was there demanding—how many costumes, how many in the corps de ballet, how many snowflakes—I actually had to plan it with Kristian, really in detail. And therefore, when I went into the rehearsal period, all I really had to do was make the architecture to fit the design specifications. And that's not very hard. It's when I'm drawing on my absolute raw instincts ... and actually I like working that way much better, I must say. But in this case of the Australian Ballet, which ended up like almost a $3^{1}/_{2}$-week rehearsal period for a full-length work, which is ridiculous, I really needed to have done all of that preparation. Sometimes it meant that I wasn't as happy as I might have been, but I churned and churned. And I worked with good people.

But the process was not hard. I just had to fit around the other activities of that huge machine, which never stop; people being dragged away to *Giselle* rehearsals and things like that. When I rehearse with my own company, everyone is there for everything. So they have a real concept of the totality of the work. And that affects the way they perform because they're part of the jigsaw, even if they're just sitting around watching the process. And of course you didn't have your principals while you were doing your corps de ballet. But I never felt like I used them like a corps de ballet. Maina was a bit distressed, I think, because she felt that they couldn't be shown to their best advantage while I was treating them like 30 soloists instead of like a mass. And I think it used to upset her when the snowflakes weren't beautifully together. But I always used to justify it by saying, 'Well, snowflakes never are!'

POTTER: What was it like returning to work with a classical technique?

MURPHY: It was not really any big deal, you know. I don't think I've ever really discarded it. I mean, we all do classical class every day and my dancers have lovely classical techniques. I didn't really think with *Nutcracker* I created particularly in the classical style anyway. If you took away the tutus and you took away the pointe shoes, I don't know what genre you'd actually say the work belonged in. Because you have classical music, tutus and pointe shoes everyone feels it's comfortably classical, but if you staged it differently, or clad it differently, or shod it differently, it would have looked quite a different work. Or if the score had been a contemporary score. It had all the comforts that people needed but enough slipping in of my sort of contemporary influences to balance the two.

I had the richness of working with older dancers and what they added to the roles. These people were sweating and puffing and I was terrified I was going to cause a heart attack. They lived it and they loved it and they thought about their characters. I enjoyed the directorship of the work. And directing the children as characters too. It involved talking about children in the fifties, which I could do. Not letting them talk in dollars and cents. They were made to talk in threepences. It was really interesting for me. It pointed out how the generations have changed and we've become so Americanised too. At the time that *Nutcracker* was set, we were just a little English colony really, looking for our identity.

POTTER: Can I ask you about your recent application for the job of artistic director of the Australian Ballet?

MURPHY: Of course, you can. One of the board members rang up actually. I didn't put in an application for the job. I wasn't really thinking about it in serious terms. And the reason I wasn't was because I do have serious doubts about that board being a board that will ever let the company fly anywhere except in the direction that they want, which to me is the equivalent of being caged. I was approached by a board member, who really most passionately said, 'Look you really should apply,' someone who had come to our performances—actually *Fornicon*, in Melbourne. Seeing an audience going wild, and young people cheering, that person said, 'I've never seen people like that at dance in this country.' So then the head hunter came and talked once or twice and, I mean, he was basically someone who was a mouthpiece for the board, but didn't really understand the medium of dance. I did welcome the chance of actually talking to the board because I felt, well, I can ask questions. They can ask me, but I can ask back because I'm not hanging on the job. I had one interview with the board where I really socked it to them. I felt like I got the point across that you *can* retain the integrity of a classical company without being moribund and in the past. You *can* encourage more creativity in this sort of country. You *can* keep your audience. I mean *Nutcracker* was a perfect example and it was nice to have that example. But they were still *terrified* that anything I touched would turn every little old lady into a screaming banshee. There was this *obsession* with the existing audience and not enough obsession with growing a new audience, which I really think is the huge danger in that company. It was a great interview. I enjoyed it. I asked the questions I'd always wanted to. How ready are you for change? Then there was a second interview. Janet and I both went to that one. And the climate had changed so much. There had been obviously much talking and decisions had already been made. And the questions!—like, what would you make the dancers wear to rehearsal? And you just knew that the small picture was all they could see. With the new millennium on the doorstep, they weren't even thinking in terms of anything except that careful continuity.

POTTER: Did you want the job?

MURPHY: I would have taken the job if for one minute I thought the job was the job I wanted. And I have to say that the job was never the job that I could have accepted or wanted. I thought about it very carefully. I think I did a very careful paper so that they could actually see the points, but I just knew that it wasn't going to happen that way. So no, in fact, under those circumstances, I never wanted the job. And yet, to me, it seems so important that someone with a choreographic background take that job.

POTTER: Do you believe then in choreographer-led companies?

MURPHY: Yes. Because otherwise, all you get is well-planned, nicely managed, supermarket-trolley shopping for good works. Basically those good works are the ones that everyone lets out. There are only five Kylián works on the open market. And every company in the world's got them. What's the point of that? I think if a choreographer's got a company, then other choreographers are often more encouraged because they know those dancers are versed in the way of creativity as opposed to reproduction of existing works, which is a real different process and gives the dancers *nothing* compared to the creation of a work on them. It gives them no ownership of the work. If you have a choreographer, not only do you get a company versed in creativity, you get other choreographers more prepared to give the new works when normally they'd say, 'Oh, no, but you can have this one.' It's a bit like, 'You can have a miniskirt because everyone's got one.' You see, *I* don't want to create on other companies either because I know that a lot of the companies aren't open to that creative process, because they're not versed in it. I wish Ross (Stretton) great success with the Australian Ballet. I hope it makes for a happy company and a creative company and an exciting company, but I do worry because it's not being led by a choreographer. Quite frankly. When you're not a choreographer, all you really do is pass on the things that perhaps you as the director, or you as the dancer, have done, and the experiences that you've had. You're not actually going, 'I've got to tailor-make something to the needs of this company and this country.' You can't control that destiny because you can't create for it.   (August 1996)

Commentators have often suggested that Murphy's particular brand of dance is quintessentially and hedonistically Sydney. 'We have outlasted every restaurant in Sydney, every whim and changing fashion,' Murphy says however, and he suggests that, although Sydney has certain claims on the company since 'it gave us birth', the company is now often appreciated more outside that city. He says that he often finds Sydney's 'avarice, appetite for the new' draining and not conducive to remounting works from his already extensive repertoire. He, like most other choreographer–directors, also has concerns about the level of funding available to his company: 'It would probably take only two bum works to push us out of business.'

POTTER: What was your vision for Sydney Dance in 1976? And, is it different now?

MURPHY: I would like the company to be far more successful than it is after 20 years. But what I see is very much more than I could ever, ever have foreseen, and that's continuity of creativity. And that to me is the ultimate miracle of Sydney Dance Company. We're still here. The new works are continuing. There's a continuing integrity about the style that we create in—how we create, the people we create for. The dancers are now their own people. They haven't ever been suppressed by a company that's been around for so long that, to get into this company, you have to be this, that and the other. They are actually a group of wildly fascinating people. But, I think, if in '76 someone had said 20 years down the track ... I would have laughed, I guess. We survived by taking every year as it comes.

I'm very nervous about the political, financial future of the company because I don't think this current government really quite understands what it takes to be a creative company. If you really understand what we're doing, you value it because what we're doing is incredibly important to this country. We make people feel good about themselves, about the country they live in, about the youth. If you come to Sydney Dance Company, you feel an optimism for the future. And young people feel it too.

The other thing is the international market—we don't tap that because of finance. We can barely tour Australia anymore. The whole climate means that sponsorship's harder, government funds are drying and much more demanding, costs of touring are accelerating all the time. We really do it hard in terms of touring because of the size of the country. Getting overseas becomes more and more impossible.

POTTER: What do you see yourself doing in the future?

MURPHY: I don't know really. I mean my last work, *Free Radicals*, nearly killed me. It was so hard. With *Radicals* I had so much pressure to create 80 minutes of score, 80 minutes of dance in eight weeks. I would have liked to have workshopped it for two months and then created the piece. But the two months was the creative process, not a workshop process. Also I doubt myself much more than I used to in the old days. When you're young and you have no measure by which to judge yourself, everything you do seems so new because you haven't done any of it before. Now the obsession with making things new, with being fresh, with not repeating yourself, becomes really draining. But there's always something on the back-burner. Often when I'm creating a work, often at the height of it, something else will flicker into my brain. I think it's a way of not letting me get over-focused on one particular work.

POTTER: Does your work have a signature?

MURPHY: You mean, you couldn't look at a Matisse and say, 'I know whose that is,' having never seen that painting. You couldn't hear a Tchaikovsky that you've never heard and recognise it? Of course, I have. I'm creating out of the depths of my soul. Not trying to one week be Picasso, the next to be Ken Done. It comes out of the deepest recesses of my subconscious, my movement, and if it doesn't relate, then I don't have a continuity within. And I think I do. I think it stems from loving the process of manipulating the human form. I adore the possibilities of the human body. I feel, okay, sometimes I've let them down but they've never let me down, those possibilities. That is why I'm still fascinated with the process of making works. Through manipulating the form, I actually get insight into the people I'm working with. I don't socialise with my dancers, I don't party with them. I'm relaxed with them. I don't have a sort of salon of young dancers. But I know them better than they know themselves in some ways.

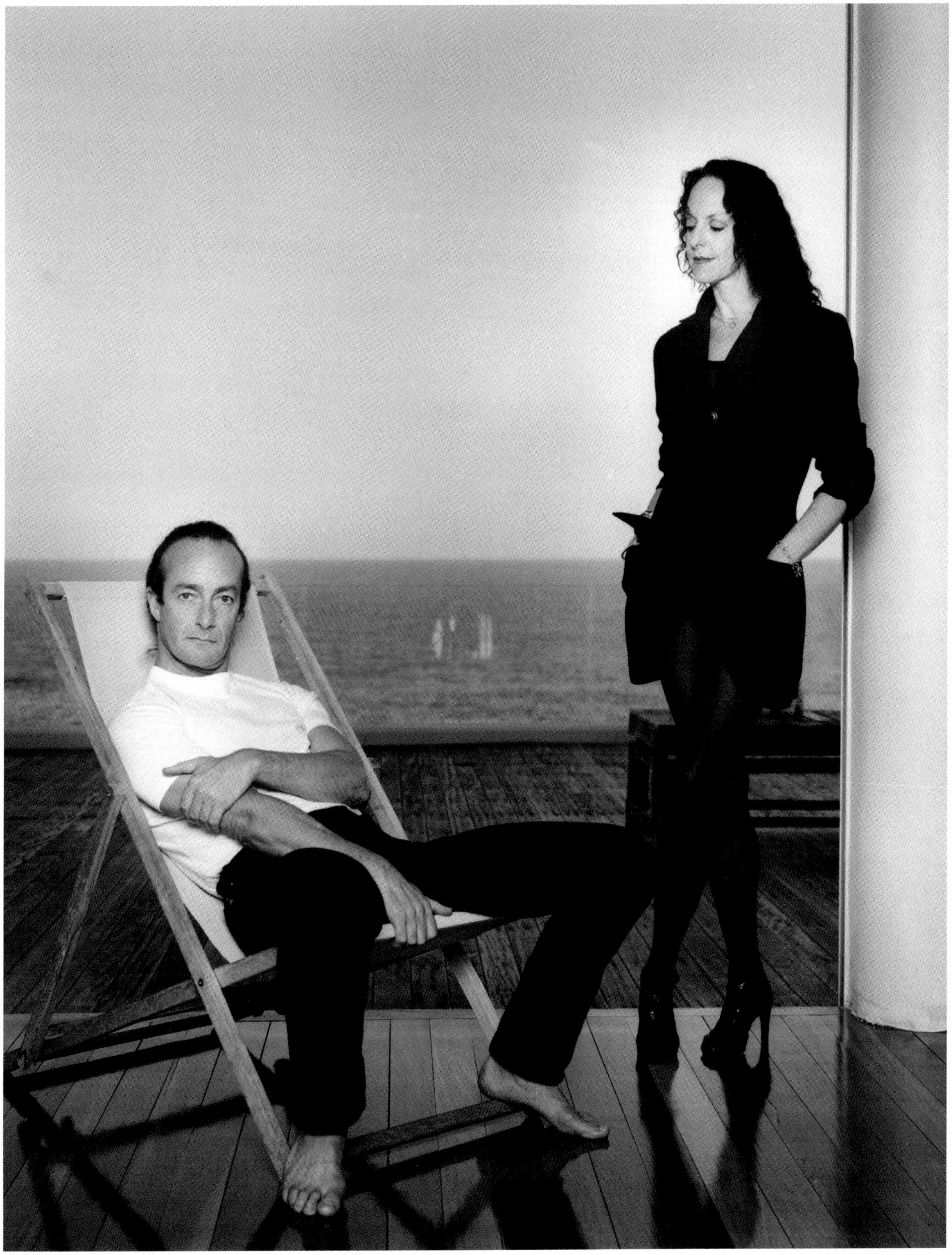

I work with fragments of their inner being. I never say to them, 'What are you thinking when you do this movement?' I don't need to do that. I want them to get the absolute guts out of the movement and I'll encourage that, and I'll indicate disappointment if I think they're just doing the shapes nicely. That's why I'm very happy with this company. There are a lot of people who actually are prepared to put that beautiful, abstract extra dimension into the work. That thrills me when that happens. Superficial motion is a revolting thing to see on stage. But emotion that comes out of movement, out of the people, out of the darkness in the theatre into the auditorium, is so fabulous.

(August 1996)

When I asked Graeme Murphy whether he had any concluding remarks to put down on the tape for posterity, his initial response was a simple 'no'. Reflecting for a moment, however, he added, 'I don't think I'm concluded yet somehow. I'm still waiting for the perfect work and then I'll stop!' But the dryness with which he offered those words was tempered by the richness of the laughter that followed, especially when the recorder was turned off. And before I began the interview, he asked me whether I liked his much-cherished orchid plant—in full, exquisite bloom in his living room—its colour made whiter by the deep cobalt blue of the wall against which it was displayed. Warm, friendly and immediately likeable in conversation, Murphy overflows with the humanity that he so richly reveals in his works.

Choreography by Graeme Murphy

Year	Work	Company
1971	Ecco le diavole	Australian Ballet Choreographic Workshop
1974	Off	Félix Blaska Choreographic Workshop
1975	Sequenza VII	Queensland Ballet
	Three Conversations	Queensland Ballet
	Papillon	Australian Ballet School
1976	Glimpses	Ballet '76
1977	Volumina	Dance Company (NSW)
	Tip	Ballet '77
	Scintillation	Dance Company (NSW)
	Fire Earth Air Water	Dance Company (NSW)
1978	Poppy	Dance Company (NSW)
	Rumours II	Dance Company (NSW)
	Tekton	Australian Ballet
1979	Signatures	Sydney Dance Company
	Shéhérazade	Sydney Dance Company
	Rumours I & III	Sydney Dance Company
1980	Viridian	Sydney Dance Company
	Daphnis and Chloé	Sydney Dance Company
	Beyond Twelve	Australian Ballet
1981	An Evening	Sydney Dance Company
1982	Homelands	Sydney Dance Company
	Hate	Sydney Dance Company
	Limited Edition	Sydney Dance Company
	Wilderness	Sydney Dance Company
1983	The Selfish Giant	Sydney Dance Company
	Flashbacks	Sydney Dance Company
	Some Rooms	Sydney Dance Company
1984	Deadly Sins	Sydney Dance Company
	Old Friends, New Friends	Sydney Dance Company
	After Venice	Sydney Dance Company
	Death in Venice	Canadian Opera Company
	Meander	Australian Ballet
	Metamorphosis	Australian Opera
1985	Shimmering	Sydney Dance Company
	Boxes	Sydney Dance Company
	Sirens	Sydney Dance Company
1986	Nearly Beloved	Sydney Dance Company
	Shining	Sydney Dance Company
	Fire and Ice	Jayne Torvill and Christopher Dean
1987	Late Afternoon of a Faun	Sydney Dance Company
	Afterworlds	Sydney Dance Company
	Gallery	Australian Ballet
	Song of the Night	Nederlands Dans Theater
1988	VAST	Sydney Dance Company
	Kraanerg	Sydney Dance Company
1989	Evening Suite	Sydney Dance Company
1990	soft bruising	Sydney Dance Company
	In the Company of Wo/Men (with Paul Mercurio)	Sydney Dance Company
	King Roger	Sydney Dance Company
	Turandot	Australian Opera
1991	Bard Bits	Sydney Dance Company
1992	Piano Sonata	Sydney Dance Company
	Synergy with Synergy	Sydney Dance Company
	Nutcracker	Australian Ballet
1993	Beauty and the Beast	Sydney Dance Company
	The Protecting Veil	Sydney Dance Company
	Salome	Australian Opera
	Sensing	ABC-TV
1994	Les Troyens	Australian Opera
1995	Fornicon	Sydney Dance Company
	Berlin	Sydney Dance Company
1996	Free Radicals	Sydney Dance Company
	Embodied	White Oak Dance Project

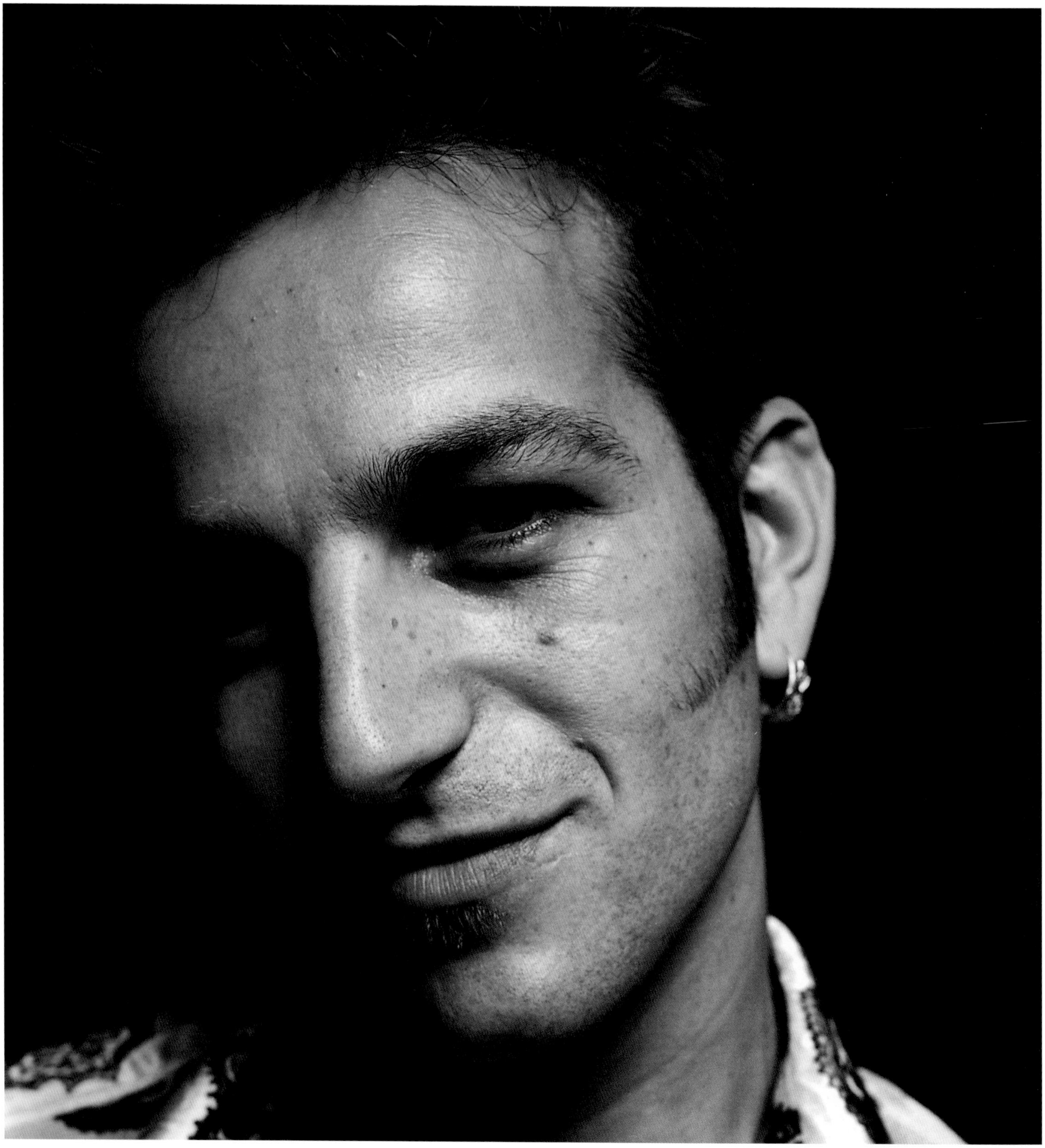

Gideon Obarzanek

Daring Dance

Interview TRC 3396

Gideon Obarzanek (born 1966), independent choreographer and director of Chunky Move, was interviewed by Michelle Potter in Sydney in January 1996

Gideon Obarzanek's career as a choreographer has already been marked by an unusually independent outlook. He currently divides his time between Australia, where he was born, and the Netherlands. In Australia he has created for the Australian Ballet, the Dancers Company, Queensland Ballet, Sydney Dance Company, West Australian Ballet and his own Chunky Move. In the Netherlands he has made a number of works for the second company of Nederlands Dans Theater (NDT2) based in The Hague. His diverse activities reflect an interest in attitudes to theatre prevalent in Europe—the 'great respect for the artwork'—and the different approaches to creating work he finds available to him there, with a genuine commitment to Australia as a source of inspiration. His Australian inspiration does not, however, come from myths and nationalistic stories but more from his particular view of the contemporary cultural landscape of Australia, and especially of Sydney where he says he feels like 'a child in a candy store'.

Obarzanek established a dance company, which he named Chunky Move, early in 1995. It emerged partly for pragmatic reasons; Obarzanek was concerned at the financial and artistic difficulties that independent artists face when trying to present a public showing of their work. He wondered what would happen if he shared a group of dancers and a specific amount of funding with another choreographer with similar sensibilities. Originating from a collaboration between Obarzanek and another independent choreographer, Garry Stewart, Chunky Move presented its first season at the 1995 Melbourne International Festival of the Arts.

Chunky Move also grew out of Obarzanek's desire to provide a space for the showing of choreography based on a contemporary rather than classical aesthetic. His methods of creating his individualistic choreographic language are eclectic, and the episodic nature of his work reflects the energetic diversity of popular culture and the rapid way in which information is transmitted in a contemporary environment.

POTTER: Gideon, I would like to start by asking you about Chunky Move, your relatively new company. What gave you the inspiration to start it up?

OBARZANEK: Oh, a number of things. I'd been working in Europe and Australia when I was thinking about starting up Chunky Move and, as a freelance choreographer, one of the things I felt was that the existing dance companies in Australia didn't really offer a very good platform, or forum, or place, for a lot of young choreographers with new material. Some of the work that I want to do, and some other choreographers want to do, doesn't really suit the more conventional dance companies in Australia. So we thought that Chunky Move would be a good company to start, that it would exhibit and perform works of young choreographers.

POTTER: What is the kind of work that you make that isn't suitable for other companies?

OBARZANEK: It is very hard to define actually. It is not that it is not suitable—in fact, I think it is very suitable for other companies in Australia. But I think in Australia particularly we have preconceived notions about what is and what isn't dance—notions of dance aesthetics and the process of making dance. When you don't follow them, or when you push those parameters by a great degree, I think a lot of artistic directors in Australia baulk. It's very difficult to get commissions unless you do have a certain kind of prescribed way of making dance. That's my experience anyway.

The other thing, too, is that after freelancing for three years I have learnt a lot about infrastructure in companies and how it affects the works that they make. I was very keen to assemble, I guess, people from different practices in the arts to make my own combination that I thought would work the best for me. The hard thing is that as a freelancer the level of compromise gets bigger and bigger the longer you freelance, because when you change from a very young choreographer to a slightly more mature choreographer your signature starts to come out in the work. I find that going from company to company is like taking two steps forward and one step back: you arrive, you have a six-week rehearsal period, you spend often three weeks of that six-week period just explaining your perception of dance, what your style is, and so forth. So, when you actually get to the work itself, you begin to question, 'How far have I really gone?' So the idea of an ongoing ensemble was a big desire for me—one I could do one work with and then get back together and do another work.

POTTER: Are you hoping then with Chunky Move to have the same dancers as much as possible?

OBARZANEK: I had a couple of different ideas. At first I thought, 'Yes, I would like the same dancers.' Then the next one was, 'No, the company would change according to the project that we were doing and what performers were necessary for each project—this leaves us artistically flexible.' I think now what is going to happen, from my experience already with Chunky Move, is that we are going to have a combination of these two. I think a core group of at least three dancers out of the current six is going to stay on and new dancers are going to come in. Our next project is a live performance project and I am trying to assemble as many of the dancers as I had in the last piece. That won't be possible but I am hoping to get four out of the six. Following that, we've got a very big film project with the ABC. We are now just starting the process of scriptwriting for it and already I have the feeling that it won't be all dancers. There may be two or three dancer–performers in the piece, but I think there will be actors as well, and people with other disciplines in this film. So Chunky Move would employ different performing artists for a project like that.

I am talking more than the questions that are being fired at me, but one thing for me that is important with Chunky Move is that in the very difficult environment of keeping companies ongoing in Australia—and it is a very difficult environment for dance companies just to stay alive—often works take the back seat. Directors and general managers are saying, 'Oh, Jesus, how are we going to keep the company afloat next year? How are we going to pay these wages?' So they try to get funding, they try to do works that will guarantee a certain box-office percentage and so forth. What I hope, and this is very idealistic, with Chunky Move is that we have an idea for a work first, and then we build up an infrastructure around that work to realise it and make it happen. That means it does a project, it may do some touring afterwards, it may present that work throughout Australia and overseas, but then it has a rest. It disbands until a new concept comes up, or a new work, and then it builds itself up for that concept. There is no desire for me to make Chunky Move an annually funded, ongoing full-time company. The work is the main reason why the company's there, not the works are there because the company has to keep going. Oh, look, ask me in two years' time, I may be saying a very different story, but I'm in a position where I can be idealistic at the moment, so I am.

POTTER: Whose idea was the name?

OBARZANEK: Mine. I'm not too good with names—well, actually for my works, I'm not too bad. Chunky Move began from a project basically—'Gideon Obarzanek and Garry Stewart present two modern dance works with six freelance dancers performing it and with three Australian composers with original scores'. It was a pretty clumsy title to present at the opening night of the Melbourne International Festival, so we figured we should really have a name. We didn't really want to have a name actually; there was no real desire to think, 'Oh, we must have a name.' But we nutted it out. It took weeks actually. 'Chunky' is a word I really like; I think 'move' just came in. I mean, chunky is the really important word for us in Chunky Move—it's chunky. We just call it

Chunky for short. You know, 'Are you going to be working with Chunky?' But Chunky Move just defines it a bit more into movement. I guess 'chunky' was a nice word because it doesn't have any held notions of professional dance or the aesthetics of dance; it's a word that really grates against it. It's nice for us because I get a feeling it frees us up. We're not held to any kind of notions of, you know, all that clean line and the ethereal beauty of dance.

POTTER: Can you talk a little bit about the first work you made for it, *Fast Idol*?

OBARZANEK: Yes. *Fast Idol* is sort of an episodic work. My main interest in *Fast Idol* was to combine, on quite a surface level, areas that I'm interested in—like popular culture influences in television that I've very much grown up with. I've been watching television from when I was a very young child on a daily basis and that has had, I think, a huge influence on me—and most of it was American television in Australia, particularly for children. Now it's a little bit different, but when I was a kid it was all pretty much American-type stuff. I'm very influenced by cartoon animation and slapstick comedy. It seems to suit the mime and language of dance for me. I'm very influenced by film and the whole genre of filmmaking. I think film, which is one of the newest visual art forms around, has had such an incredible impact on Western society this century. It's definitely had an impact on performing arts, I think—live performing arts and how you dish it out. So *Fast Idol* kind of deals with that.

It also deals with a slight fascination I have with the relationship between someone who's idolised and the idolisers. That is both in a religious sense and in a sexual sense, and in just everyday life. These scenes in *Fast Idol* are very theatrical and they're easily recognised. I use devotional music; they're very different in tempo from television and they're much more emotional. I'm very sarcastic, very dry often, very ironic, but deep down I feel like it's just a veneer to cover up this almost acute sensitivity. I've always been interested in unearthing the thoughts of the vulnerable and sensitive human condition that lies behind this veneer of popular pulp that you see these days. I guess *Fast Idol* dips in and out from one to the other. I like that juxtaposition; I like multiple facets within people. I feel like I have multiple lives myself—it's not schizophrenia, but I think everybody has this type of thing. So *Fast Idol* deals with that. I mean, how well it deals with that, that's very arguable, but that's sort of the premise behind it.

POTTER: So, in order to realise these ideas, what sort of movement vocabulary do you work from?

OBARZANEK: Movement vocabulary is very important to me. With Chunky Move the agenda of finding and developing and building the language is actually part of our mission statement. We have used a number of different ways in the rehearsal process. This is an ongoing process—one of the interests for me as a choreographer.

One the problems I see is that there's a certain conventional language in movement. You go to see performers and you think, 'Uh huh, it's modern dance. I can tell by the way they're moving or by the type of music that's played and so forth.' Like classical dance, modern dance has moved to where there's a certain language that you recognise as contemporary dance. It's very annoying as a choreographer.

I've begged, borrowed and stolen certain styles or methods of finding movement as well as worked on my own. One of the borrowed ones has been a nine-point improvisation, to my knowledge originally used by William Forsythe—I'm not sure if it was used before—where the space around a body is carved up in a certain way and where you have certain tasks. It doesn't really make you come up with material and it doesn't really choreograph it for you, but it does help you to lose a conventional sense of moving. It compartmentalises the body.

One of the things you learn as a dancer is to use the body in one block or to use the energy in a coordinated fashion so you have a certain sense of weight and the using of weight. Classical and contemporary dance, any dance, is the way you shift weight. With very coordinated sportspeople or dancers you see the whole body moving in a fluid manner. The weight shifts in a coordinated fashion through the body allowing it to wield itself and move itself in a very efficient and powerful manner. Nine-point kind of breaks all that up. It kind of goes, 'Well, okay, every single part of the body is different and you can point them in a multiple number of directions.' It becomes very mathematical and, after about two hours of it, you get this kind of loose-limbed rather than fluid type of movement. Often we'll do that and then we start working. Other movement just comes from me and my experience as a dancer working in different styles. I mean, movement now seems to have reached extremes and when it's rigid, it's really rigid and broken down and compartmentalised; when it's fluid, it's very fluid.

In my works I often have acting sections where there's a very efficient kind of miming to tell you what's happening, and then there's a dance section. I don't like that kind of dancing with someone twirling over to this corner and kissing somebody, and then someone twirling over there and stabbing somebody—the kind of narrative ballet-type thing where the steps are just a pretext to deliver an absolutely basic story to an audience and it takes you two hours to do it because the dance got in the way. I'd rather write it on an A4 sheet of paper and just hand it out and say, 'Well, I think this is much more efficient. There you go.' Dance is not efficient in narrative, not in that kind of very detailed storytelling. Dance is very good with emotions and the body itself. So often that takes over in my work.

POTTER: One thing about you that keeps coming out in the press is that you need a lot of rehearsal time. Do you want to elaborate on that, because the processes you've been talking about seem to be intensive?

OBARZANEK: Well, I don't think I need a lot of rehearsal time; I think I do works really efficiently. I work my butt off in an eight-week, ten-week rehearsal period to produce a work and I think what we come up with is very efficient. But it doesn't seem to suit the conventions here at the moment about how long it takes to create a work and then what kind of money you need to pay wages for that certain period of time. So, if you say to a funding body, or anybody, sponsors or theatre festivals who commission you to do a work for a festival, 'We need ten weeks' rehearsal,' they go, 'Come on, other people create works in six weeks or five weeks, why can't you do it?' In Europe—in Holland and in Belgium and in Germany—ten weeks is very standard, eight weeks to ten weeks or more.

I think one of the problems with these very short rehearsal periods is that if you are working on a narrative, or you've written an abstract, what tends to happen is you've got this certain amount of time in the studio. People prepare their music, they prepare their scenarios and they often prepare their designs, their set designs and so forth. So when they go through a rehearsal period, they go, 'Okay, the design's going to look like this, the music's this and the basic plot of the work, whether it's abstract or narrative, is this.' It's like, 'Okay, darling, you're the king and you get very jealous and then you die and dah, dah, dah, dah,' and then the choreography becomes this secondary medium. It just becomes this thing to get people around the stage. I get back to narrative because it's easier to talk about, but I mean that also for abstract works. We tend to rehearse dance in Australia with very similar rehearsal schedules to theatre schedules. You'll often rehearse a play for five or six weeks or two or three or four weeks. I don't know, for some reason people keep forgetting that they're holding a big fat script in their hands that's taken, sometimes, a number of years to write. In dance you don't have that script, you are writing that script at the same time as you're rehearsing. People must be aware that that is a fundamental difference between dance rehearsals and creating a new dance piece, and creating a play where a playwright can spend a long period of time writing a play and the rehearsal period is often quite short. In dance, choreographers write their work and inscribe it on the bodies of performers in a rehearsal studio. That takes time, particularly if you want to produce quality.

I would rather, like Chunky Move endeavours to do, work on one work a year and then do a lot of performing of it and invest the time and money into one work than feel that we have to do two or three or four new works a year that have very little time and effort put into each one. They're all rushed. Australian dance works just don't last very long, you know. They go on the stage, you see them for about a year or so and they go off, and there's a new one. People don't see it as an investment of money and time in a work that you can actually use for a long period of time.

Wim Vanderkeybus in Belgium, for instance, he rehearses for six months on a work—which maybe is a little bit too long— and then tours it for six months around the world. And the next year, a new work. DV8 in London, a very similar process— a very long rehearsal period, then extensive touring and then a very high budget film made as a product, kind of rescripted, reworked and then made as a film. They may do only one work in two years or one work a year. It's just a different way of working and I think it's the only way of working for choreographers who really want to create

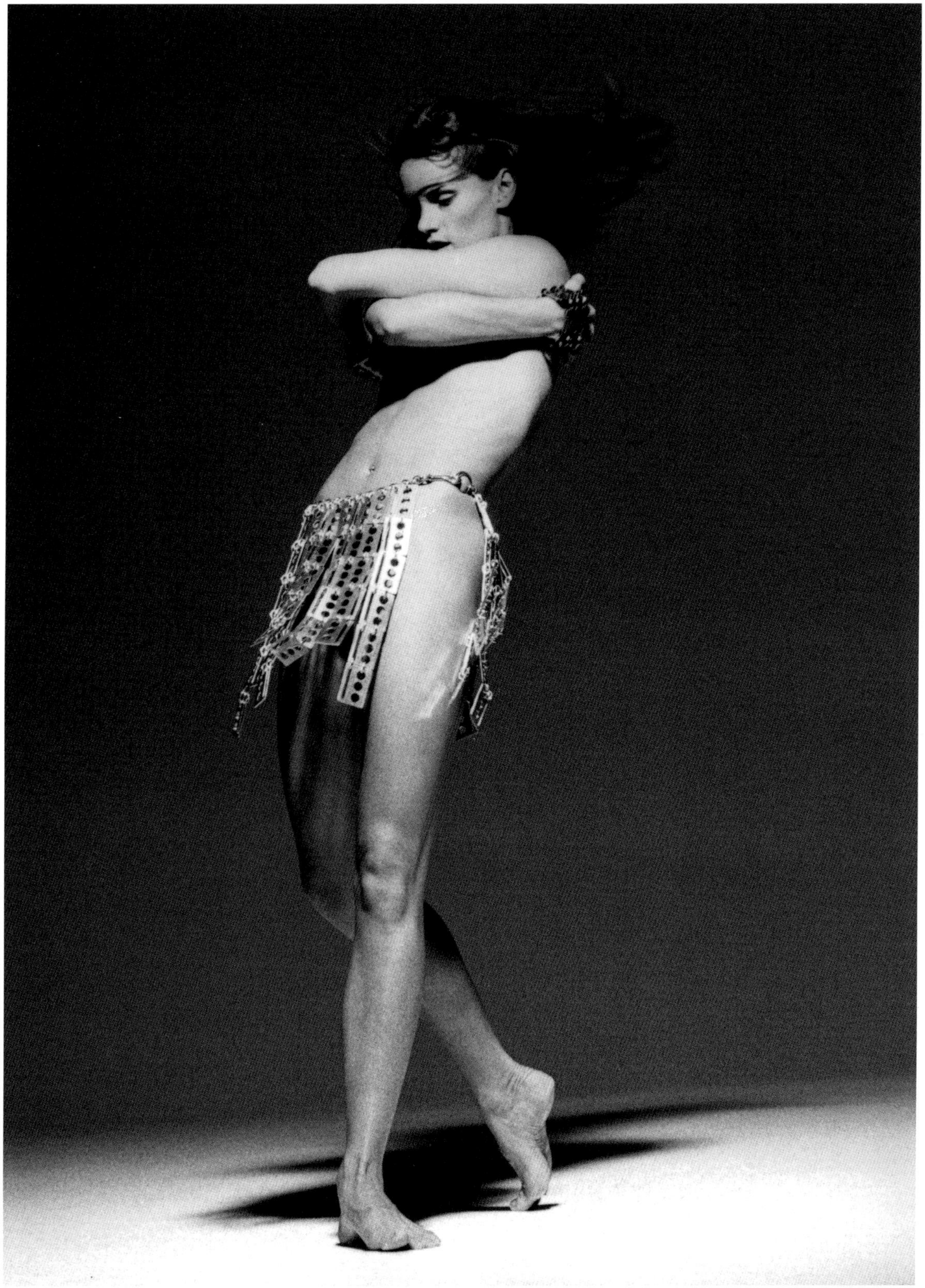

works—I mean real works that are comparable to writing and to visual arts.

POTTER: Is there a kind of ambivalence in your thoughts or in yourself between this European way and the Australian way, because you've spent a lot of time working with Nederlands Dans Theater?

OBARZANEK: No, I don't think so. I very much like aspects of both worlds, and they are almost two different worlds. I think if I really got off in Europe and the way you produced work there, I wouldn't be coming back to Australia at all. I now have a lot of opportunity in Europe and I can stay there but—I know it sounds very corny—it took me living in Europe for a year in '94 and into '95 to realise that I was very Australian. I liked it, I liked it very much—the wilderness, the type of people around me, the environment. I missed it very, very much, to the point where I couldn't stand being in Europe anymore—I had to go back. And most of my inspiration comes in Australia. For most of my works, even for Europe, the seed is always sown here and ideas gestate in my mind here in Australia. Then I take it over there and I develop it. What I like very much about Australia is there's a certain kind of raw vigour, a certain naivety, in a positive way. And also our New World type of culture—what could almost be argued by Europeans as this culture-less culture that becomes a culture of its own, this cultural-less-ness.

But Europe's taught me a lot, an incredible amount. There's a great respect for the integrity of the artwork and the importance of the development of choreography. And the low entertainment quota that you have to put into works, unlike in Australia, to please audiences. Going to the theatre is not necessarily to be entertained. It's actually to watch work that is discussed. It's sort of studied and pushed a lot further. That has had a big influence on me. So, yeah, maybe I have a slight arrogance coming back because I think, yes dammit, I need ten weeks. I need a designer to be designing in residence during the making of the choreography of the work in the studio; I don't want designs before I start the work. And the same with composers. I want to incite people, as I want to be incited by them as well, so we all create the work simultaneously. That's definitely an influence I've had from Europe.

For me, one of my biggest inspirations—and I'm going off the subject a bit here, but it's sort of related to it—has been the work of some recent film directors: Jim Jarmusch with *Stranger than Paradise*, then *Down by Law* and *Mystery Train*; Hal Hartley with *Trust*, *The Unbelievable Truth* and *Simple Men*; and then followed by Quentin Tarantino a number of years later, in a much more commercial sense, with *Pulp Fiction* and *Reservoir Dogs*. Quentin Tarantino is known for *Pulp Fiction*, but I think Jim Jarmusch and Hal Hartley were the first pulp fiction directors. And what is meant by pulp fiction is the ability to use popular culture, to appropriate it like pulp and shape it in your own way, to use it as an art form. So you're not a victim of popular culture, you actually begin to use it, deconstruct it and assemble it, and use it as fodder, as a material, as a communicative language. There's no point for a person of my age, or from my background or my culture, to be using classical aesthetics and classical sensibilities to communicate. It doesn't make any sense to me.

So, going back to the thing about Europe and Australia, the appeal about Australia—and for me to work in it is exactly that—I am surrounded by this popular culture fodder, and particularly in Sydney. That's why I live in Sydney—I love it, I'm like a child in a candy store. I just rip everything off, reshape it and spit it out again. I didn't feel that in Europe. I'm surprised how little influenced they are by popular culture there. I was relieved as well, but I realised that's where I get my excitement from, that's where I get my buzz from.

But despite his overwhelming interest in popular culture and contemporary aesthetics, Obarzanek's early dance background was classical. At the age of 15 he took some jazz classes in Melbourne and then, on the advice of his teacher, took ballet classes as well. Even though he had a sporting background at high school and was clearly physically proficient, he found the classical classes challenging—'it was so difficult, I liked it'. They led to his auditioning for and being accepted in the Australian Ballet School, where he also choreographed his first pieces.

Between the Australian Ballet School and Chunky Move, Obarzanek worked with the Queensland Ballet, which he joined in 1988, and then with

Sydney Dance Company in the early 1990s. The seeds for his independent career were sown during this period, partly as a result of a certain unease he felt with dance company lifestyle, and partly out of frustrations he felt at not being offered enough opportunities to choreograph. But it was, nevertheless, also a period of choreographic creativity that resulted in a number of successful works for major companies including *Sleep No More* (1991) and *Saccharin Suite* (1994) for Sydney Dance Company, and *Sand Siren* (1992) for the Australian Ballet, and his first work for NDT2, *Petrol Head Lover*. It also saw his first foray into filmmaking, an avenue that he confesses he would like to pursue further.

POTTER: You actually have had a classical background?

OBARZANEK: Yes. I started off when I first went to dance classes doing jazz ballet at the local community centre type thing. To go there took a lot of courage, I think, and a lot of prodding from my mum. I was 15, going on 16. It was in Melbourne and I was a real suburban kid. But I got into it and I enjoyed it very much. Before long, I really was convinced I wanted to become a commercial dancer or a professional dancer of some sort, and my teacher convinced me that I should do some classical classes as well to improve my discipline, my sense of coordination, my strength. I wasn't too keen on the idea, but I listened to her advice and I went. I found that very, very difficult, particularly as I was now 16 and doing high school at the same time. But there was a challenge there, you know—it was so difficult, I liked it.

Then I finished high school and I went to the Australian Ballet School. That was a total classical scene. I was 19 in my first year there and a lot of the dancers there were much younger than me. But I was lucky. It was a bad year, I think, for auditioning for the Ballet School and there were a few guys in there 19 and 20 and 21, and we were all pretty shonky. That was great. I'm glad that that was that year because if it was another year, maybe I wouldn't have lasted. I think there were just certain teachers who made me feel that it was really worth going on and really pursuing. My classical teacher was Kelvin Coe and my modern teacher was Gayrie MacSween. They were very inspirational—the two individuals that basically pushed me through ballet school. It was definitely not the institution of the Australian Ballet School at all. I thought it was a totally shocking place. I already had earrings and the whole thing and was taking drugs and drinking and I drove a car—and I was known for it as well, you know, it was not a hidden thing. And they were very conservative. I didn't see that it should have an effect, my private life, as long as it didn't affect my work life.

I think, over the three years at the Ballet School, that indoctrination and that kind of insulation that happens by being a student there had a real effect on me, and by the end I really wanted to become a very good classical dancer. And I wasn't the best classical dancer at that time—I got better later on—and I didn't make it to the Australian Ballet. I got offered a contract with Queensland Ballet and I took it. It was a good basis to start with because, being in a smaller and more regional company, you had to do very different works and very different roles. You were thrown on stage continuously, rather than being in a corps for a long period of time. By the end of first year in the Queensland Ballet I was in contemporary works, I was doing lead roles, and then in the second year I was doing lead roles in classical works. But really, contemporary was just so much more interesting and, the longer I was away from the Ballet School, it just became more and more evident. You know, it was just very clear. I was already choreographing in the Ballet School and no work I was choreographing was remotely classical. So, I don't know why, I felt I had to prove something, you know. I had a very huge sporting background when I was in high school, a very competitive edge at that time, my physicality was very competitive, and so being in a classical dance environment, I felt some kind of compulsion to do it well and to get big roles and so forth. And I don't know, then I just got totally over it and saw the light and dropped the whole thing.

POTTER: What inspired you to choreograph in the first place?

OBARZANEK: I'm not sure at the time, I can't remember. I remember my first choreography very clearly. We had Martha Graham classes three times a week with Gayrie MacSween and she believed it was very important for us to produce some of our own works. The School would not give any time in its curriculum for composition, the study of composition, of choreography and so forth. So Gayrie

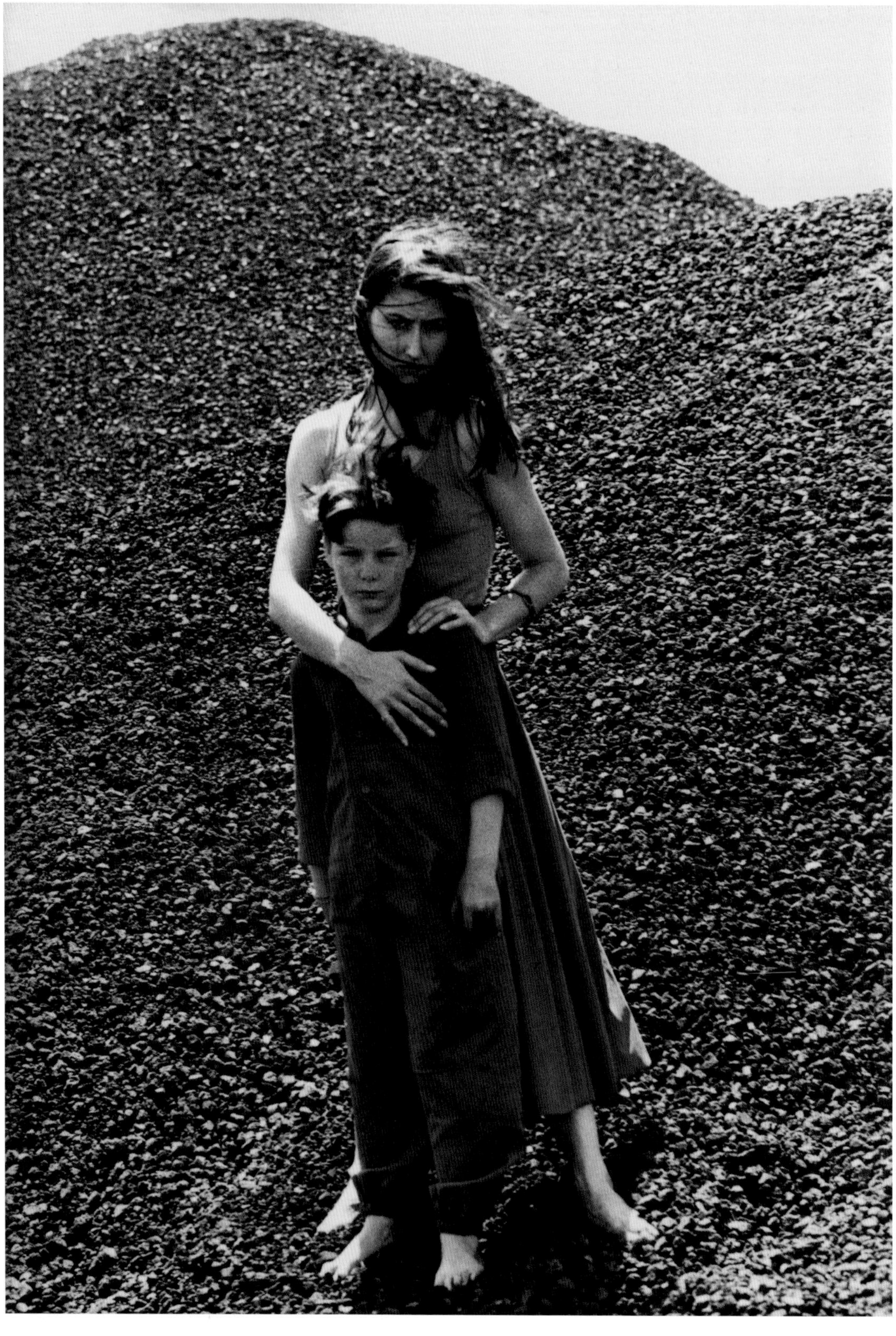

encouraged us—I was in first year. A few of us really became interested. She basically talked me into it. She was so positive about it that I thought, 'Okay, this classical thing's a real dog.' It was very difficult for me and I thought, 'Well, I'll do some of this as well.' So, during our lunchtimes and after school in our own time, we started working on very small pieces. I did this piece with music, a percussion piece, by Peter Gabriel. I was embarrassed about choreographing because I felt all the dancers were better than me—they were more experienced, they'd been dancing since they were eight or nine. I ended up actually choreographing in my bedroom at home and then I'd bring steps back, kind of combinations, to school. The piece I did was very exciting and it was for four men. We had this showing and the audience just went wild over this piece. It was kept and it was performed again, and then it was used actually with the Dancers Company.

POTTER: Oh, is this *The Heat*?

OBARZANEK: Yes. So, really, what started me choreographing was success. I'm sad and embarrassed to say that I just sat there so stupefied. I mean, I was just amazed at these people going off about this piece that I was very shy about, choreographed in my bedroom—which was very small. It made me very interested; I was very keen to try something else. So, yes, it started there. It never stopped. I was always really keen to choreograph.

When I joined Queensland Ballet we had this choreographic workshop in my first year. I did this piece and it went very well, and I was commissioned by Australasian Drama Studies Association Conference to do an opening piece for them, and then by Queensland Dance School of Excellence, QDSE, to do a short work. It all kind of came from doing this piece at this workshop. So I sort of thought, 'Well, I want to do more, I want to do more.' I directed a film in my own spare time. I lived in a warehouse in Teneriffe in Brisbane and one of the people who hired out the warehouse for a band practice was thrown out of the Australian Film and Television School the year before in his second year. He was kind of a keen, crazy filmmaker, so we got together and made a film, because I was already getting bored with doing classical works. To get our money back, we put it into this film commission, the Queensland Film Makers Awards, and we got an award for it and Graeme Murphy saw it.

So there was always this one thing leading to another. Then I had these grand ideas. I wanted to choreograph more, I wanted to choreograph for the Queensland Ballet and I used to just nag Harold Collins (artistic director of the Queensland Ballet, 1978–97) the whole time—I must have been the biggest pain in the butt for him, you know, continuously going, 'Harold, Harold, I want to do this piece, dah, dah, dah.' He just didn't have time for it, and my ideas were very contemporary and modern, and Harold's weren't. And I didn't have the patience, either. I think if I had have stuck it out, I would have gotten opportunities, but I'm a very impatient person—I have to do it now, yesterday. I left; I left Queensland Ballet. I think I would have been in Queensland Ballet longer had I had opportunities to choreograph, but Harold was interested in me as a dancer and not that interested in me as a choreographer. One of the reasons that I left the Queensland Ballet was this incredible frustration.

POTTER: So you went to Sydney Dance Company after that?

OBARZANEK: Yes, went to Sydney Dance. Graeme saw that film we made—it was called *Mr Crowther and the Wallflower*—and he liked it very much. It was choreographed actually for Grant McLay and Larissa Wright. It was sort of a duet done in different environments, sort of a narrative, because a thing was happening in an office between a businessman and a secretary. It was very arty. I couldn't bear looking at it now. It's one of those student films. You know, when you're 21, you make these incredibly dumb, powerful, deep and meaningful films that are just crap. But, I think, for its time, yes, it was a fine film to make, it was an adventure, it was a totally naive jump into filmmaking.

But anyway, Graeme saw that and he liked it very much. I was on holidays in Sydney—I was doing some classes with Sydney Dance. I'd just been given my first big, big role in a classic rep of Romeo dancing with Rosetta Cook as Juliet; it was the first thing we were starting with Queensland Ballet after the holidays. For me that was very nerve-racking, because it was a very big bite for me as a dancer to do at that stage. So, during the holidays, I was just doing classes all the time and doing as much as I could. I wanted to be really strong for it, really strong for the big full-length. So I was consequently in Sydney doing classes there. And I think it was a combination of the film and me doing classes and stuff, but Graeme asked me what I was doing. I was getting more and more frustrated with Harold not really giving me opportunities to choreograph. I wanted to go overseas, actually to Europe, and start really getting into more contemporary dance. I chickened out. I think Graeme offered me a safe place, a good contract in Sydney, and I wanted to go back down south from where I came. I was very much over Brisbane from the day I'd got there. I found it a hard place to work, I found it culturally really depressing the whole time I was there. So I chickened out big from Europe. I took the Sydney Dance contract thinking, 'Okay, I'll do this for a year'—the old 'I'll do it for year, I'll make some money, I'll get some more experience, and then I'll go'. So, 2½ years later, still in Sydney Dance, I finally left.

Sydney Dance was a really interesting period of time for me. I think I became the most cynical about professional dance and company-style dancing during my time at Sydney Dance Company. And also I learnt a lot—I learnt a lot about the business of dance, very much the business of professional dance, the business of marketing, the business of charisma. It's a very hard time to talk about. I actually think, and having talked to Paul Mercurio and Stephen Page and Kim Walker and Dale Pengelly—all friends of mine, all ex-Sydney Dance people—it's amusing how, a few years down the track, we've shared very, very similar feelings that we've never really discussed with people. I think I was there for a much shorter period of time than, say, Kim and Paul and Stephen, so I wasn't as affected, but I really felt stripped of my pride, of a sense of creativity. You joined a stable of thoroughbreds, you know—that's what you were led to believe. You were all these great, beautiful, handsome, sexy, aesthetically pleasing, cat-like-moving dancers. The company worked very hard to create an illusion of grandeur and we worked very hard to believe it. You were going on great international tours and doing great fantastic things, and Graeme does the most huge and amazing works. You worked so much there, you were so involved with Sydney Dance, it was hours and days. When I joined, we spent only three months of the year in Sydney, or four months in Sydney—and even that was only like a number of weeks—and then we'd be off again. You lost contact with people outside of Sydney Dance Company, because you were this travelling troupe, you know.

But, nevertheless, I was very keen to choreograph all the time and that never stopped. Graeme was not so keen for me to choreograph. Again, if I had the patience, I think I would have been doing more for Sydney Dance than I did, but I wanted to do more there and then. I became very disillusioned with dance after doing a period of just fast-lane Sydney living, young guy in the Cross. I got a scholarship from the Marten Bequest—I actually received it just before I joined the Sydney Dance Company and I'd deferred it for a year. The minute I joined Sydney Dance, I was very busy doing really great roles and my dancing was elevated to no end from Queensland Ballet, hugely. I was seen as a very special dancer at Sydney Dance when I first joined, a very exciting new recruit, and it was a very exciting time to be there.

But then I travelled to New York and I travelled to Spain and I went to London for a short period of time. It was such an eye-opener, like having seen NDT when they were touring, when they came to the Adelaide Festival in '86 and they were using the Australian Ballet School studios for their rehearsal rooms. They came to Melbourne at the Princess Theatre and they had no rehearsal room, and they were working on a new program while they were doing their program at night. That was one of those times when it was just total revolutionary for me—this ballet student, missing my classes to wedge the door slightly open and sit there for hours watching all these fabulous modern dancers hurling themselves in the studio. Again, this Marten Bequest scholarship was like another one of those times. It was one of those fast-track learning periods. It was very hard after that to go back to Sydney Dance and the ego. Opening night functions were as important as the show itself, and all this. Brunch with Bill and Dallas Hayden at Government House, all this sort of stuff, and embassy functions. I became very cynical of the whole thing.

Then I had a really bad injury to my knee which had been playing up for quite a while. Finally my knee—my left knee— gave in at the Caracas Festival in Venezuela in the early nineties and I had to have quite a big operation on it. At that time I got a commission from the Australian Ballet to do my first commissioned work outside of Sydney Dance. Graeme didn't want me to do it because I was pegged to be this special performer in his new full-evening work. I asked for three months' leave and we got into an argument, and in the end it just totally broke down and I very much clearly saw the direction I wanted to go and left.

But the injury, I think, really gave me no choice of returning. I was very scared of leaving, I was very scared of not performing. When you perform for a while it begins to define you, it becomes so much a part of you that not performing is like a part of yourself gone missing. It's like people who get married when they're 18 or 19 and they're with somebody for 20 years—they build each other, they are part of each other and, if one person leaves for whatever reason, it's like a part of yourself goes. I think similarly it is with a performer. So that was very frightening, and then I got over it. I do perform every now and again, and I don't feel this obligation or this real 'I'm going to melt and disappear if I don't perform'. Well, I did then, but the injury helped me kind of go, 'Okay, well, you haven't got a choice.' I was on crutches for a long time and rehab for a long time. It was very good, it was very good for a dancer at that stage to be forced—or, preferably, not to be forced—but not to dance for a period of time. It clears your head and if you go back in to dancing, you do it so much better. And often if you weren't doing it for the right reasons, you *are* after that. That was very much the case with me, both with choreographing and performing after my injury. There was the before and after, which was great.

POTTER: But you must have come back to Sydney Dance Company to work because you did *Saccharin Suite* in 1994.

OBARZANEK: Yes, that was a couple of years down the track, after I left. I had done my first work with NDT2 already by that stage and Graeme saw a video of that. I think I was not pegged to do that work with Sydney Dance; Sydney Dance was hoping to get Ohad Naharin back and do *Arbos* again. Ohad had done a second version on Cullberg Ballet after its world premiere with Sydney Dance and didn't want the original version done by Sydney Dance—he wanted only the new version done. He didn't have the time to come and teach it—it was part of his thing that none of his works are done without him personally rehearsing them. So he left Sydney Dance in a real lurch—they couldn't actually do their own work, *Arbos*, which was originally done on them.

I was around and I'd just finished doing this successful work, *Petrol Head Lover*, with NDT2, so Graeme asked me whether I'd do a new work, and I did. I don't think *Saccharin Suite* overall is a very successful work, although I like it and a lot of people liked it. But it was a very important work for me. There are certain works for choreographers that may not necessarily be as successful as others, but they're very important works. It did open a new door. It was a style that I had not used before. Now in *Fast Idol*, I can see *Saccharin Suite* is definitely the baby, the before, and *Fast Idol* is a much more grown-up version of it. It's interesting, I do that style in Australia. My European style is very physical. I get very influenced by the people I work with and, with the Australian people I work with, the humour comes out. My suburban background just comes out for some reason. The European works are much more involved with dance, you know, pure investigation of dance and movement and not very narrative. Also, in NDT2 I work with very young dancers and it's hard work for very young dancers to approach works like *Fast Idol*—impossible, I think actually.

Born in Melbourne in 1966, Obarzanek spent his early childhood in Israel. His memories of and reflections on the Middle East have fed into at least one of his works, *Sand Siren*, although he suggests that he has well and truly moved on from the romanticism that fuelled that work. His hopes for the future suggest that he will continue to produce work that is daring, diverse and of its time.

POTTER: Do you have pleasant childhood memories?

OBARZANEK: Yes, I do. When I was one we moved to Israel and I grew up on a kibbutz called Gal-On and I was there until I was eight. So my early childhood memories are from the kibbutz. They're very pleasant memories for me. The kibbutz was very small. It was like a huge farm, I guess, with about 80 members or so, like a collective. We had a children's house—it was for 12 children. Every afternoon you'd have siesta, and after siesta you'd go to your parents' house and you'd spend the whole evening there, and then they'd come and tuck you in, but in *your* room, which was the schoolroom.

We mainly grew cotton. We were an agricultural kibbutz—we had cotton and wheat and a lot of citrus, so it was all based on the seasons and all based on irrigation and huge farming equipment. It was totally 'boys with toys'. I was totally into trucks and things. My father was a welder there and worked in maintenance on big, huge harvesting equipment, so I hung around. It felt very exciting. The men, I remember, built our whole playground with swings and slides and a huge rocketship thing with a staircase and things. Yeah, it was just a total child fantasy time. Even during the Yom Kippur War when I was there, it was still a bit of fantasy. Even with the air raid drills and bunkers and my father being away for long periods of time in the army, it felt very exciting.

When my parents decided to move back to Melbourne, they lied to me and my brother; they said, 'We're going on a big holiday and we're going to be away for two or three months.' And we were away, and we were away, and we were away, and then finally my brother and I realised we weren't coming back. That was really tough at that age. I really didn't want to stay in Australia—Australia was such an alien environment. I think if we'd moved to the country in Australia, it may have been slightly different, but we moved right into Melbourne. That kind of city and that kind of suburban living and that kind of lifestyle I had never experienced before at all. And a different language— I didn't know a word of English; I could read, write and speak Hebrew. So that was very difficult; and going to this kind of red-brick state primary school. I knew every child in the kibbutz so intimately, so well—every single person by their first name—and I'd grown up like that, and to be hurled into a school of, what, 400 total strangers! And for the first time, actually coming in contact with the cruelty of children, how cruel they can be to each other, which I'd never experienced before—I don't know why that didn't come up in the kibbutz. It affected my brother and I differently. I think I coped better than my brother—my brother totally shut down at one stage and he refused to speak any English or anything for over a year and a half or something. He was a bit younger than me and he found it very difficult.

We also found Australia really dead. We found the people really, really dead compared to Israelis where there was always a lot of commotion. I think, in the Middle East in general, there's just that kind of things are happening, people are out in the streets, people are outdoor people. But I got used to it. I was fortunately physically not huge, but big, and I was playing football for my primary school pretty quick.

POTTER: Did the kibbutz experience provide inspiration for *Sand Siren*?

OBARZANEK: Yes, yes, very much. *Sand Siren* was one of those concepts or way of working that I never work in at all now, where it came to me like a vision. It was like really corny. It was just a series of ideas that built up very quickly when I was listening to Arvo Pärt's *Cantus, Tribute to Benjamin Britten*. It was all very romantic and it was still in the heady days of being in Queensland Ballet, still dancing classical roles. God, I can't believe it's the same person, because it's quite a classical approach to dance, *Sand Siren*. It's a very romantic work, it's a very idealistic work. I'd find a work like that very difficult to watch now, whether I choreographed it or anybody else choreographed it. But yes, it was like romantic idealism about death and war in the Middle East when men were men and women cried. I'm really, really glad that *Sand Siren* is no longer performed; that's all I can say about it.

POTTER: How did *Sand Siren* come about, that commission?

OBARZANEK: *Sand Siren* came about because we were doing *Shakespeare Dances*, which was in Sydney Dance Company where I think seven or six choreographers—dancers in Sydney Dance—were invited to choreograph short pieces based on Shakespeare works. I did a work, *Sleep No More*, which was loosely—very loosely—based on Macbeth. Maina (Gielgud) saw it and liked it very much. Then the Australian Ballet was having a workshop, a choreographic workshop, which was an in-house workshop similar to Sydney Dance. I expressed frustrations that I wasn't doing much at Sydney Dance, as much choreography as I wanted to do. I wanted to do more and would it be possible for me to be part of the workshop? She was keen for me to come to the Australian Ballet and be part of the workshop, and it coincidentally fell within our vacation at Sydney Dance. So, during my holidays I went straight to Melbourne and worked on this short 12-minute piece (*Siesta to Dusk*) which was later a part of *Sand Siren*. This piece went really well in the workshop and Maina said, 'Look, there's a window, there's a gap next year, we've got a work that's fallen through. Do you want to expand on this short piece?' I said, 'Yes, sure.' So that's how *Sand Siren* came about.

POTTER: Where do you see yourself going in the future?

OBARZANEK: That's a good question. Well, I definitely want to keep batting on this Chunky Move wicket for a while. It is a lot of hard work, it's much harder work than commissions and working with dance companies where there's a certain format—once you understand it and you're in the scene, you can keep doing it. Otherwise very few people will stand in your way, but very few people will really help you either. It's very much up to you. That's a challenge. You know, if any good works are going to come from me, I think most of them will probably come under Chunky Move because I will try to create the environment I need to continue my works.

I feel I'm finding a voice, I'm feeling more comfortable. I'm feeling more daring too, more challenging—I strive for that. I feel that dance, comparatively to other arts mediums, is really behind, it's really verging on a joke kind of medium, it's really a lagging kind of thing. There's a few people who are really into it. I think it's a medium with such potential, such incredible potential—if it's a little bit of a mixed medium, it doesn't really matter. I really want to push that at the moment. I've no idea for how long. I'd hate to be this old, fat, drunken, middle-aged choreographer with a dying-in-the-arse company pontificating to young choreographers about the days when we were a bloody revolution—I just hope that that doesn't happen to me. But I don't know how to avert that. I'll probably go on to something else.

The interview with Gideon Obarzanek took place on a warm, Sydney summer evening. Towards the end of the interview the light began to fade but, rather than disturb the pace and the energy of the conversation, we continued in the growing darkness. Obarzanek had only just returned to Sydney from the Netherlands, and the question of the differences between a European and an Australian way of working was very much in his mind. He is an exuberant talker and was generous and thoroughly forthright in his answers to whatever questions were put before him.

Choreography by Gideon Obarzanek

1987	The Heat	Australian Ballet School Choreographic Workshop
1988	Drift Office	Queensland Ballet Choreographic Workshop
1989	Mr Crowther and the Wallflower	Australasian Drama Studies Association
1991	Sleep No More	Sydney Dance Company
	Siesta to Dusk	Australian Ballet Choreographic Workshop
1992	You've Got Me Floating	Victorian College of the Arts
	Sand Siren	Australian Ballet
1993	Sweetheart	Dancers Company
	Slow Me Up, Speed Me Down	Kibbutz Contemporary Dance Company
	Petrol Head Lover	Nederlands Dans Theater 2
1994	Saccharin Suite	Sydney Dance Company
	While You're Down There	Melbourne Dance Theatre
	Play Dead	West Australian Ballet
1995	Cool White Fridge Knocked Over	Nederlands Dans Theater 2
	Fast Idol	Chunky Move, Melbourne Festival
1996	Lurch	Nederlands Dans Theater 2
1997	Bonehead	Chunky Move, Sydney Festival

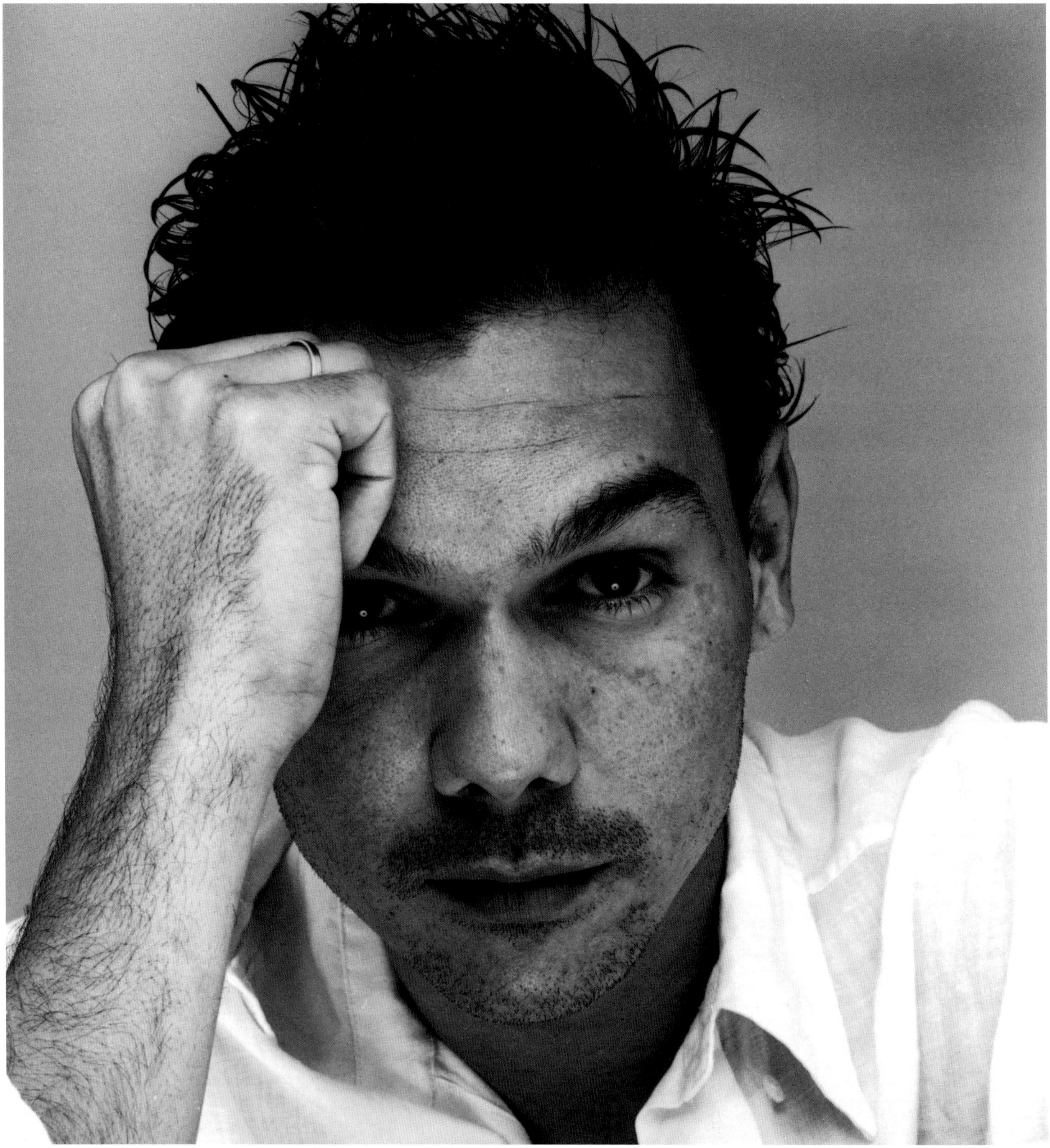

Stephen Page

Feet to the Earth

Interview TRC 3397

Stephen Page (born 1965), dancer and choreographer and artistic director of Bangarra Dance Theatre, was interviewed in Sydney by Michelle Potter in January 1996

Stephen Page, whose work combines both traditional Aboriginal and strong urban influences, is the first choreographer of Aboriginal descent to have achieved major national and international recognition. He is currently artistic director of Bangarra Dance Theatre, a company established in 1989 by graduates and staff of the Aboriginal Islander Dance Theatre, the performing arm of the National Aboriginal and Islander Skills Development Association (NAISDA). Page has, however, choreographed an eclectic range of works for an equally eclectic range of theatrical and non-theatrical organisations, which range well beyond indigenous dance companies and include the Australian Ballet and the Australian Football League.

The timing of Page's arrival on the professional, theatrical dance scene coincides with a particularly momentous period in Australian history, a period of growing recognition by non-Aboriginal Australians of the traditions and culture, not to mention the rights, of indigenous Australians. This emerging public awareness of Aboriginal arts, strongly promoted in the media, has given Page a particularly significant status in Australia. Page himself sets his career in this context when he refers to his various achievements as 'breaking down barriers'. He also emphasises his conviction that the recognition of indigenous art is long overdue when he says that he is frustrated that government support for a dance company like Bangarra did not happen long ago.

Brisbane-born, Page is the tenth in a family of 12 children, six girls and six boys. His Aboriginal ties are to his father's community, that of the Munaldjali people of the Yugambeh tribe whose traditional land in south-eastern Queensland extends from Charleville in the west across to Surfers Paradise in the east. But his upbringing was urban and he grew up in what he calls 'the Bronx of Brisbane', in a family for whom urbanisation meant poverty, but whose lifestyle was still able to centre on what Page sees as indigenous cultural values, including the close bonds of kinship and the non-separation of art and life.

POTTER: Stephen, can you tell me a little bit about your background—your parents and any particular memories you might have of your childhood?

PAGE: No traditional Aboriginal language was passed on in my family, except for a lot of the day-to-day words that were used that my father had hung on to from his grandparents. You must understand that in the southern part of the country, with the onslaught—it's not a very nice word—the reality of colonialism and settlement at that time was that people were not meant to hang on to their language and take it further. So for me, I suppose, my childhood was just about surviving. My mother and father were people who were very much in the lower class in terms of settlement. It was very much a struggle in a way because we just had to make do with what necessities we had. It was basically, I suppose, a lot of humour and love and great communication amongst the family. It was very hard for my father to actually feel proud of his culture, not having much to pass on because such a lot of it had been broken up. So, I suppose, we just created our own sort of urban tribe living in Mount Gravatt in Brisbane. Having older brothers and sisters was good for me because we were able to observe the struggle and the opportunities that they didn't have as they were growing, so there was a sense of respect there right from the beginning, a mutual respect amongst the family.

I was always involved in the arts, I suppose naturally, because I believe my mother tap-danced when she was quite young, and my father was very much into music—at their local gatherings he was always wanting to be the song man of the party. But my mother, I never knew much about my mother in terms of her background until I was a lot older. But a lot of the art was passed on naturally through the sisters' experiences in terms of what music they were interested in. I suppose the boys became the guinea pigs. The girls were the artistic directors and choreographers, they would practise on the boys. So we were like their models or their actors or their dancers. They would create on us. We used to perform in the kitchen and then we got promoted to the laundry roof. We were always spending a lot of time within the family environment.

I think, to me, that reflects very much the form of any tribe or community. I think that it was very much an urban one, but I believe it had the essence of a traditional tribe, how it would work. It was family bonding—the family were very close, and still are very close.

POTTER: Did you have any formal music or dance training while you were in Brisbane?

PAGE: No. Like I said, it was probably much more natural home talent that was passed on to us. My sisters were very clever. They were very creative. The majority of them were very in tune with their bodies and very athletic, very physical, because they worked at a young age just to help the family survive. So they were strong women. And they had an interest in a great diversity of styles of music, from the blues to jazz. My mother and father were into jazz and the blues and very much the vaudeville times of Ginger Rogers and Fred Astaire. My sisters were interested in Elvis Presley.

So a diversity of music and rhythms was always floating through the house; you got connected with that naturally. The younger members of the family would have been influenced a lot more than, say, the older members of the family. I sympathise with the girls because I always feel like if it was the boys first and the girls coming later, what sort of person would I be today? Would I be just a landscaper, concreter, living in Brisbane and raising a family, or living on a farm? So time is a real issue for me in terms of what guides are there at the time. But, I think, the natural interest in performing arts was just passed on through my mother, father and my sisters.

Page began his formal training as a dancer in Sydney. He left Brisbane to attend NAISDA College after being distracted from his job as a trainee law clerk by an image of a dancer on a poster advertising the Aboriginal Islander Dance Theatre. NAISDA was a major influence on Page's life. It was there that he had his first encounters with traditional Aboriginal dance. It was there, too, that he began to consider the political implications of his aboriginality.

POTTER: Was it a huge step leaving your family and coming to Sydney?

PAGE: I think naturally, yes. Emotionally it was. But I used to defeat that because at times it's all too much to be that close-knit into a community. I might sound like I'm contradicting myself, but at that age I had seen a lot and taken what I wanted to take. I think I had the strength and I was quite confident and very eager. I don't think my mother and father challenged that in me; I think they had known that, by the time I reached 12 and got to high school, I was pretty much the good boy of the family, so to speak. I'd never asked my mother and father for anything and I never got into any trouble, so they were quite supportive I suppose, and there was a wonderful respect. I think my father was more nervous than I was; I was quite confident. And at the same time I think he was quite proud that I could break away, because I was the youngest to leave—well, the youngest in age to leave at that time.

POTTER: What was it like coming to NAISDA? What kind of technique were you being taught?

PAGE: I think NAISDA would have been going for seven years then—seven or eight years—so they were obviously still in an evolving stage of their curriculum and in a stage of determining how the academic side would work with the performing arts, the dance side. So it was very much an exciting process, an evolving time. In my application I can remember I wrote stories about my experience and my upbringing. The student officer at that time, Graham Mooney, I can remember him and I talking about my application many years later and he was stating that I didn't say I had jazz lessons or anything like that, it was very much driven from the natural home talent of how I was brought up. And I believe most Aboriginal and Torres Strait Islander students very much had the same experiences, obviously because it was too confronting to even go into a ballet class or a music class where they felt a minority. So I think most of them would not have had any formal training.

The forms of dance were jazz, tap, ballet, modern—whether it was (Lester) Horton or Martha Graham—and classical ballet. Then you had the priority styles of dance, which was some form of traditional Aboriginal dancing and some form of Torres Strait Island dancing. So the fruit salad of all that. And you *know* a NAISDA student when they come out, you *know* that style. Now within Bangarra it's moved on to the next level, which is much more of an independent, professional level.

POTTER: When did you become aware of a traditional part of your life? Did that happen at NAISDA?

PAGE: I went to Arnhem Land in the first year I was there, because each year in the College you go on a remote tour—whether it's in the Kimberleys or the Central Desert or Arnhem Land or the Torres Strait depends on the course at that time and where they want to send the students. But all the students would go at the end of the year to a remote area and, for me, it was fortunate that it was Arnhem Land. That was the first time I came in contact with any form of traditional customs or values or lifestyle. So I was very culture-shocked—it changed me completely.

It's very confronting if you're brought up in an urban situation and then you've got a traditional elder there teaching you your own dances. Whereas everything else, if it was classical or tap or jazz, we were much more immune to because we had an urban upbringing—that's what we were used to, the contemporary world. So it was just an amazing moment to learn any form of traditional dance. I think when I did discover traditional dance, or the essence of it, and the groundedness behind it, it then influenced and inspired me to choreograph and to bring my experiences all together. So that's what it is, I believe, when you choreograph and create—it's just a fruit salad of your experiences, and that becomes your style.

POTTER: What is the essence of traditional dance for you?

PAGE: I just believe you've got to have a sense of self-respect and self-focus. I mean, I will never understand a traditional upbringing. I made the decision that it was an experience that I should really respect. With Aboriginal people, their life is art really. It's like the hunter stalking a prey, it's a dance. Anything they do—the gathering, the hunting, it's all those survival skills and those life experiences—they put it all into their music and their song and their dance, and their storytelling especially. That's what the dreaming's about. It's cyclic, it's ongoing and then they pass it on. It's a bit like a tree and it's got 17 branches to it—everyone should be able to have 17 branches and be that diverse and be able to feel like that, be able to look into life like that.

So, for me, I think the importance of going back to the traditional style of dance was that I was able to observe and watch our traditional teachers, not just for the dance steps but to be aware of what environment they came from, what their landscape was like geographically, and to try to understand their kinship and their customs and their values. Then that made me understand why they're so grounded, and made me understand the dreaming and the mother earth and just all the myths and storytellings behind me. I believed that there had to be some core to that. It is a sense of self-essence that we have to focus on. Hopefully I can pass it on to my son and he will be able to somehow experience a lot more than me in that area and then he will pass it on. So there's a sense of continuity. It's being consistent about the belief too. Yes, it's an interesting one.

Once I started to observe the traditional values my father was very interested in it. I had brought it back home in stages. Then my father started to open up and reveal a lot more. He started to tell a lot of stories then and pass information to me bit by bit. But it was very painful for him, so I'm going to have to take like a whole two years off just to rekindle his thoughts about his past and his culture, his traditional values. There's information, there's a lot of research to be done there, but it's going to be quite an emotional journey for me. But maybe I'm my father's messenger—I'm meant to go on that journey to help bring back and rekindle his past.

But once I joined NAISDA I had huge revelations in terms of how I was brought up. Once you met someone from the Kimberleys

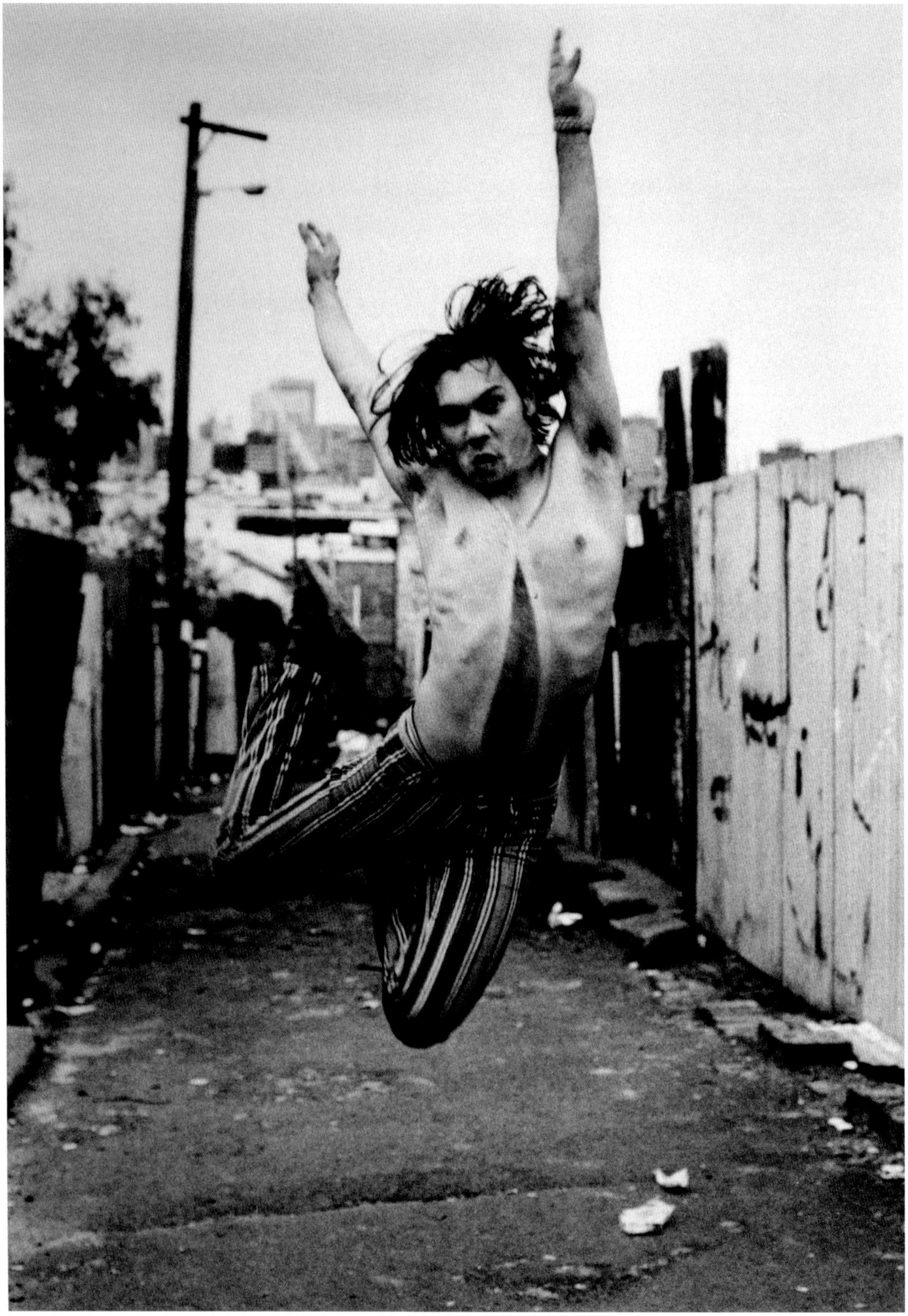

or the Central Desert or Arnhem Land or people from the Torres Straits, they inspired you to get in touch more with your roots and more with your traditional background, or just your cultural background. It was all based on language, whether it meant language in dance language, in hunting language ... But it was almost like, for them, it was important to maintain their language and to try to live two worlds, so to speak. For me, I was a bit saddened by that, because then I started to get angry and started to get a bit of a radical. You know, I was anti-white. I became a racist-type person. I think it's between that age of 16–21 or whatever—some people never let go of it. But I was quite angry actually at that time. I think I laid a lot of pressure on my father at that stage because I'd only go home once a year for the superficial Christmas times.

POTTER: When you say you were something of a rebel at NAISDA, what exactly did you do to give vent to this feeling?

PAGE: I was just very confident, I was always very confident and at the same time very quiet. So, when I say 'rebel', at times I could be very arrogant and quite witty and quite abrupt. I was probably ugly in a constructive way, if that makes sense. I always knew what I wanted and I always had a sense of purpose for what I wanted. So I think when elders or mentors see that energy in a young adult, they tend to try to steer it. So that's where I say I had good mentors who could see that. I think that what they saw at that stage was a young leader. And when that's pushed in your head all the time—that you have the energy and you have the tough goanna skin to actually be a leader—I think the more you hear it, the more you start to believe in it. I was hearing it from a good source, but what I had to do was remind myself to respect it. I don't know, I just think that was a natural instinct at that age, to get the attention to make sure that you got what you wanted.

POTTER: Did you have a vision for your career at the end of NAISDA?

PAGE: I didn't have a vision but my guides had a vision, if that makes sense. It's almost like everyone's got two sides to themselves—I believe that, I totally believe in that—there's a positive and a negative in everyone. I think I was very much into the negative side of things. I was just totally confused and frustrated about human rights and justice, not so much the dance or the arts, and the only way that I thought I could get out of that frustration was just basically to use the motto that life is art and go back into my creativity, which would make me understand and appreciate and pull myself out of that rut. I was very fortunate that I had a lot of support and I respected it. But, at the same time, I was frustrated with my own culture and trying to resolve it somehow. So that was a tough one. I romanticised with a vision, if you know what I mean, and I think at that age it was very romantic in terms of how I saw it. But I really believe that there is a strong guide that I have. I really believe that it was directing my vision.

From NAISDA, Page joined Sydney Dance Company but, after some time with the company, returned to NAISDA to teach and direct. This period on the staff of NAISDA opened up his choreographic career, which was also nurtured during a second period with Sydney Dance. The return to NAISDA also marked the beginnings of his career as a director and paved the way for him to be offered the directorship of Bangarra. Page joined Bangarra as its principal choreographer in September 1991, and was appointed artistic director at the end of 1991.

POTTER: Did you go then straight from NAISDA into Sydney Dance Company, or was there a transition of some sort?

PAGE: I was at NAISDA for three years and it was actually Janet Vernon who saw an end-of-year performance called *Stomping Ground* in '85 and invited me to do classes. Classical wasn't my best style, but I think both she and Graeme (Murphy) just saw something. She saw me as a performer and when I did class, she was a bit confused why my classical technique wasn't as advanced as my performance skills. So I think that that was interesting to them. About two weeks later I went through a bit of an interview on how keen I was. Once again I was very confident and said yes. And then I just worked, I worked very hard. That was probably one of the hardest stages of my life, because I moved from the house of identity into the house of discipline. The spirit was different, the energy was different. It was a professional company. It was very much every man for himself and look, learn and listen at the same time—but for yourself. And very competitive—things that probably weren't introduced to me at the College or through my family. Those sorts of emotions were just different, so it was hard to keep my feet to the earth. I've always reflected on my upbringing and where I'd come from. It was a bit of a culture shock just going there and moving away from that, from what I was brought up with.

Sydney Dance had been in the mainstream for a bit of time then, so it was very glamorous. It was very rich in a different sense from my other experiences, so I behaved like that. You know, the different peers, your peers had come from very different and very well-off upbringings, and I wanted that. At that stage I think I wanted the red Ferrari and I wanted the glamorous white girlfriend. I travelled overseas with the company in my first year, when I was 19—I was the first child to actually go overseas. I remember ringing my mother from Athens in Greece and I just cried to her for the most expensive phone bill I had in my life. And that's, I think, when I touched base, went back to the source of my mother. That's when I started to realise that I really missed the cultural side of things. But then I was in Athens and I was performing at the Herod Atticus near the Acropolis. So, once again, I was having revelations there, reflecting on my own heritage; then trips out to Delphi learning about the Greek gods and comparing them to my leaders.

So I realised that my confidence and all that keenness in the early stage of my life had thrown me into deep water. I had to learn and have quick tastes and combine that all together and then work out where my next journey would go. I started to sum that up quite quickly—not to get caught up in the company hype and look at the bigger picture. My father's always had an image about the bigger picture, a little myth that he's passed on, so it always stayed in my head. I think that's wonderful to have a sense of another voice reminding you to push forward.

POTTER: Are there pieces that you remember working on? I know Graeme actually made *Late Afternoon of a Faun* on you; or was it more the experiential thing that you got from Sydney Dance?

PAGE: I think it was more probably the experience but, once I did have the role in *Late Afternoon of a Faun* with Graeme and Garth Welch—I mean, at that stage I didn't fear anything—I just went ahead. I had known little about Garth Welch. If I'd come from the Australian Ballet School, I probably would have been a nervous wreck, but because I did not know ... And I didn't know much about Graeme, either. I just thought they were running this dance company and it was normal. I didn't get into the whole foundation, growth, and that they were national ambassadors—they were huge, you know. I was still just coming from having my own elders and their experiences. So it *was* the experience. And then I did *Afternoon of a Faun*, but I didn't really think about that until I actually left.

In Sydney Dance I felt like my feet were taken from the earth and I was floating almost, so I felt I had no control in a sense of my experiences, you know. They were just coming in waves and it was just like being in *Star Wars* or something, just sort of ducking from battleships and stuff—not that dramatic, but once again it was just up to me to take what I wanted to take. But when I look back now, that was very brave of Graeme. It was very brave of him to put me in that role and to take me through that deep-water process. And I respect that now, but at the time I was very much more paranoid than anything. You know, why me?—is it because I'm black? is it because I've come from somewhere else? why has he chosen me? I don't have the experiences they do. I felt like a little bit of a guinea pig really, and I stayed very quiet about it all—I was quite emotionless really. I never showed any of my frustrations in that company. I was very respectful in terms of what was theirs was theirs, and what was mine was mine.

But I was starting to long to come back to my cultural base. That would have happened after probably two years of being in Sydney Dance. I can remember Graeme asking me what I was going to do to renew my contract and I said I actually wanted to go back to work at the College as a teacher and a choreographer. I think it was just the fact that I wanted to share it, I wanted to go back to the College—and not so much brag about it, but just to share the experience, you know: 'It's not a bad initiation. You can all do it.' So that was sort of my attitude at that stage.

POTTER: And is that what you did—did you go back to NAISDA?

PAGE: Well, I had a bit of pressure from the College. You know, if he was a traditional black man, would they have taken him in? Because he's urban-looking, he's safe. There was a lot of political-type issues about my whole move. I can remember having letters from people in the Department of Foreign Affairs and people from Aboriginal Affairs congratulating me. It was like Cathy Freeman running with the flag. Then your peers on the other side are throwing the black politics at you. I became the sort of meat in the sandwich; it was a hard one to come to terms with. Then 1988 was coming up, the bicentennial year, and a lot of elders and people that I respected were against it. Graeme was about to do *VAST* for the country, this sort of nice political statement on the bicentenary, and that edged me to leave before the bicentenary.

But then when I did leave, I got to tour with a performing group of NAISDA, graduates that were coming through. This was the birthing probably of Bangarra. I basically came back there and realised that my potential and experience were very beneficial and that I should come back and try to pass that on. I still acted like a little bit of a rock star for the first six months, but that was just me releasing the excess luggage from where I'd come from. But I tell you, my peers really grounded me quite quickly and knocked that out of me, and that's what I needed. Then I was able to share like I was told to in my upbringing. So, once I started to share, I started to choreograph, I started to tour overseas and just take my responsibilities.

In '89 I was doing a lot of teaching for the College for all the students and I had this wonderful rapport with the students because I was able to bring experiences quite fresh and raw and they could relate to that. I was a teacher and director at that time. It was the first time, I think, they actually had a director who'd been through the College to direct their end-of-year show, which in '89 was called *Kayn Walu* and was at Belvoir Theatre.

But the wonderful thing about that is that I had to prove the responsibility. I did a small synopsis of what I wanted to do for the show and they had a huge creative meeting where I was just a teacher, and then I just popped my head up and said, 'Well, I want to direct this one and here is the synopsis and this is what I want it to do.' And I think they were quite shocked, because there was no other Aboriginal or Torres Strait Island teacher there, so the school was very much working with people from the outside—with a lot of expertise, or the right expertise. So, for me, that was a breakthrough of my life to feel confident to say, 'Well, I will direct 40 students and I'll take them through to Belvoir Street.'

They said, 'Sure, take the responsibility'—and it *was* a responsibility. I mean, 40 students, that really woke me up because I started to see myself in 40 ways. And that was very successful for the school, because it was storytelling through a different set of eyes and creative minds. It was raw, it was very raw and unique. I look back on it now and, creatively, it was definitely the one that broke through. It broke down a lot of barriers in terms of letting the Aboriginal and Torres Strait Islander choreographers actually direct their shows. So, once again, I felt a bit like a guinea pig. But that was a great experience.

That was when I first invited David (Page), who was working at CASM—the Centre for Aboriginal Studies in Music in Adelaide, part of the University of Adelaide—to work with me. He had been down there studying for three years, so his is a very similar story to mine. I wanted him to supply some original music for one of my choreographic pieces. And I was also fortunate enough to have another of my brothers, Russell, there. He was in his fifth year at the College and he danced in a lot of the roles. So, once again, I had my family working there with me, so there was an amazing energy and strength surrounding me and that was a wonderful boost to my confidence.

That took a lot out of me. By the end of that year I just wanted to dance again, I just wanted to concentrate on myself and dance. So I rang Graeme and Janet and I went back to Sydney Dance for two years. I was a completely different person. They had realised that I had gone through some strong initiation of responsibility, and I was very confident and just knew my body so well and I was able to adjust my attitude to anything. They saw a huge change. I was a real asset to the company at that stage and I must admit that I had a much better time then than I did the first time around, and that's always the case. I don't know how many people do that in their cycle, if they actually go back to something that they didn't quite complete, but I felt like

I had to complete and resolve my time with Sydney Dance, and that's what I did. I was able to choreograph for the company—*Mooggrah*, which was part of *Shakespeare Dances*—along with Gideon Obarzanek, Kim Walker, Adrian Batchelor, Graeme Murphy and Alfred Taahi. So, that was fantastic because I was able to demonstrate my style on a group of dancers that had such strong techniques.

At that stage Bangarra was just developing. Then they heard I'd choreographed for Sydney Dance and they thought I was the magic boy behind *Kayn Walu* in '89, and Carole (Johnson) was contemplating whether or not I'd be the responsible person for artistic director of Bangarra. So I took some time off in New York, went to New York and did some classes and did a few auditions. I was about to get a call-back on one audition and Cheryl Stone, who was a founding member of NAISDA and was the operation's manager for Bangarra at that stage, called me in New York and said, 'We want to offer you the job as artistic director.' I wasn't sure because I really wanted to stay in New York. I felt very strong in New York, I felt the universal state and city and I wanted to be universal at that stage. I really wanted to feel that I could connect my feet to this landscape here, but at the same time wear those 17 branches, and I wanted a taste of it there and then. But what happened was, there was something pulling me back to the bush and again, I believe, that's where my guide stood up and took over me. Once I came back to Sydney I choreographed, and then it was just me being able to give the foundation a strong vision. So it all started in the end of '91, beginning of '92, and I've been with Bangarra since then.

POTTER: Can you articulate what your vision for Bangarra is, for its future?

PAGE: I think Bangarra was necessary just to house a strong indigenous foundation that was able to be accessible to the rest of the nation, whether you were black or white, whether it was community-based or mainstream. It was storytelling from indigenous eyes and ears and mouths and minds. It was a resource for all performing arts or all across-the-board arts to be a part of—whether it's song, dance or storytelling—because I really believe our style, and Bangarra style, is very much the combination of all those styles, those art forms.

The interesting thing for me was to set a vision statement that made Bangarra very much a contemporary meeting place.

It was really meant to be quite diverse and at the same time able to nurture a respect for the traditional culture. I'd love to think that this resource is the bridge between traditional and urban lifestyles. I'm interested in housing a foundation for the next generation. So the opportunities can only get better, we can only go forward, and I'm just fortunate that it's at this time. But I do get frustrated with the fact that it should have been done a couple of centuries ago, and the people that fought for that had picked up all the other dirty laundry and knocked down all the other barriers so that it could be here for me to be responsible for helping to maintain.

There've been a lot of founding members that have always supported that vision for Bangarra, that it is a resource, it is a house for indigenous professional artists. As far as I'm concerned, it did need a leader and it did need someone with a vision and someone that had a tough vision, that could actually see the bigger picture. I believe I had that. So it's just for me now to be consistent and always be evolving and just maintain the integrity and the respect and ensure the artists of Bangarra are speaking the same language that I am, and are riding in the same boat so that there will be the sons and cousins of Bangarra in 20 years spread across the nation, and the world maybe, I don't know.

Page's choreography, like his vision for Bangarra, usually melds urban and traditional motifs and ideas. His first foray into this kind of choreographic fusion occurred during his second year at NAISDA when he made a piece, *Warumpi Warumpi*, for an end-of-term workshop. Following the lead of Warumpi Band, who were fusing traditional Aboriginal music with rock and roll, Page did the same with traditional and contemporary dance styles. 'That's when I knew that I wanted to continue,' he says. Since then his wish to blend dance styles is perhaps epitomised by *Ochres*, a piece co-choreographed with Bernadette Walong in 1994 which has been extensively toured in Australia and overseas, whose four parts express the spiritual significance of the ochre colours of yellow, black, red and white.

POTTER: When you choreograph, how do you go about making a piece?

PAGE: In terms of our workshop and our process, it's very much a lot of storytelling, a lot of debating issues—contemporary issues today in our society. Before we do any form of physical movement, it's making sure everyone understands the dance language or the dance intention before we even practise it. I believe it's healthy for them and it stimulates the work every time it's performed, because you can keep pruning it and adding to it—I tend to be a bit like the acupuncturist where he actually comes in and keeps stimulating the blood to the work. I think that's one of the best methods of working. I really like to come much more from the human base. I let them have a voice before they actually start throwing their body around. So that's how we work really. By the end of the day I'll make the last decision on what it should be, but it's very collaborative. And I'm learning too, I'm just experiencing like them—it's total professional development the whole time. I still need that stimulus too and their feedback with me is very good. I think what I made sure I did was knock the barriers down between them and me, the artists and me, and just put us all in the same boat. If I respect myself first, then they're naturally going to respect me; and if they respect themselves first, I'm naturally going to respect them. That's just going back to very much traditional ways of working in our culture. It's just adapting that and bringing that to the nineties. I think it's very healthy for the company.

POTTER: Tell me why the landscape is important to you?

PAGE: The landscape, well, I believe each country has a sex and I believe this landscape is very female. I think she's mother earth and I believe she's very much responsible for the nurturing of this landscape. If I had no Aboriginal blood in me or had no connection with Aboriginal people or acceptance about traditional Aboriginal lifestyle, I think it would confuse me why this landscape is so different to the rest of the world. I just have a real belief in those creation myths and I'll make sure that my son will understand that as well. Man-made things will always go through an experimental phase, and they'll succeed, but at the same time what is underneath them will always stay forever. I really believe in strong indigenous cultures—they're the landkeepers, they're the ones talking to the land and making sure the land is preserved and looked after.

I've travelled around the world and, every time I come back, the smell and the beauty of the land, and how raw it is and how it's maintained, is quite amazing. So I realise that working in this country we're very fortunate, anyone in this country is very fortunate to have this under their feet. To be aware of that is quite amazing, I think.

This interview was conducted in the Bangarra studios on the top floor of an old factory in the inner Sydney suburb of Leichhardt. The factory is directly over the Sydney airport flight path and the oral interview is punctured at regular intervals by the sound of jet planes descending and ascending, a fact that somehow seemed incredibly incongruous as Page spoke about the nature of the landscape and of his belief in and respect for Aboriginal culture. Perhaps the most distinctive feature of the interview, however, is the manner in which Page, a quietly spoken man, returns over and over to certain images. He constantly refers to the earth, and the need to have one's feet firmly planted on it. Other recurring images are of a tree with 17 branches representing diversity and the 'tough goanna skin' that Aboriginal leaders must assume in a modern world. Despite his vision to straddle urban and traditional cultures, Page is firmly 'grounded' in his Aboriginal heritage.

Choreography by Stephen Page

1984	*Warumpi Warumpi*	NAISDA Choreographic Workshop
1989	*Kayn Walu*	Aboriginal Islander Dance Theatre
1991	*Trackers of Oxyrhyncus*	Sydney Theatre Company
	The Marriage of Figaro	Australian Opera
	Mooggrah	Sydney Dance Company
	Up Til Now	Bangarra Dance Theatre
1992	*Niki Nali*	Expo '92, Seville
	Praying Mantis Dreaming	Bangarra Dance Theatre
1993	*Opening Ceremony*	World Youth Soccer, Sydney
	Black River	Feature film directed by Kevin Lucas
	Pride	*Seven Deadly Sins*, ABC-TV
	Grand Final	Australian Football League, Melbourne
	Black Vine	Sydney City Council
	Ninni	Bangarra Dance Theatre
1994	*The Wedding Song*	NIDA (National Institute of Dramatic Art)
	Ochres (with Bernadette Walong)	Bangarra Dance Theatre
1996	*Olympic Flag Handover Ceremony*	Sydney Olympic Games Organising Committee, Atlanta, 1996
	Alchemy	Australian Ballet

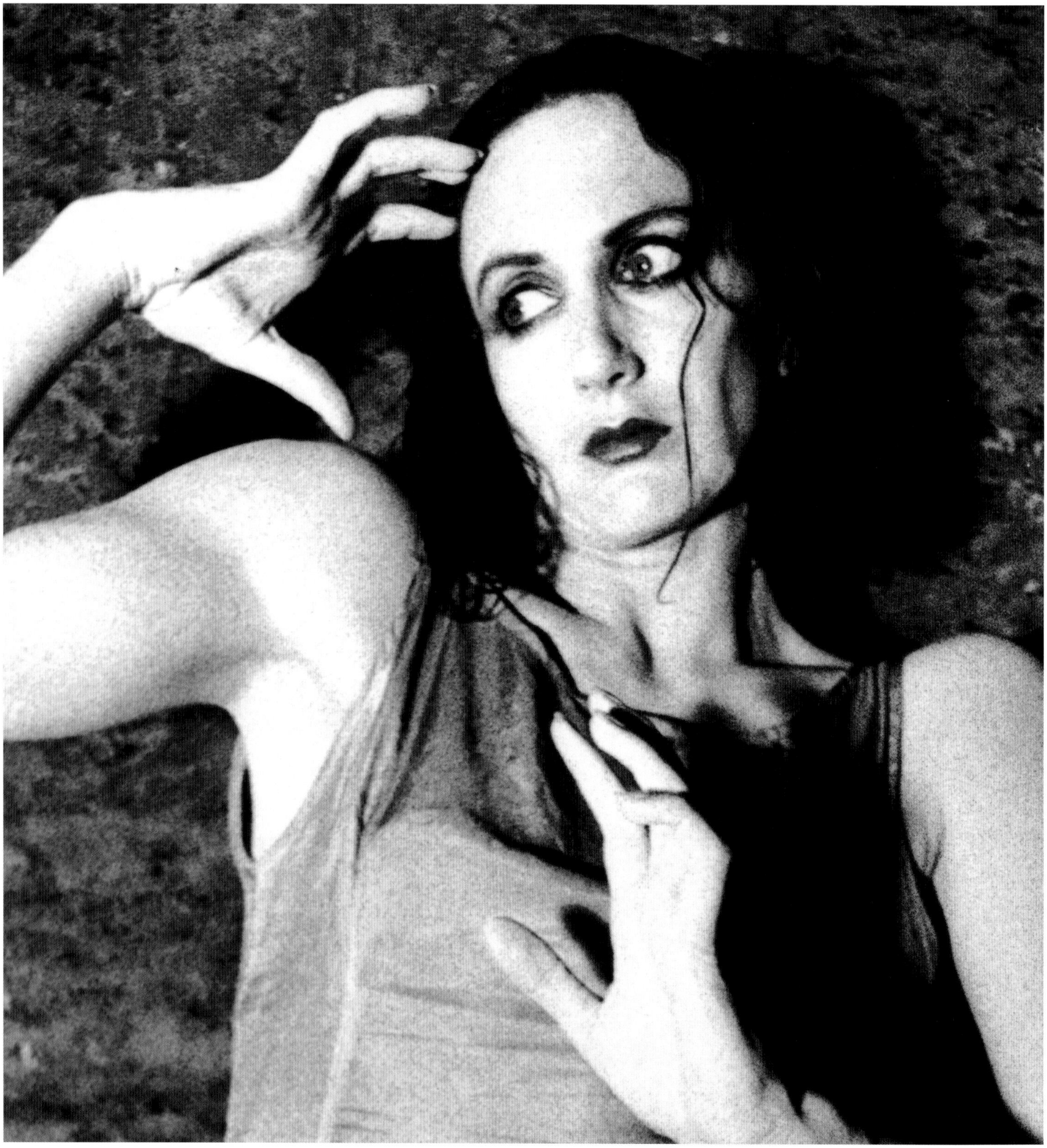

Meryl Tankard
Touching the Heart

Interviews TRC 2602; TRC 3477

Meryl Tankard (born 1955), artistic director of the Adelaide-based Meryl Tankard Australian Dance Theatre, was interviewed in Canberra by Shirley McKechnie in July 1990, and in Melbourne by Michelle Potter in July 1996

Of all the Australian choreographers whose profile has been consolidated during the 1990s, Meryl Tankard is perhaps the most individualistic. Uninterested in commonly prescribed artistic boundaries, her pursuit of dance that crosses styles and forms has been a constantly evolving one. In addition to works created for traditional theatre spaces, Tankard has created site- and event-specific pieces. Her vocabulary has drawn on a diverse range of movement from classical ballet to unique steps that have emerged during workshop processes, from folk dance to movement inspired by the forms of jewellery and sculpture. In her eclectic repertoire of pieces to date, she has asked her dancers not only to dance, but to speak—in *Chants de mariage*, they provide a narrative comment throughout the dance; to sing—in *Songs with Mara*, they perform a specialised style of Balkan 'open throat' singing; to perform acrobatic feats—in *Furioso*, they perform while suspended from free-swinging ropes; and to consider non-Western dance styles—in *Rasa*, they collaborate with Australian–Indian dancer Padma Menon.

Tankard's work has not been without its controversial elements—critics and audiences alike have suggested that some of her works are 'not dance'. But Tankard's skill is to be able to transform her innovations and cross-art form experiments into choreography that is never merely a vehicle for the display of movement. Her choreography emerges from a strongly emotional base; it bombards the senses and besieges the emotions, while still having the capacity to engage the mind.

Tankard, the youngest of three sisters, spent her early childhood in Darwin and Melbourne. When she was ten her father was posted to Penang, Malaysia, where the family lived for 2½ years before returning to Australia to live just out of Newcastle. Her childhood recollections and experiences, including her dance lessons, which began in Melbourne but which she continued in Malaysia and, on her return from Malaysia, again in Australia, have provided her with source material for a number of her works. In particular, Tankard's solo piece *Two Feet*, at once both hilarious and deeply moving as it examines the obsessions of the dance world, draws partly on her experiences as a child learning to dance. Tankard suggests, too, that her memories of childhood and adolescence, along with the influence of her father, have also had a more general, more subtle influence on her work.

TANKARD: I was born in Darwin in 1955. I lived there for three years. We have many, many photos of the whole family—the three girls and my mother and father—driving down in an FJ Holden to Melbourne. Then we drove back up again, and then we drove back down again. I can't imagine what it was like in 1958, to do that. I think my father was very adventurous, and we've got photos of us sitting next to Ayers Rock with underpants on our heads to keep the flies away and things like that. Then we lived in Melbourne. That was where I started dancing with Bruce Morrow—he was my first ballet teacher.

Then my father was posted to Penang; he was in the air force. That was just incredible, going from Ringwood to Penang. We lived there for 2½ years and we had the most amazing houses, gardens, servants. That time had an influence on me; I'm only starting to realise that now. All these processions, all the colour and dancing and movement that we saw all the time, we just took for granted. I mean we would run out of the house to see a funeral procession, and there were people balancing poles on their heads, and mourners, and great big festivals all the time. That's what I remember most, from Penang; and again this driving around. My father loved to drive everywhere so we drove up to Bangkok. That was an incredible experience because it was in '65, '66, so it was quite dangerous really to be driving around those areas.

MCKECHNIE: Your father seems to have been an important figure in your life. Where was he born?

TANKARD: He was born in Melbourne, and my mother too. Yes, I think he was important because he was the one that made these decisions about where we were living all the time. We were constantly changing. He was in the army in the war. He had gone everywhere. He went to Africa and New Guinea and all those places. Never, ever, ever spoke about it, but had about 12 medals or something. He was in Crete in the motor transport section. I didn't find that out until I met a cousin, just in the last few years, in Brisbane, who told me these stories about my father being a sort of hero when they had to evacuate. All the Germans were coming in and apparently my father wouldn't stop pulling the engines out of the cars so that the Germans couldn't use them. It was really very interesting to find all this out. I thought what an incredible experience; and never having talked about that, never, ever. I think that's very Australian. When he died, when I was 16, I realised I missed out on all these things.

MCKECHNIE: So let's just talk about your mother for a moment. Did she have a career of any kind?

TANKARD: No. My mother must be, I think, the perfect mother. She was there for the family, totally. She still is an incredibly thoughtful person.

MCKECHNIE: When you were a little girl, Meryl, can you recall particular things that gripped your imagination?

TANKARD: I always liked making things, more so than dancing. I just had a lot of energy, I guess, and I liked to create, so it didn't matter what it was, whether it was cutting out dolls' clothes, or sewing dolls' clothes. I loved doing things with my hands. My mother finally sent me to ballet. I mean, I look back and think I probably would have done acting, or been an artist, but in Ringwood there weren't schools for artists and there weren't schools for actors. There was a ballet school. That was really our only creative outlet. Ballet was where my imagination could run riot. When I think about it, it was the end of the ballet class when we got to improvise that I waited for all night.

MCKECHNIE: Did you read a lot, or were you read to as a child? Do you remember stories being an important part of childhood?

TANKARD: Not really. It think it was the landscape really. I do think it was space, and when I look at photos of my childhood in Darwin, we had this backyard—it was just wild. It was bamboo, grass right up to our waist. Even when I went to Ringwood, my father would be making toys for us constantly. He would go to the tip and he would make bicycles. They were made out of junk. We had all this stuff in the backyard. And I can remember sitting out in the front garden and just turning, doing somersaults right around the whole garden while my father hosed or something like that. So I think it was a sort of outdoor thing that was important.

MCKECHNIE: Meryl, what about ordinary education? Did you go to school in Ringwood?

TANKARD: Yes, to a Catholic school, Our Lady's. I went to all-girls schools always, except for Malaya where it was an air force school.

MCKECHNIE: Do you recall particular things from school days?

TANKARD: I just remember church. I think I was very religious—until my father died, and then I sort of gave up. But I remember going to church and praying to Our Lady that we would go to Penang. I mean, we were up for the posting and, because of Vietnam and all these things, I thought maybe we wouldn't go, and I would go in there and put my hand on that painting, photograph or whatever—painting I guess, just a print—and pray to Our Lady. Ask her every day. I can remember my father—he'd come from the station in his uniform with his bag—and I'd wait outside the house and run down the street to meet him when I saw him at 6 o'clock. I remember that day when he came and told us. I can remember going in that evening and telling them at ballet that I would not be coming back because I was going to Penang.

MCKECHNIE: Were you able to keep up your dancing lessons in Penang?

TANKARD: Yes. I had a really strict Chinese teacher, very strict. She used to have this big bamboo stick and she'd hit the ground. And she had suitcases and we'd have to do *pas de chats* over the suitcases. If our ballet shoes, the laces, came out we would get fined 20 cents. If our pleat on our tunic— a white tunic with a red belt—wasn't ironed the correct way, we would get fined 20 cents; if our hair fell out—another 20 cents. She would check us every day before the class.

MCKECHNIE: So when you came back to Australia, who did you take dancing lessons from in Newcastle?

TANKARD: Well, I started with Tessa Maunder and then I went to Elaine Morgan. My father—that was around the time when my father died—had started to build me this ballet studio in the backyard. I don't know why. I mean, he never saw me dance.

MCKECHNIE: I think that is very typical of Australian fathers.

TANKARD: Yes. And not showing you love in a physical way or talking about it. I mean, he was changing the garage, putting that on the other side and then building this dance studio with the best floor. He researched it. He was out there just teaching himself how to do it. And he didn't finish it when he died. There was the floor and there were the walls, and then all the air force guys came and got in and finished it for him.

That year I'd made up my mind that I was going to do the elementary, intermediate and advanced ballet exams in one year. I was going to go to ballet full-time for a year. I gave up school in fourth year, which was a big thing. I was dux of the school. The nuns were going mad. The nuns said, 'You're going to be mentally frustrated for the rest of your life.' I think about that often and it does happen to me, too. I mean there's something in what they said.

Anyway, that year I said, 'Okay, if I can pass all those exams, I will go on to ballet and I'll go overseas and I'll try and do something. If I don't, I can still come back to school and do sixth year, Higher School Certificate, in one year, and I haven't lost anything.' I had it all worked out. I thought, 'I'll try this dancing because I'm young and I won't be able to do that later.'

MCKECHNIE: What kind of mental processes were pressing you to do this?

TANKARD: I think it was such a challenge. I don't think it was the beauty. I don't know what it was. But it was hard, it was difficult. With school I knew I could pass those exams and get A's, but I would still get on the barre and it was still difficult. It was still something I hadn't conquered, I guess. It becomes an obsession. That's what my piece *Two Feet* is about. The obsession just takes over, I think.

I wanted to be strong and put up with any sort of pain. With *Two Feet* there's a whole scene where I talk about torture. I used to think as I was doing those *grands battements* or *sautés* that if I could do a hundred of them, or whatever, or if I could keep going for two hours without breaking down, if a war came I could be tortured, and I would never, ever tell the secrets, never. So, you know, I could be used for lots of things, lots of important things. I used to think lots of things. If I could do this, then my mother would be very happy and she'd have a long life, you know, make up little things like that as I was doing them to stop myself breaking down. Then I started travelling on the train from Newcastle to Sydney— three days a week, I think, I went—to learn from Joan and Monica Halliday. It took about four hours to get there. I'd travel up there, work all day, dance all day, then get the train at night; come home.

Then I started this little ballet school with the studio my father had built. Wednesday nights I'd teach women jazz and the whole day Saturday I just had classes. It got so popular. I had classes all day from little babies to, again, women at the end of the day on Saturday. I don't know how I did that. I was 17 or 16 or something. *And* I was doing—no, I had done elementary. I was doing intermediate, advanced and solo seal. They were the three exams I was doing, sorry. I had done elementary the year before.

But going to Sydney, I remember my mother. We would get up in the morning, she'd cook steak for me, steak and eggs.

I'd get the bus at quarter to five and I think I'd get to Sydney at 9.30 or something and I'd be falling asleep. I could never do that again. I think it was my father dying, I felt I had all his strength. I just felt I had to do this for him, you know. On Sundays I'd be in the studio practising solo seal, all by myself. I'd go in there with a tape recorder and I'd just stay there all day, alone. I could never do that now, never. I hate going into a room by myself. I'd be in there going through every dance, you know. Mad, mad. Absolutely mad. (July 1990)

Having passed her three major exams, Tankard continued her dance training at the Australian Ballet School, for which she auditioned successfully at the end of 1972. Tankard says she was 'quite good at picking up things' and while at the School she occasionally replaced injured dancers from the Australian Ballet, notably in Frederick Ashton's *The Dream*. She was taken into the company in 1975 at the end of her two years of training.

It was while she was with the Australian Ballet that her choreographic career began. Her first piece, *Birds behind Bars*, was made for *Dance Horizons*, a program of new choreography performed in July 1977 as a tribute to the former and founding artistic director of the Australian Ballet, Peggy van Praagh. Along with *Birds behind Bars*, the *Dance Horizons* program also included *Hello?* by Julia Cotton, *Monkeys in a Cage* by Don Asker, *Rapid Transit* by Paul Saliba, and *Tip* by Graeme Murphy, and Tankard appeared in the pieces by Asker and Saliba.

On a study trip to Europe, however, Tankard's career took a dramatic turn when she encountered the work of German choreographer Pina Bausch and her Wuppertal Tanztheater. Tankard became one of Bausch's most admired performers during the early 1980s, dancing and creating major parts in the Bausch repertoire.

MCKECHNIE: So what were the events, or the circumstances, or the thoughts that made you eventually leave the Australian Ballet?

TANKARD: It was Anne Woolliams, artistic director of the company. I loved it when she came. She had this energy and vitality, and everyone gave her a hard time. She did lots of things to bring people together. Like, she had these games around the motel when we were on tour, had parties, and everyone sort of laughed about it. But, at the same time, there we were doing all these swimming races and things, and there was a nice feeling amongst the people.

She really encouraged me to be a choreographer. *Horizons* was coming up for Dame Peggy. And it was quite difficult because you had to get people to rehearse out of work time. I was also in some of the pieces. I don't know how I did it. For *Birds behind Bars* I got this Soweto music—the Dark City Sisters—and I put the girls on pointe with bird costumes and they were doing cha-chas and sambas. It got good reviews, encouraging reviews. Then the Australian Ballet Society gave me $1000, a little award or something. So I thought I would go to Europe in the six-week break, I would go to Europe and look at all the other companies. I met up with some Australian dancers while I was there—I bumped into Leigh Warren on the street in Rome, just walking on the street in Rome. He said to me, 'You have to go and see Pina Bausch.' Then I went to see Shane Carroll in the Netherlands and she said, 'You have to go and see Pina Bausch.' So Shane organised everything and she organised that I would stay with another Australian dancer, Jo Anne Endicott. There was a performance that night—I took the train. I saw *Renate (Wandert Aus)* which was a $3^{1/2}$-hour work. I could not believe it. Here it all was—great costumes, a great set, the talking, the acting, the crying, the laughing. It was just like, 'Thank you, God. This is the miracle.'

Jo Anne said, 'Audition, audition!' I said, 'I can't audition. I've just signed a 12-month contract with the Australian Ballet. They've given me this scholarship. I can't leave them.' Anyway I did audition, just for the experience. Pina was incredible. She pretended she did not speak any English at all and she said I had to join in the rehearsal. And I could see that she liked what I was doing. So she then had to take me into a ballet room and after the rehearsal I did a classical class.

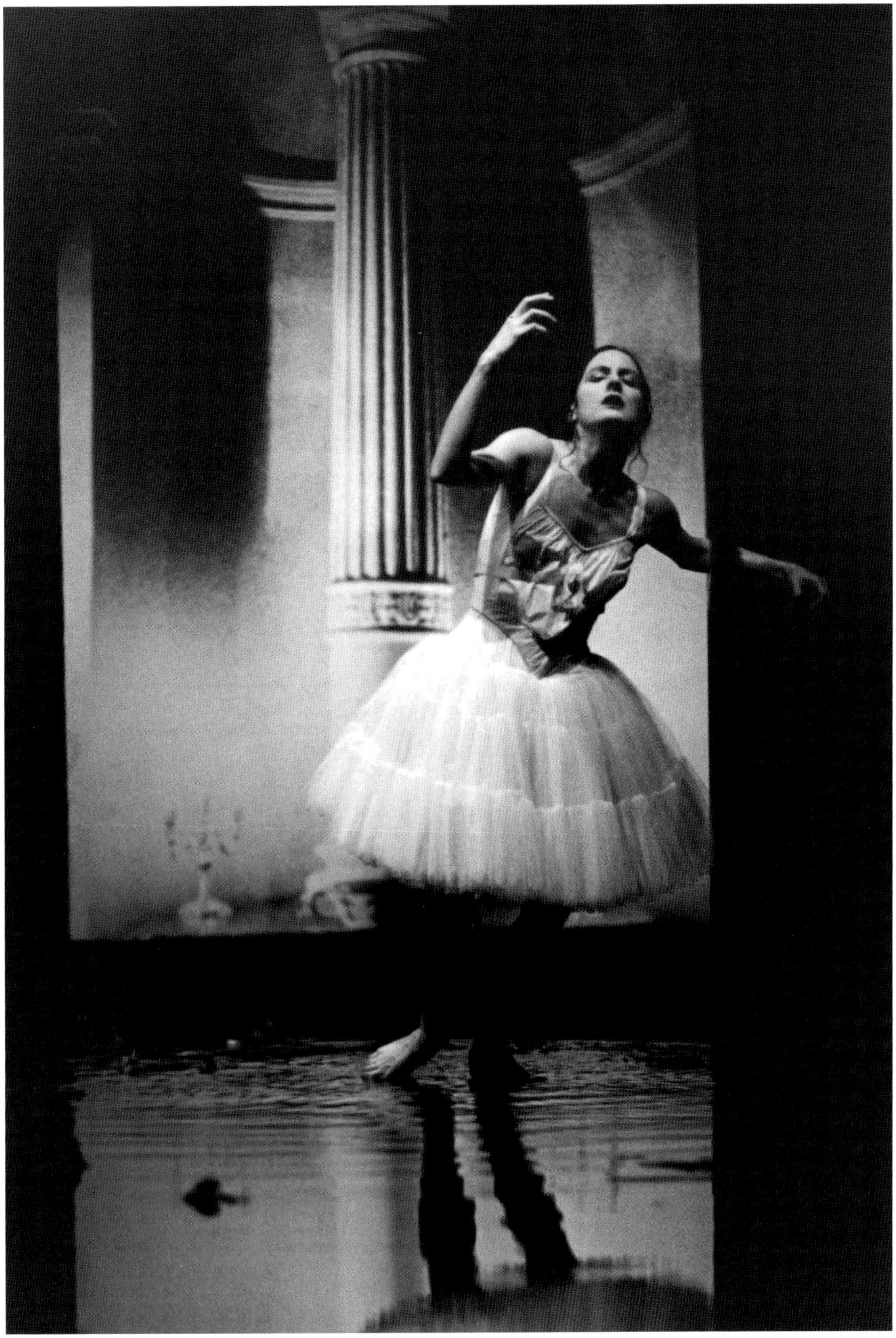

MCKECHNIE: Did she take that class?

TANKARD: No. She sat there on the floor reading the newspaper. Horrendous classical, and then these movements from *Sacre* (*Le Sacre du printemps*). I had never bent my back back like that before. Then little parts of the piece I had seen the night before. And then at the end of this three-hour audition, it was about 11 o'clock, 11.30, she said, 'All right. I'll take you into the company.' And I said, 'Oh, I can't. I can come in 12 months' time.' I just could not believe that she had said she would take me because she had not even looked at me—she was just reading the newspaper.

Anyway I went back to Australia and I said, 'If I go there for a year, just let me take a year's leave of absence.' They would not let me go for ages, and finally there was this funny opportunity to choreograph a hair show in Tokyo. It came through the ballet and they gave it to me. So I got my trip. I did this hair show in Tokyo and I said, 'Look, I'm going now.'

So I got to Pina and she straight away put me in this piece with five of her own people. She gave me a hard time. It was not easy, even though she put me in as a soloist. She was really critical of everything I did. Every movement I made was corrected and corrected and corrected. She would take me on her own for *Sacre*. I realise now that was quite an honour, because she does not do that at all now. At the time it was very hard. I came with lipstick and nail polish and greased-back hair and bright colours and she used to stare at me in those rehearsals. And she said, 'You wipe that make-up off your face. I can't rehearse with you looking like that. I can't rehearse with you in a pale pink leotard. It's too pretty.'

I remember in *Sacre* she thought that I had dyed my hair because it was so black and curly. I had to sort of straighten it out and I had to put dirt in it. I had to look real, look earthy. It was just this sort of gloss or fashion stuff that she really knocked out of me. But then, as she got to know me, that was what she loved about me—there was that brightness and I brought that to a lot of pieces. But the work was everything, everything I had ever wanted to do. I could not believe this. I mean, I could create all day. The way Pina works is she asks you questions and you answer them. So every question she asked, you know, I was just in my element. And as she got to know me, she saw that I was quite funny. So I did a lot of comic roles, but I think I used the comedy, too, in a really interesting way. The audience would be laughing and the next minute I would have them crying.

MCKECHNIE: What kind of questions did she ask?

TANKARD: Many questions about love. Every time we did a piece we would go, 'Oh no, not that question again.' But I mean it was just another area of it. It was often, 'If you are in love with someone, what do you do, how do you show it, or how do you hide it?'

MCKECHNIE: When you talk about love, was there a strong erotic element in that for her?

TANKARD: No. It didn't feel that way when I was performing. But in a lot of the work you felt like you were being raped. In *Kontakthof* I just had to stand there while all the men in the company gave me their tenderness, were affectionate to me. So they have all got little gestures that they do on my body. I just stood there. Pina told me to do nothing. So I did nothing and they were just all over me. It was so horrible. It just got too much, that they were actually enjoying being tender to me. I mean it became something else. That is why her pieces always took so long. She managed to sort of change the whole scene, without you realising it, into something quite different. We repeated things all the time, all the time. I did everything full out. I was just, I guess, wanting her to love me. I wanted to do it well, even in rehearsal. All these emotional things that were really hard to do. I mean, if we had to cry in the piece, we rehearsed that constantly—crying, crying, crying.

Pina never explains why she does anything. She never explained anything and she never said, 'That was good', 'That was bad'. You know, when you were improvising, nothing is right, nothing is wrong. It is what she chooses to select and put in her piece. I think I developed such an eye because we were watching this stuff all day. It was really good experience to work out what I liked and what I would do.

I think what I learned most is how powerful a small movement can be. I had worked with choreographers before. They taught you the step, they taught you the movements, but, gosh, you could do those movements in so many different ways. I felt very confident in Pina's work. I knew I was right there; I knew I belonged.

MCKECHNIE: Of all the works you danced in while you were with the company, is there a role that stands out as having been particularly difficult or particularly rewarding, or maybe both?

TANKARD: I think *1980* for me was a very special piece. Pina's designer, Rolf Borzik, whom she lived with, had created the most amazing sets, landscapes. I felt very close to him because I had always wanted to be a designer. So we would go out and buy costumes together, or I would pick costumes for the girls or for myself. He died—he was 36 and he had cancer. It was just so sad, you know, because really he was just such a part of the work. Then we had to do this piece after the funeral and all this sadness. It was so hard to get going and we had six weeks. Pina usually takes three months to do a piece and she really didn't think she could do it. I just remember getting this sort of energy and it was like it was dedicated to Rolf. This piece was for Rolf—we were going to do it for him. No-one said that but, you know, that is what it felt like. Pina always says the piece is very special to her.

Pina used to select things for me that I never liked. That is what I find interesting. I'd do a lot of improvisation and then it was up to her to select. Some of the things that she liked, I just had real difficulty with. Once I did this lady who was talking about her shoes, talking about her hair, talking about this, this, this, trying to impress people or something. And of course that is the one she picked. That is in *1980*. I talked and talked and talked, and I was really quite mad. Do you know what she said after? She said that woman is like someone trying to forget something. It was interesting.

She never told us what things meant at the beginning. It was difficult for us to be always emotionally there and try to remember exactly how we did that first improvisation, with that spontaneity. I always think it took months before we really understood the piece.

MCKECHNIE: Meryl, once you had done an improvisation that she had selected for incorporation in the piece, did she require you to modify it or to retain it exactly? Or was it always an improvisation in performance?

TANKARD: It was always set, but we had to still keep it looking like it was just done on the spot. That was a discipline I think I learned. Towards the end of the six years I felt like I wanted to be told something. I wanted to be changed in some way. I felt like I was giving her all this stuff and not really being helped with the way to develop it.

We worked incredibly hard. I mean we rehearsed from 10 till 2.30, and then we'd come back at 6 o'clock and we worked till 10.30, 11 at night. And that was six days a week. And then she'd ring you up on Sundays. Then, you know, the company got really successful and we went everywhere. I was in everything—a $3^{1/2}$-hour piece where I got mauled by men and was thrown around the stage and had to scream. And using the voice was incredible. And then having to dance incredibly fast afterwards, and not really ever learning a technique of breathing. And never being told how to speak on stage, and yet all my characters spoke quite a lot. So I thought I'd come back to Australia and just have a break, you know. Get away for a year or something and try and create my own work.

MCKECHNIE: Was Pina distressed about you leaving the company at that stage?

TANKARD: She was very upset. And we had a big fight about how much each one had given to the other. I said, 'I feel I've given you so much, I'm absolutely exhausted. I feel like a dish rag.' And she said, 'You should feel lucky that you've been able to give it.' And, do you know, it was funny because when I came back to Australia, here I was with all this experience and all this energy. Nobody wanted anything. I thought, 'That's what she meant.' It was true. (July 1990)

POTTER: What is it in your own work that comes from Pina?

TANKARD: With Pina we could do anything. There didn't seem to be those rules. People made mistakes and she said, 'Oh, that's great.' I became really in tune with the kind of energy that was not the main event, but the angst before the event or the feeling after. I think it's being really sensitive, being really open to what is touching, moving in a particular situation. With my own work I still find it weird when people say, 'Oh, but they're singing.' So who cares? Who cares if they're singing? Who cares if they're crying? People are so wanting to put things in a box. I'm just trying not to put it in a box. Everybody wants to market it and say, 'What is it?' But I'm saying it's only interesting when you don't know what it is. If you can tell me exactly what it is, then I would think it's dead. (July 1996)

Tankard freelanced in Australia between 1984 and 1988, during which time she made *Echo Point*, *Travelling Light* and *Two Feet* and performed on television in *Dancing Daze* and in Robyn Archer's *Pack of Women*. She also frequently returned to Bausch's company, touring with it as guest artist throughout Europe and in Canada and the United States.

In 1989 she was offered the directorship of a small professional dance company in Canberra. As Human Veins Dance Theatre, this company had been led by Don Asker since its foundation in 1979. On her appointment Tankard renamed it the Meryl Tankard Company and between 1989 and 1992 created an astonishing range of works, drawing on her experience with Bausch and, again, often using memories as a catalyst in her creative process. In Canberra her works were also inspired by the environment in which Tankard now found herself. Her pieces developed what she has referred to as 'an earthy tone'.

TANKARD: Anyway, I came to Canberra and suddenly I was living in this house, beautiful little house, with a garden full of rosebushes. Opposite was a park full of these wonderful trees. And parrots and rosellas, and all of these birds were just coming into the backyard. I could not believe it. Cockatoos. Suddenly I started to feel very close to the trees, nature, and I really felt Australian somehow.

VX 18504 was the first piece I did in Canberra. *VX 18504* was the dog tags my father had, the number of his dog tags in the war. I got a lot of music from the Chieftains. I also found some beautiful Scottish songs. We were living near the War Memorial, which was a really strange thing because I'd just met a man who had known my father during the war and was suddenly told all these stories about the war that my father had experienced, that he had never, ever told me. I visited the War Memorial and the material there was just so overpowering. These photographs of young men at war and all their little objects that they'd managed to keep; and here they all were under glass. It was just such a moving experience and some of these photographs, in all that pain and anguish, were so beautiful. There was an incredible beauty there, out of this horror.

So I thought, if for *VX 18504* I could somehow have a set with this mood, one that shows this pain, and somehow people really coming together, and that closeness, and the loneliness of the women and the longing and hope—all these emotions that seemed to be in this little building. I wanted these dead trees. I had seen this beautiful—well, quite horrific—photo, I guess, of dead trees in France. We went out to Lake Eucumbene and we got real dead trees and we set them up in the theatre. Then I felt there had to be something about being home, about the family waiting and what they were going through. It wasn't just the men out there fighting. Somehow the men had their battles and their glory, but the women really didn't seem to have much at all. So I got a grey fence—my backyard suddenly had this grey fence, and that reminded me so much of my childhood in Ringwood. Then I got some chickens and we had these chooks up the back—little white chooks—and then junk, like rubbish, just around.

The piece started with photographs really because, somehow, photos became so important. I mean, in the War Memorial among a lot of the articles left from the soldiers, there would be a photo of their wife, or their child. That's all they had. Nothing else. So *VX 18504* began with groupings that represented photos, and they were photos that were actually from the dancers' lives. I mean, I asked them about when they went on holidays with their family and we set up the grouping and they would come in and just say, 'This is me with my mother and my twin brother' and they would stand there for a minute and you would just see this image, and then they'd go on to the next photo. I used that photo thing again in the second half, but with the men, just the men, representing photographs that I had actually taken from war books. For me, that was such a special part—those men just standing there.

Then with this beautiful Irish music I started to get into folk dancing, because I felt there was this big community thing—everybody got together in war somehow, everybody was working together and so close. It wasn't really folk dancing;

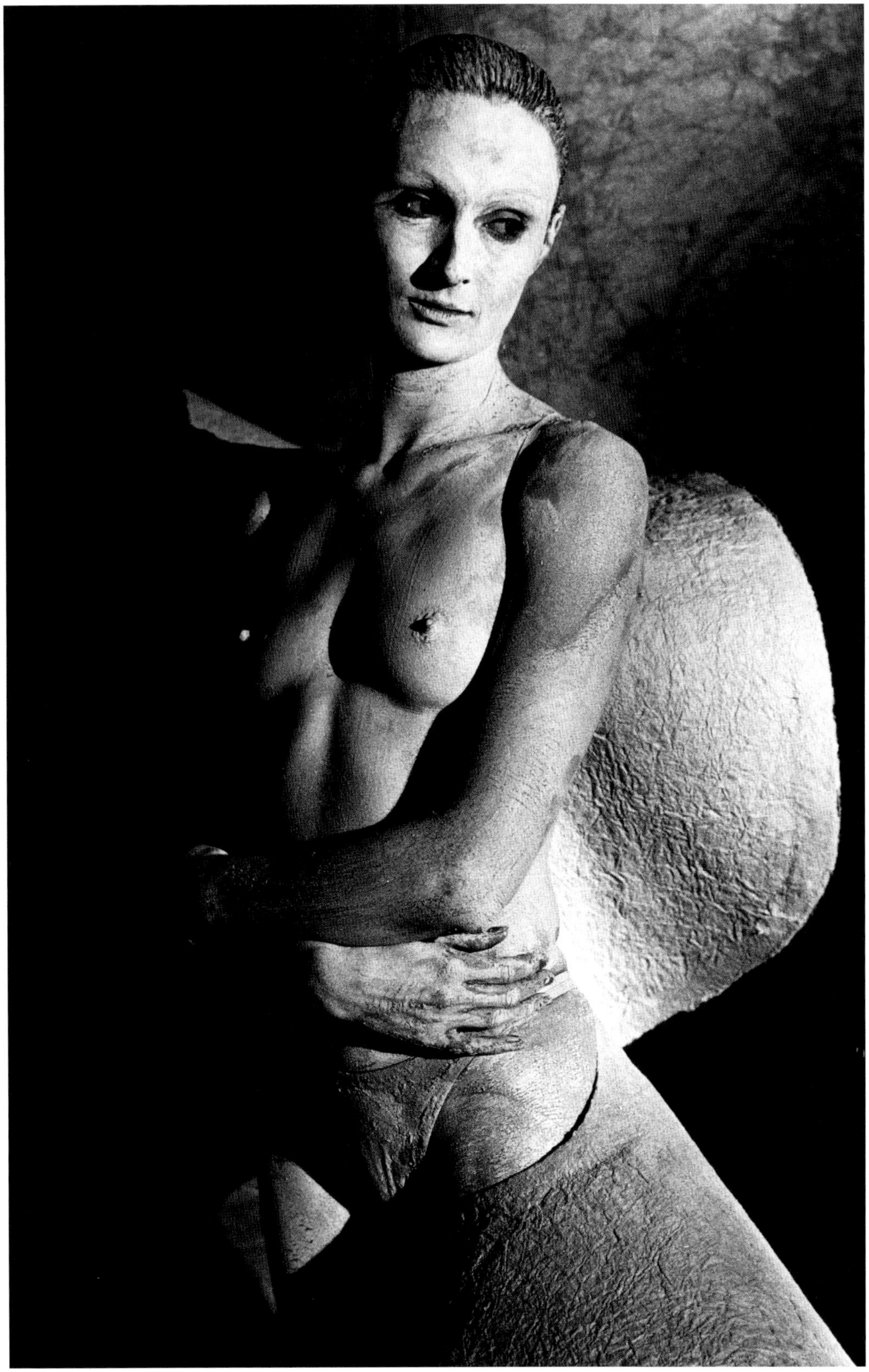

it used circles and it used lots of feet and steps that went into the earth. With one of the folk dances I asked the dancers how they'd polish medals, or awards, or little cups you get when you win something. So I made this dance up out of all these funny little movements where they're blowing and polishing and being proud because underneath polishing a little medal is that incredible pride. I think that's all that keeps you going in a war. I mean, it must be. Why did all these guys go?

I've got one scene where the women are just right on the side. The men are running like a big competition and they're winning. They're running and they're winning. And the women are just on the side sewing. There's another part. They never touch each other, really, through the whole piece until one part where the women are standing on the stools and each man comes to the woman and they embrace each other. That was very special too, for me. It's very, very simple, but I always felt there was something quite sensual about that.

MCKECHNIE: This must have been in very great contrast to the piece you had done the year before. I understand you did *Two Feet* the year before you came to Canberra. I wonder if we could talk about *Two Feet*.

TANKARD: *Two Feet*. The original idea, I mean, it was so strange. I'd read about Olga Spessivtseva when I was in the Ballet School in a book called *The Sleeping Ballerina*. I was astonished that no-one had ever told me about this woman. I mean here was this ballerina who was locked away in a mental asylum simply for being obsessed by dance. And just her photos. This frail beauty, and her legs. I mean, she seemed much finer than Pavlova. I think she was just not fashionable. This very thin physique, it just wasn't 'in' at the time.

I wanted to do a piece talking about dancers that had actually come to Australia. I'd read about Lola Montez doing this spider dance for these men out in the goldfields, and then there was—it wasn't Loie Fuller—someone who copied Loie Fuller that came out and did a fire dance. They all seemed such extraordinary pieces, and extraordinary women too. Then, as I got going, Olga got more important really. And I had Jane Campion come in and try and work with me at the beginning. She made me talk about my whole ballet experience. She asked me all these questions and she said, 'Why don't you talk about that?' And I said, 'God, Jane, that's so boring. I can't get up there and talk about my ballet experience.' She was very impressed by Olga and all this madness. And somehow these two characters ... it seemed there was a relationship. I felt there were lots of little girls that just went nuts too, that just could not cope. I mean, I felt very close to the edge at times, being sort of obsessed by this dance and not really knowing anymore if you loved it or not. I mean, it just became an obsession. So I thought, is it possible to put these two together? Even a little girl that was never famous has the same sort of problems. So I started to work and it was an incredibly difficult process just working by myself.

Anyway, we eventually got this piece together. I wanted to contrast this little Australian girl that was so used to the open air and space. Actually it begins with Olga really—the very first image is Olga like a little ballerina in a music box. She is dressed in her favourite dress from *Carnaval* and she's just turning. That's all you see of her. Then we go into Mepsie, which was my name—when I was little, they used to call me that in Darwin. She's learning a little dance from a book. Then you see Mepsie sort of growing up, and growing up, and growing up. It got a bit difficult, physically, to zap out of Mepsie who, I insisted, have no tights and no shoes, just little underpants and a dress and the hair out, into Olga who had pink tights, a tunic, pointe shoes, a hairnet.

Then Mepsie sort of ends at that point where, I guess, *my* classical ballet sort of ended, in that whole ballet school environment or company where the whole obsession was food. There's a big scene, I call it 'Mepsie's Christmas Dinner', and the girls are talking about the food they eat and trying to vomit, and cooking meals, and inviting other girls in and forcing them to eat it, so they'd get fat. The whole audience is laughing, but it's really not very funny.

MCKECHNIE: I was going to ask you about that, because the humorous element is clearly what is the first response, and then people have this other response that you clearly intend as well.

TANKARD: I like to do that. I like to surprise people, I guess, just put them in a situation they don't realise they're in.

(July 1990)

Two of Tankard's most innovative works made in Canberra, *Banshee* and *Nuti*, were created to accompany exhibitions at the National Gallery of Australia. In these two works Tankard and photographer Régis Lansac began to experiment with the use of slide projections as a part of the choreography rather than as a visual adjunct to a piece.

MCKECHNIE: How did it come about that you did *Banshee*?

TANKARD: Well, the Gallery had an exhibition of Irish silver and gold, which was jewellery and a lot of things, but the gold jewellery was particularly interesting. It was so ancient, nothing like you'd imagine Irish to be. It looked like big, gold, African necklaces. They were wonderful shapes and wonderful objects, and the material was amazing. So I thought, 'Oh well, this is the Gallery, I can experiment. It's this little theatre and there are just three shows.' I felt in a way I could indulge a bit.

We said, 'Okay, let's try slides.' Régis had photographed me; he did a series of portraits where he projected images onto my face, often a painting, quite a well-known painting, and because there was this real person underneath, it really became something else. So, you know, he said, 'Why can't we get this moving?' So Régis photographed a lot of Celtic symbols, often these carvings in rocks, and we projected them on the dancers. It just looked amazing. It looked like the room was full of coloured liquid, fluid. Quite magical. So then I got paper costumes. There was a woman (Dorothy Herel)—I knew she'd made paper dresses before—and I said, 'Why can't you make them more abstract?' So we worked together and got these curves happening just like the spirals in the necklaces. We had dancers in clay. I decided to put clay on their bodies, so they really looked like the rocks. And Colin Offord was going to create the music.

Then I thought, 'Oh dear, it's all so superficial.' I just couldn't start. I just had all these outside things. So I got some books on Irish folklore and found the banshee and found lots of other, often female, characters in their folklore. All the movements the dancers do in the piece come from these stories of the banshee. Then Colin was wonderful. He created some amazing sounds with these instruments that he makes, like conch shells, that really sounded like the banshee screaming. And I thought, 'They're going to hate this.' Do you know they loved it? I just could not believe it. We had such a response. It was packed, the Gallery was packed for those three days. I was thinking it was quite abstract, quite spooky, esoteric and there they were—young, old, punks—sitting there. Four punks waiting for the show to start half an hour before. And now I just did *Nuti* for another exhibition, *Civilization: Ancient Treasures from the British Museum*.

MCKECHNIE: With *Nuti* have you not also taken very clear images from some of the visuals in the exhibition?

TANKARD: Well, not actually the exhibition, but of a lot of research I did on Egyptian mythology—like an image of these women throwing dust over their heads when someone has died. So there's one scene where the girls are just throwing this dust. And there was the arch, the backward arch. It was called the death leap, and this death leap they did when someone died. I read about these transformation dances—I mean, I have no idea what they must have looked like, but they tried to look like trees or like animals. So I worked with that a lot. In very simple ways you can distort the body. It doesn't have to be amazing ballet technique or any dance technique. I guess that fascinated me.

MCKECHNIE: In *Nuti* it is a dance we're seeing. From the beginning to end we're seeing a dance that looks like a ritual, and it's also very sculptural. I wondered, once you had small motifs of movement as you have described, do you have a particular method of putting those together? Do they just accumulate as you go along, or do you have certain structures that you use to develop that material?

TANKARD: I still feel I'm finding those structures. I still feel often very scared at the beginning of a new work. I have an incredible fear of just being out there in deep water because I'm still developing that technique I feel. What I've done to myself though, which sometimes I really hate, is that I'm determined not to just go in and say, 'I want you to move like this.' I just get it out of them and they may not even realise they're doing something. But I feel like I have got to have this honesty. I feel if I go in there and show them, I don't know, it feels a bit obvious. So I get a movement from here and a movement from there during the rehearsal period and

I have put them together, or ask them to do it in slow motion, or ask them to do it with their foot or with their elbow. It's much more interesting if I don't tell them where I want that movement to go, if I keep a little bit of magic there.

(July 1990)

Tankard left Canberra at the end of 1992 to take on the directorship of the Adelaide-based Australian Dance Theatre. Adelaide provided her with new inspiration and her first piece made there was *Furioso*, in which her dancers, attached by harnesses to ropes suspended in the performing space, were airborne for large sections of the work. The developments begun in *Furioso* were pushed further in *Possessed* when the harnesses were removed after Tankard wondered what would happen 'if the ropes were attached to one limb—their arm or their foot, their wrist or ankle'. *Aurora*, her witty and touching look at love inspired by the ballet classic *The Sleeping Beauty*, also grew out of her experiences in Adelaide, although the tap-dancing fairies, men in tutus and limping gardeners with which she peopled the piece were often the source of bitter criticism.

POTTER: What made you leave Canberra?

TANKARD: In 1992 I was approached by the board of the Australian Dance Theatre in Adelaide. They were looking for an artistic director and I was approached by the board to apply for that position. The company had probably five times more funding than the company in Canberra, so I was able to have double the amount of dancers, a bigger space and be in a bigger city. I wasn't that enthusiastic about it at first, because I felt that I'd built up something in Canberra that I wanted to see grow and develop. But I looked at the Canberra situation and thought, because of the population, we're never going to be able to really have a big company there—we would never get the funding.

POTTER: Looking back, what do you think were the positive and the negative things about Canberra?

TANKARD: I always liked living in Canberra, even though it's a tiny, quiet place, because it was the first time I had the opportunity to have a group of dancers of my own. The thing that was interesting, too, was you had access to the embassies. You had those people coming in and out of town, so there was quite a cosmopolitan feel in a way. I always thought it could be a great city for dance festivals. You were right in the middle of Melbourne and Sydney. And at the time I had all these hopes that I could build something there that could be a centre for dance. But on the other hand, you've got this small-town mentality too. I don't know, there's something in Australia that the bigger you get, instead of people getting proud of that and wanting to own you, they actually get a bit jealous or something. So there's that thing about a small town that I've realised, and I'm realising it in Adelaide, too—it's the same. They don't like you to get too big. So it was like we'd got as big as we could get there.

POTTER: Since moving to Adelaide has your work changed?

TANKARD: Well, I had just five women in Canberra. I had three dancers come with me to Adelaide from Canberra. We got another two and we got five boys. So it was really exciting for me to have male and female energy. So that was entirely different. But a lot of the new dancers were out of the Victorian College of the Arts, and I know there was just a little bit of trouble. They didn't really know what it's like to be in a company and I don't think people are trained now to work with other people. So it took a while to get that ensemble feeling. There was this feeling that they're all individuals and they're all soloists. And that's a little bit in the teaching now, I think, from the feeling I'm getting. So that took a while. Everyone had to get to know each other and work together. But now I feel that we have got a strong group of people.

In Canberra we had a tiny studio. In Adelaide the space is fantastic—we've got a huge space, a high ceiling. The first major work I made in Adelaide was *Furioso*. The dancers reworked *Nuti* and reworked *Kikimora* and that was almost like a training they went through, of just having to learn something that existed. Then there was that freedom of creating a new work. And when you see *Furioso*, it's so different from Canberra. I felt I wanted to use every bit of air in that rehearsal room. So we did. We used right up in the ceiling. We used that air and had the dancers flying on ropes. And it was as if I'd just burst out of something, I think.

POTTER: Did the ropes come only from that increased sense of space that you had? Or was there some other tradition or heritage that you were drawing on there?

TANKARD: No. Nobody I know, nobody I've worked with, has ever worked on ropes. But when I was doing *Sloth* for the ABC film *Seven Deadly Sins*, which I made in a quarry outside Canberra, what I wanted to do was defy gravity and have the dancers floating. With film you've got that opportunity to turn the wall upside down, the floor upside down, to make the wall the floor. I'm not particularly happy with the film because I was forced to compromise greatly. I was not actually allowed to do the shots I wanted to do. But, in a way, that's how *Furioso* started. Why can't we have the wall as the floor? So I got ropes in, so they could actually walk on the wall. But one day a rope was hung in the centre of the studio and people just started jumping on it, and then it just got so exciting. There was a different energy. I think there was that male energy I hadn't had and I think I was wanting to explore that.

POTTER: Can you talk about what inspired you to do *Aurora*?

TANKARD: I had the idea, I guess, in 1992. I had actually wanted to make a version of *Sleeping Beauty* as my first piece in Adelaide and I'd started asking the dancers questions about it. But I felt they were not really ready to act like that. So the next year, after *Furioso*, which is more of a dance piece, I came back to those questions. Then I felt they'd been working as a team for a year. They'd grown together. That's when we started doing *Aurora*. I had this fascination with the idea of whether I could do a ballet. And could I do a ballet with ten people? And how do I make ten people look like 60? There were all these challenges. I'd just gone to Europe; the French Government had just given me a grant to go to France to meet choreographers, to see their work. I came back thinking how much Pina has influenced the whole world of dance. But what I felt was a lot of people were taking Pina's concepts and using them in a very superficial way. It became all this violence and angst and boots, and women falling down and getting up and throwing themselves on walls. I just felt often it wasn't done sincerely. And I just felt, 'Oh, surely we can dance for joy and happiness.' That, for me, was a big challenge to do a piece that was really about love, happiness. And I also felt Australia is a happy country. It's bright. The sky is blue. The grass is really green. It's not grey and muted and faded. It's all really clear, like crystal. So I think that was the inspiration, saying 'This is my country, this is where we live.' It is actually a very happy country, joyful. And it was great because I had what, for me, was a narrative, which I'd never worked with before. It was good to work within a plan like that.

POTTER: What were the questions you were asking?

TANKARD: There were all the obvious ones, like how would you impress a princess? How would you test someone for marriage? But then there was one that I think was the most important and the one that really went right through the whole piece, became the basis for the whole piece. I asked the dancers to put the palm of the right hand on the three most sacred parts of their own body, thinking that they'd all do the same thing. And they didn't! Some people put their hand under the soles of their feet, some put it on their heart, and even if they did do the same, it felt quite different. So then I started to explore how we could make movement out of those simple gestures. It was amazing; it was just endless, endless. And, I find, if you hit the right question, everyone gets involved and they treat it very seriously. And they did. They were very sincere and a really nice atmosphere came over. So the movement vocabulary came from those gestures.

Originally I wanted *Aurora* to be like a little cartoon, a little magic fairytale. But I wanted to use traditional things like star cloths and cycloramas—things I've never, ever used in the theatre. And they just sort of fell into place. Like the silhouettes at the beginning of the second act. They were inspired by the little silhouettes that illustrate a lot of fairytale books. It started out to be so that it looked like there were more people on the stage, but it became something else. They became the labyrinth, the men searching for love, enduring all these strange things, caught up in a maelstrom trying to find their princess. It was just like the prince in the old fairytale chopping down the trees and overgrown bushes.

POTTER: You introduced tap dancing in *Aurora*. Had the dancers already learnt tap?

TANKARD: No, only Michelle (Ryan) and Tuula (Roppola). But, I don't know why, they were doing these little steps, like little cockroaches, little insects. And I listened to that music and I thought, 'I'm sure tap shoes would go with Tchaikovsky!' And I think they do actually.

POTTER: I think you got criticised for putting the boys in tutus in some sections.

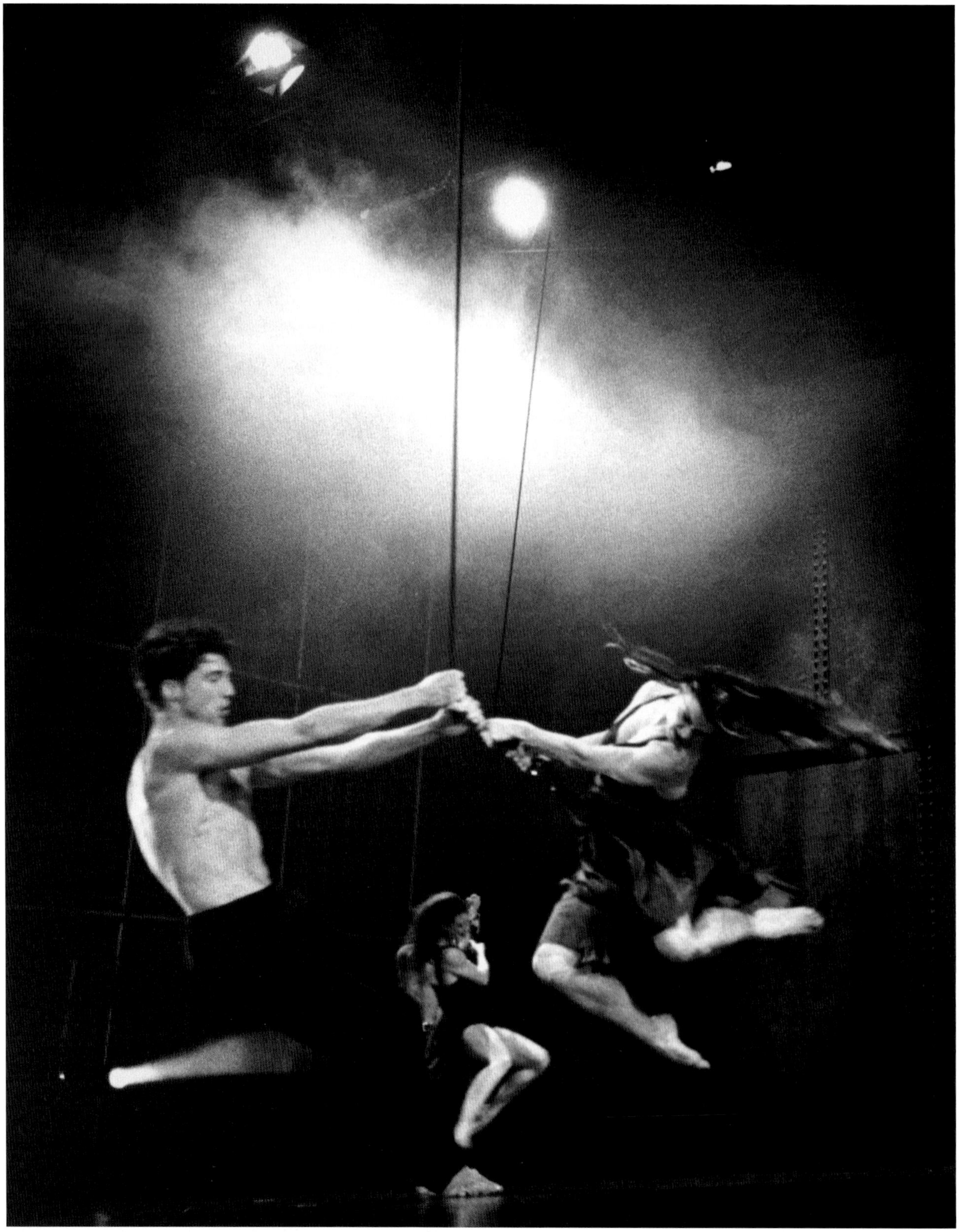

TANKARD: Oh, yes. People in Adelaide wrote to the newspaper and said that it was bad enough the boys wearing tutus, but it was Miss Tankard's fault for forcing them to wear them. So the boys wrote back saying they loved their tutus! In Adelaide, too, we had a little girl on the poster, a four-year-old girl, a friend of ours, who was dressed up as a fairy but was not wearing a top. Letters went everywhere saying that the poster was pornographic. So, for future productions, we decided to change the poster—I mean, this piece that came from really pure innocence. I found it fascinating that critics reacted in such a way. They've almost been repulsed by it. And I find it quite interesting because never in the whole creation of it was there anything evil or nasty or hateful. It's as if it irritates some people. I've never had a reaction like that from critics where they're so angry. I just think it's a fun, happy piece. It's like they won't allow themselves to get into that. But the audiences are always so warm, and that's who we do it for really. (July 1996)

Since returning to Australia from Europe, Tankard has continued to try to find her own voice in dance. She has moved away from her initial balletic training, although she is always aware of the discipline that such training instils. But it is, nevertheless, an emotional power that she looks for in her search to make work that will inspire audiences and touch their hearts.

MCKECHNIE: Are there any aspects of the working process that really get you down?

TANKARD: Sometimes that I just start in there with nothing. It's just so scary and, you know, I say, 'Why can't I just go in there and do arabesques and first position and second position?' I would almost like to have this little box of steps that I can draw on. I often try to do it and I hate it so much and I get really angry with myself. So this is a constant struggle.

I do what I feel. I don't do it for myself, though. I'm doing things where I think I will move people, but I can only judge it myself. I know that I have to be really aware of that—just keep following my instincts, not give into doing what you think people are going to like.

MCKECHNIE: What restricts you most?

TANKARD: Well, I think the culture. In Australia people are just not used to going to the theatre. They don't realise that they could actually get something out of this. I don't think you have to have a great knowledge of the arts or dance or anything. I do feel that I'm trying to create steps that you really don't have to have any knowledge of dance to appreciate. I want to make dance just for normal everyday people. (July 1990)

POTTER: When you moved to Adelaide you added your name to the name of the company which had always been known simply as Australian Dance Theatre. There was some discussion about whether this was appropriate or not.

TANKARD: It had nothing to do with me. The board said they wanted to change the name. For me, my name is just like a product name. It's the best way to describe the show. I don't really want to put 'dance' because then, if I don't dance, I'll get into trouble. So I'd rather not say dance. I'd rather not say 'dance theatre' because that conjures up some other thing for people. I really think the best way to describe everybody's work is just to put the name of the person there. It's ultimately that person's personality that's going to come out. But Australians are still so weird that they think this is some ego thing. I think it's hideous because I get the blame for everything. If someone's bill hasn't been paid, who do they blame? Meryl Tankard. She's in the office. She's doing everything. She's typing, she's signing the cheques, she's sewing. I've actually lost my name. I feel like I may as well be called Palmolive or something.

POTTER: Are you a choreographer then?

TANKARD: I don't particularly like doing steps. I see a whole thing. I can see the whole piece. Sometimes I think it's like designing a dress. Maybe you don't actually do the running stitches on the machine. For me, it's a much bigger thing. I feel in time that what I would like is just to do films and maybe someone else will choreograph sections of that.

POTTER: What is it about film that's so attractive to you?

TANKARD: Well, you can direct it exactly where you want it to go. Often on the stage there's a really tiny subtle moment that I look out for every time. But people come to the show and they don't even see it. That's why a lot of people often come back a second time and say, 'Oh, you've changed it.' And I say, 'No. I haven't changed a thing. You're looking at it differently.' So often, for me, the more subtle thing that's happening in the corner is more interesting than the big thing in the centre. I guess in film you can take that person right there. And little tiny movements and textures and things you can show in film. I'd like to work with texture. And I'd like to make the stage have a texture. That's why, I suppose, it's nice to go out in a bullring, which is where we performed *Rasa* with Padma Menon. Then you sort of feel like the people are part of the stage, more than in a theatre where there's that big separation.

POTTER: Do you think you'll stay in Adelaide?

TANKARD: I don't know. It's again this thing in Australia—and I do have to say it. I just think there's some major problem. As soon as you start to get successful, people do start to knock you. I mean, we're just starting to build up an audience. We're going to New York. We've got a European tour planned with fees. We could really, really be an international company. And I don't know if there are that many companies in Australia getting invitations from Paris and New York. But I'm always made to feel that that's not that important. You know, we can't even get a national tour. There's no real system in place to take us nationally. They tried this year, but we're marketed as a contemporary dance company, and we're *not* a contemporary dance company. If you don't again fit into a box, if you don't fit into the marketing person's head, it's like you don't exist. I'm trying to push myself creatively and it goes against me. If I did something that they could actually sell and say it's the story of such and such, then they could market it. But I'm not sure the work would be good.

POTTER: What are your hopes and aspirations for yourself and your company?

TANKARD: I guess that when people hear my name and the name of the company, they would hope that what they'll see is going to be something exciting, hope that it is going to move them. And it doesn't matter how it moves them. It can move them with Bulgarian singing or with people on ropes. And hopefully it will surprise them. Hopefully the next piece will not be like the piece they saw before. (July 1996)

During Meryl Tankard's extraordinary period of creativity in Canberra between 1989 and 1992, the press dubbed her 'La Tankard'. She contributed to the city's artistic life in a way that constantly engaged the community. In her interviews a similar sense of engagement is apparent. Her eyes are expressive and she gestures frequently. Her voice is coloured with emotion and rises and falls evocatively. As in her works, there seems always a desire to connect with people's emotions.

Choreography by Meryl Tankard

1977	*Birds behind Bars*	*Dance Horizons*, Australian Ballet Choreographic Workshop
1984	*Echo Point*	Independent work, Sydney
1986	*Travelling Light*	Independent work, Sydney
1988	*Two Feet*	Independent work, Brisbane World Expo on Stage
1989	*VX 18504*	Meryl Tankard Company
	Banshee	Meryl Tankard Company
	Death in Venice	Australian Opera
1990	*Nuti*	Meryl Tankard Company
	Kikimora	Meryl Tankard Company
	Court of Flora	Meryl Tankard Company
1991	*Chants de mariage I*	Meryl Tankard Company
1992	*Chants de mariage II*	Meryl Tankard Company, Adelaide Festival
	Songs with Mara	Meryl Tankard Company
	Sloth	*Seven Deadly Sins*, ABC-TV
1993	*Furioso*	Meryl Tankard Australian Dance Theatre
	Orphée et Euridyce	Australian Opera
1994	*Aurora*	Meryl Tankard Australian Dance Theatre
	O Let Me Weep	Meryl Tankard Australian Dance Theatre, Barossa Music Festival
1995	*Possessed*	Meryl Tankard Australian Dance Theatre, Barossa Music Festival
1996	*Rasa* (with Padma Menon)	Meryl Tankard Australian Dance Theatre, Adelaide Festival
	The Deep End	Australian Ballet

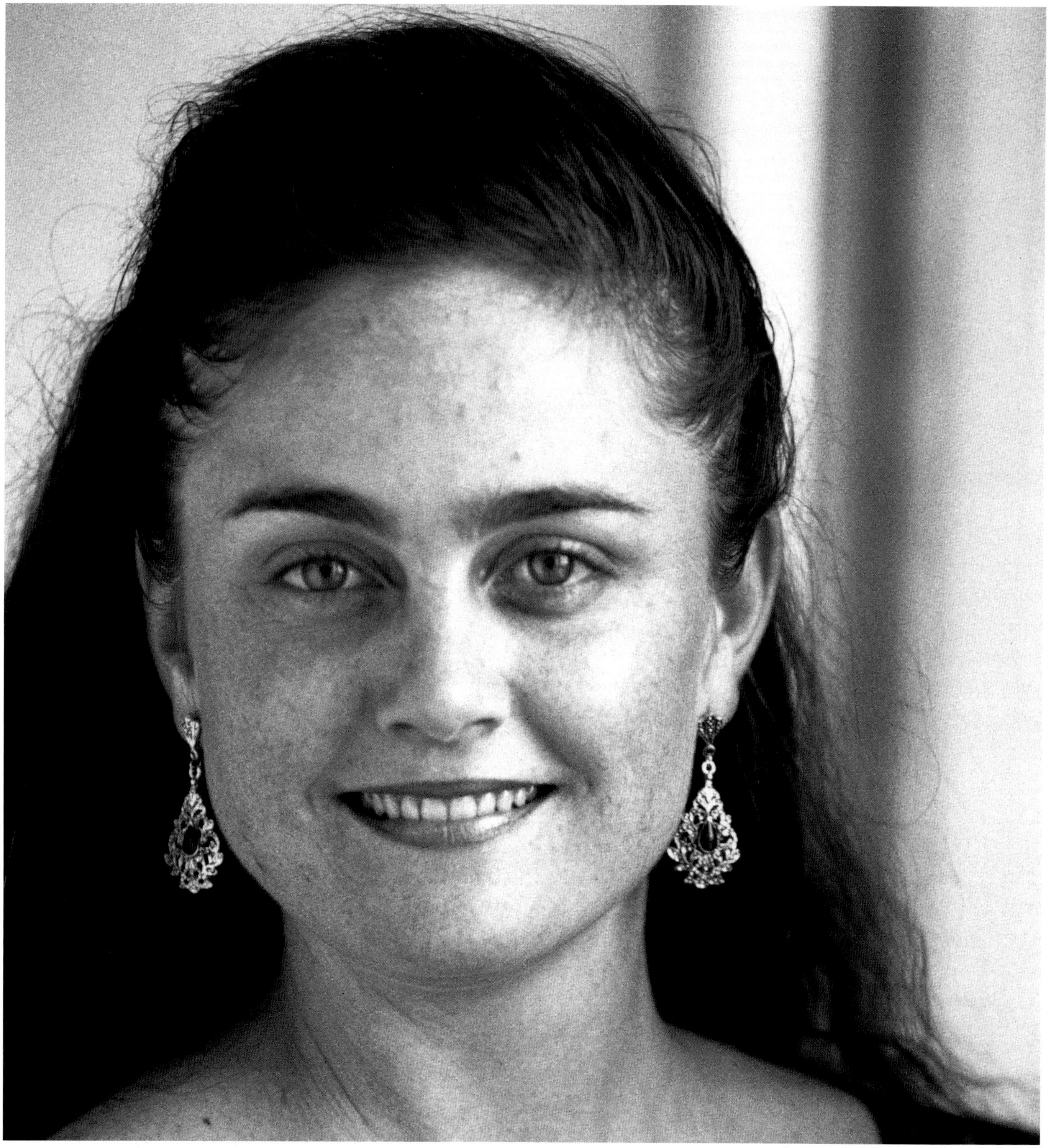

Natalie Weir

Textures and Layers

Interview TRC 3320

Natalie Weir (born 1967), independent choreographer, was interviewed in Brisbane by Michelle Potter in August 1995

As an independent choreographer Natalie Weir has worked for a diverse range of companies and organisations including the Queensland Ballet, where she was choreographer-in-residence for two years, the Australian Ballet School's Dancers Company, the West Australian Ballet, Dance North and Expressions Dance Company, as well as for a range of tertiary institutions for whom she frequently creates pieces for graduation seasons. Although her work is distinctively her own, her choreography necessarily spans a range of styles and techniques to accommodate the needs of dancers with different training and backgrounds, and companies with different expectations of and attitudes to dance as an art form. Working independently also involves Weir in a constant search for opportunities and has its difficulties, not the least of which is a lack of financial security. But although she dreams of eventually having her own small company of dancers to create on, rather than having 'snatched moments' with other companies, Weir continues to work independently because, at present, it is the only way she can pursue what she calls her 'passion' for choreography.

The eldest of two daughters, Weir was born in Townsville, Far North Queensland, and educated at Townsville Grammar. She says she had 'a lovely childhood, no dramas to report'. Her early dance training was with Ann Roberts in Townsville and she performed in and toured with Roberts' North Queensland Ballet Company, the precursor to Dance North. The seeds of her choreographic career were planted during her time with the North Queensland Ballet Company, when she had the opportunity of dancing in works especially created for the company by choreographers who included Ronne Arnold, Maggi Sietsma, Anthony Shearsmith, Andris Toppe and Merrillee Macourt. Her choreographic career began in earnest, however, when she was a dance student at the Kelvin Grove College, now the Queensland University of Technology. It was there that she eventually decided, happily, to give up the idea of performing herself and to concentrate fully on creating.

POTTER: Natalie, I'd like to start off by asking you what your current projects are.

WEIR: Right. At this particular moment I'm working on two things: one is a ballet for the Queensland University of Technology; and the other is, I'm preparing to go to the West Australian Ballet in three weeks to do a work for them. The work for QUT is called *Narcissus*. It's a collaboration with Bill Haycock, the designer, and we're looking at ideas, such as the beauty myth, that are sort of relevant in modern society and trying to translate that into dance. It's a 40-minute work for their graduation season and involves 20 dancers. The piece I'm doing for the West Australian Ballet is a work called *The Collector* based on a novel by John Fowles, who wrote *The French Lieutenant's Woman*. It's an observation of an obsession. The book's written in two parts—one from the male point of view, and one from the female—and I think that's really quite fascinating and I'm hoping to take that kind of approach in the ballet. It deals with issues such as materialism, ownership and values, and the conditions of attachment, which I think will be interesting to explore in movement.

POTTER: The one for West Australian Ballet is some kind of fellowship that I think Barry Moreland offered. Would you like to explain a bit about that?

WEIR: Yes. It's called a national choreographic workshop. What they want to do is to create new work using the classical vocabulary. I applied with this idea, which was a work that I had done for the Queensland Ballet five years ago. I thought that it would be something worth redeveloping now that I'm a little bit older. I got the job along with two other Australian male choreographers. That was fab.

POTTER: Have you worked for the WA Ballet before?

WEIR: No, I haven't. I think, for me, it's quite a nice step forward and a great opportunity because they're beautiful dancers over there. There's not much opportunity to work with classical dancers and I really feel that my work does very well with the classical technique. So this is a real chance to experiment and develop. My understanding of the West Australian workshop is, I guess, that it's an experimental season. They say that if the works are successful, they will take them on board into their repertoire and put more money into them with regards to the design and production of the work.

POTTER: What about the music for this work?

WEIR: I'm still in the throes of trying to find it. When I originally did it, I did use some Elgar, but I feel that that was too sort of big and grand and sometimes overpowered the choreography, so what I'm looking for is something that can be played by an orchestra but something that is perhaps modern, that has been written more recently. I've got a few things I like but nothing that's sort of startling yet, so I'm still looking. The endless search continues.

POTTER: When I look at the things you've done for the Queensland Ballet, and I look at the music you've chosen, you've often used a kind of collage of music and it's often been quite a startling juxtaposition of musical styles—quite classical composers with modern works. Do you like working like that with the music?

WEIR: I do. I find it hard to find long pieces of music that say the things that I want to say, so I tend to use a lot of short pieces that grab me. The music has to inspire me. I'm hoping with this work to use just one composer and a longer piece of music so that there is more of a sense of continuity in it, and that's why I think I'm having trouble finding it, because I tend to like shorter things that sum things up. For the work for QUT I have a composer, Andy Athurs. That's fantastic because I can actually talk about my ideas with him and then he takes them on board and they come out in the music. I'd like to have a composer that followed me around full-time. Make life a lot easier.

POTTER: You had a classical dance training in the Royal Academy of Dancing (RAD) system. Did you have any thoughts about that system, or did you just accept it?

WEIR: As a child it was just acceptance. It's only looking back I think it was good because, I suppose, it teaches you discipline, although you have to have that discipline yourself. As a young child I was very classically orientated, you know; I didn't know there was anything else out there. It wasn't until I started to work with other choreographers in the North Queensland Ballet Company that I sort of went, 'Oh right, your head doesn't always have to be looking there' and all of those sorts of things. It was very strict, very locked in, everything had to be in a certain place. I don't know that that is so healthy for artistic expression, although it certainly probably trains the body very well. I don't know, it's not something I work with anymore and it's not something I'm really up with, so I wouldn't know now. But back then it was very difficult, against my body completely—my body just didn't agree with it. All classical dance is inhuman in a way.

POTTER: But despite all that, you still maintained a kind of interest in the classical vocabulary, haven't you?

WEIR: Absolutely yes, I mean RAD is what taught me all of the classical steps and it is beautiful, it is. The lines are extraordinarily beautiful. I mean, you can't get away from your background—I was trained as a classical child. My work's not that classical anymore but I use a classical base, that's where the understanding has come from. It's something that my body has known. I like to use it when I'm working with classical dancers—it's better to use what they are so good at, rather than fight against them. Often I have very short periods of time to do things, so I can't teach them how to fall to the floor or how to feel heavy into the floor. They're very light and pulled up, so it's better to work with them rather than against them.

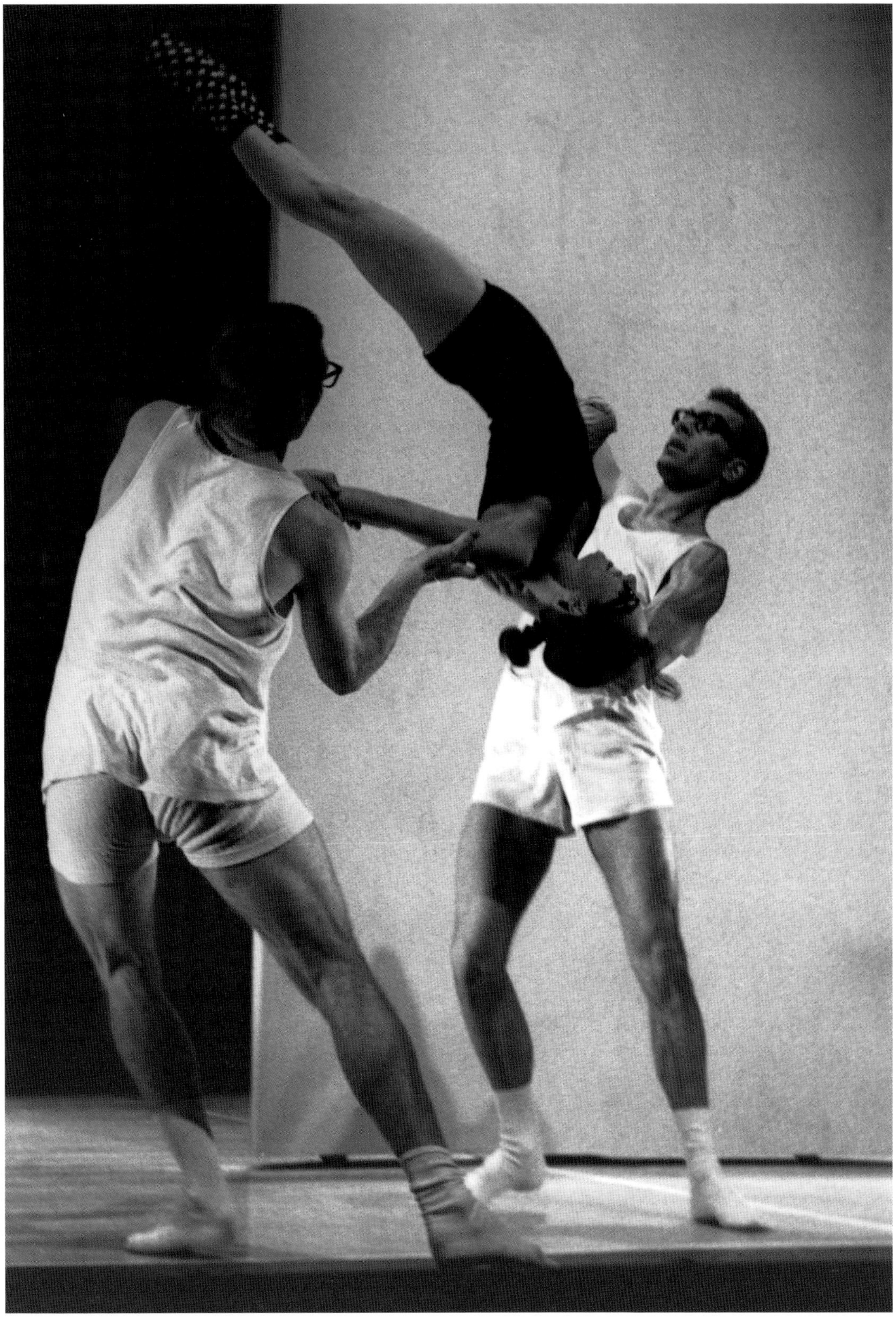

POTTER: Do you often use pointe work for the women still?

WEIR: Not that often. Now and then. Either when I'm asked to or I have a specific thought or idea that I think pointe work would express the best. It's certainly not something I love. I find it a little restricting at times. But for partner work, it sort of allows you to do turns and things that are not possible without the shoes, so I use it when I think it's going to help me.

POTTER: Have you always had this idea of being a choreographer in the back of your mind?

WEIR: I think it's something that I fell into, that I was doing before I knew I was doing it. As a young child, I remember that I wanted to be a dancer, but I didn't know that I'd ever be able to, and that used to worry me. I used to choreograph because I was asked to or there was no-one else to do it. But it wasn't until I got to the uni here that I considered it as a profession.

POTTER: Well, what made you decide to audition for QUT?

WEIR: At school, I remember I was very dissatisfied learning about maths and economics and things that I really didn't feel like I was going to be using in my later life. I remember I was in the library one day and I opened a drawer and found out about this uni—it was Kelvin Grove College then— and asked Mum and Dad if I could apply, and did so. The director at the time was Anne Sylvie, I think, and she came to Townsville to audition as they still do, and saw me in Ann Roberts' end-of-year concert. That was basically my audition and I was accepted in. I did not complete Year 12. I left school at the end of Grade 11 to go on to this, which was something I thought was more focused on what I'd be doing later. It was the best decision of my life really, and one that Mum and Dad approved luckily, God knows why. I was only 15 at the time, I was very young, but that's the way it went.

POTTER: You said that you didn't think you'd be a dancer, but you nevertheless were accepted. On what grounds do you think they accepted you?

WEIR: I've never thought about that. I suppose when I was younger and very slender, I was sort of an okay dancer. Maybe they saw some promise in me, but I don't think I ever had a star quality, I really don't. I had short achilles tendons. I was a bigger person. I was very stiff. I had a lot of things that I was battling with myself. Even during that first year I was still keen to be a dancer. It was only during the second year that my mind completely did a turnaround.

POTTER: What happened to make your mind turn around?

WEIR: I remember at Ann Roberts' I was always one of the better dancers, but then Townsville was a small place and it depended who was going through the school at the time. At QUT I was suddenly right down the ranks compared to other people. I found this frustrating and I was just becoming very dissatisfied. I was doing contemporary classes but they weren't working for me either, so it was all sort of working against me. Then we did choreography as part of our course and I did my first piece and found that it was really quite good and interesting. I was fascinated by creating movement I'd never seen before and I remember that fascination because, now that I'm more experienced, the fascination's still there, although it's not quite as wondrous as those first few works were when everything was something new. So I suppose that wonder kept with me. The fact that the first work was very successful and they took it into one of their productions as the only student work along with all the lecturers' choreographies was very encouraging for me. So I guess things just started to happen from there.

POTTER: What was the first work?

WEIR: It was called *Phaedra*, it was very short. It was only about four minutes and it was the first time I'd ever created partner work and I have a love of partner work that seems to be getting worse as I get older rather than getting better— I just adore doing partner work. So I was doing interesting lifts and interesting sort of intertwining and that was all very new and exciting to me. The second work I did was called *Lovestruck Serenade*, which was a piece to some Dire Straits music. It was a similar sort of exploration of partnering and solo work. So it was mainly those two pieces that I did in the time.

POTTER: Did you give up your ideas of being a performer yourself then?

WEIR: No, not completely, although I was sort of very fortunate in that Maggi (Sietsma) started her company, Expressions, the year I left the university, the year I graduated. She asked me to choreograph for the company as well as perform in their arts-in-education program, which was just a small company, three of us who went into primary schools throughout Brisbane and Queensland taking dance into schools, putting on small performances with the Arts Council. But I never performed in the main Expressions seasons, which obviously I would have loved to have done. After a few years I basically opted out. I didn't want to do it anymore; I just wanted to choreograph. It wasn't anything dramatic and it wasn't something that upset me or anything like that. It was just sort of the way things went, something I was really happy about. I found something I was better at and I was really happy with this, so that just happened.

POTTER: When you were at QUT, did you have classes in the craft of choreography?

WEIR: More or less. They were all taken, when I was there, by Maggi Sietsma. We learnt simple things about composition that have been very, very useful, but that was it. The course was just starting so it was only one a fortnight maybe, but at least she got us to practise our craft ourselves, to try things out. She got me up and moving. I would probably never have thought to choreograph something otherwise. Now they do a lot of composition work and it's very, very good. Sometimes I wish I had learnt more, but I wonder if I'd been taught more about composition, if I would be more inhibited, because I would be aware of all the things I could be doing wrong. It's a very hard thing to teach and just getting in there and doing it, you know, by the seat of your pants is the way you find out what works best. Not being afraid because you don't know that that's totally the wrong form or the wrong structure to be using.

POTTER: What were the kind of technical things that you learnt in composition classes?

WEIR: Canon. ABA form or ABC form. The power of stage, you know, the strongest parts of the stage being centre and the strongest diagonals and all of those sorts of things, which have been very useful. And like writing a structure for your work so that it has high points and low points, that it is well structured and doesn't go on at one level the whole time—how all of that integrates to make a finished work. That you can do two things at once—where the focus is; where you want the focus to be. So that was really good, but it was just the basics. They were taught very, very well, but they were taught in the time that Maggi had to teach them. She's taught me a lot more since then. Most of what I've learnt has come just from watching her work. Sometimes too I've watched Graeme Watson do a work here. It's things like that that help, seeing how other people create. Not necessarily taking any of it on board, or maybe taking some of it on board and trying it yourself. The way I work in a studio is very different from Maggi or Graeme, but at least it sort of opens your mind to different approaches.

Weir's sources of inspiration are varied and her understanding of the choreographic process has deepened and flourished since her early experiences as a student. Now she works frequently with Brisbane-based designer Bill Haycock, and from him, from her actor–husband and from a developing self-awareness and maturity, she has learnt techniques that she says give her works different textures and multiple layers of meaning.

POTTER: What are your sources? Where do you look for your inspiration?

WEIR: Everywhere really. It's so hard to say. Lately a lot of my inspiration's coming more from life, I suppose, from my experience, from things I see happening around me—from death, from having a baby, from all of these things. Earlier it came more from poetry, from ideas in books, a novel, and less from life, I think. I was more narrative as a young choreographer whereas now I tend to be more abstract and I'm more interested in emotional content now than I was back then, if that makes any sense.

The last piece, or the piece before last, I did for Queensland Ballet was *Burning*. It was, to me, my most successful, my most precious work. It was the first work that was a complete invention from nowhere. It came totally from the imagination of Bill (Haycock) and me. It was about the human condition and was about life and experience and loss of love. I found that it was affecting people emotionally, which had never happened in my works so much before. The images sort of had a lot of layers to them. People could read many different things into the work and were affected in different ways.

Sometimes my husband writes poetry for me which I use as inspiration—which is wonderful—or I do something and he writes a poem to go in the program. I can't think of what else. Many things, anything. I'm not sort of closed off to anything; a lot of times the music is the inspiration, or a thought or a feeling.

POTTER: What does your husband do?

WEIR: My husband's an actor, which makes a very unstable life for us both. I have a son called Maitland, he's 18 months old—he's the best creation we've ever had, he's lovely. So Peter works for Queensland Theatre Company quite a lot. He does a lot of bits and pieces to help pay the bills, sort of street entertainment, very entertaining. He's had small roles in movies and mini-series and things like that. It's an absolute passion with him as is choreography with me. So we have to be very fair to each other so that we both get a go. Obviously money's not going to be a steady, stable thing because we're not in a '9 to 5' job. That's probably our biggest problem. So it's just trying to balance all of that out. He's my biggest support and my biggest inspiration, I suppose.

POTTER: What is the process that you go through when you're choreographing a work?

WEIR: Trauma—I'm a mess. A lot of my work is done hands-on in the studio. I prepare what I'm trying to say or I see an image, and then I'll go in and work it from the dancers. I don't prepare steps or movements at home at all. I did once when I was younger. Now that I'm more confident, I don't need to do that and it works much better because the dance comes from the people you're working with, which makes every step unique to the dancer that you're creating it on. I guess that's the most important thing I've discovered as a choreographer. So it's confidence that allows you to walk into a room with 20 dancers standing there looking at you and to be able to throw yourself in and start working.

The music plays a huge part. For me, I listen to the music for hours and hours and it takes me months to collect the music. The music certainly has a lot to do with the inspiration and the dynamic of the movement and the way the movement is headed. Lots of thinking. I write things out on cards, my images, and get them into an order that I think's reasonable and hopefully says what I want it to say.

POTTER: Do you use cards to organise the structure of your work then?

WEIR: Yes, that's only a recent thing. Bill Haycock taught me that. Because he's a designer, he draws everything and he likes to have everything out on separate pieces of paper. So we did that with *Burning* for the first time. Yes, it's a great way. You write down what you want to say, and include any images you have of the work—perhaps it might be an image from a magazine or a phrase from a poem, or words that inspire a particular thought or feeling, or perhaps a drawing—and then you sort of mish them, mash them around and you get like a storyboard. Bill gets images out of magazines and books and from looking at photographs and things. So I'm sort of always doing that now and I end up with a big, thick collage, I suppose, of stuff that I just sort of put in a book and I have it all there. And my husband taught me that as an actor you fill your mind with every bit of information about your part—filling the bottle, he calls it—even if it's off on a different angle. Then you just forget about it and you go in there and do it knowing everything you could possibly know. Then it has to come out right, it has to come out informed, and it has to come out in multiple layers because you've got all that information stored away. Using a card is probably the most valuable tool I've learnt to structure a work. I can talk for hours about a ballet and where it's come from and what it means and stuff like that. I can talk to the dancers because I know where it's come from. And they know where your mind's coming from and they can help you get what you want in the end.

POTTER: Is there a lot of back and forth conversation between you and the dancers when you're choreographing?

WEIR: Yes, it's getting more and more. I used to shut them out and that was insecurity. In *Burning* I had a few raves about what it was and I found that they responded extremely well; they said, 'We want you to talk more about it.' I found it a little bit difficult in *Burning*, because it was largely inspired by a girlfriend of mine who had an asthma attack and died. A lot of it was very personal, so I wasn't happy sort of ranting about it. And there's also that feeling of fright that they're not going to accept it, that they're going to laugh at something that's so dear to you. But that didn't happen. They were very, very keen to take it on board. Since that time, I've learnt that the more you tell them, the better it is, because they'll say, 'Something like that happened to me. Is it like this?' I mean, it becomes personal to them, which means that they're going to perform it in a way that's truly their own and that means something to them. So now I start telling them everything; in fact, I talk too much. So that's really good because you get a far better work and you get them sort of putting all their input in as well, which just makes it a far more textured and more layered piece. It has a lot more meaning than you could have possibly thought up by yourself. It's a vital thing, but it has to come with confidence, I think.

POTTER: Have you worked with other designers, apart from Bill, over a long period of time?

WEIR: No, Bill's the only one I've developed, I think, a proper relationship with. I've worked with Greg Clarke and I think he's really fabulous—he works very differently to Bill. Bill's the only designer I've worked with who's interested in the process itself, who's interested in collaborating and helping with the ideas and helping with the structure and all of that that goes with it. We talk endlessly, and sometimes get nowhere with it. But it's all that feeling involved.

POTTER: You've mentioned *Burning* as perhaps your most memorable work for you to date. What are some of the other pieces that you feel have made some kind of impact?

WEIR: I suppose you always think your most recent's your best, and I just did a work with Expressions called *In-sight*, which was inspired by an Edward Hopper painting. It was wonderful to use something visual as a source. I felt that it had a similar feel to *Burning* in that it had a lot to do with turbulent human relations. I felt that it was a very focused piece with less in it rather than more, which is something you can't do until you're confident. It was very clear and simple and I was really thrilled with it. I did a piece called *Medea* for Queensland Ballet years ago—that was my first ever big commission, I suppose, for a company the size of the Queensland Ballet. I felt that it was a turning point in that I'd developed a style, but it didn't work for me. I went on to do another work called *The Studio* which was along similar lines, but still I hadn't quite got it. Then I did a work for Expressions called *Proof Sheet* and I think I got it right, and from there I've been following the same path of exploration. It's sort of integration of narrative and abstract, and the last few pieces have worked very well. Got it round my head now.

POTTER: When you say an integration of narrative and abstract, do you mean in the meaning of the work or do you mean choreographically somehow?

WEIR: I sort of mean that the work tends to follow, I don't know if it's a story, but an understandable path if you want to view it in that way. But it tends to take all of these sidelines that can be abstract but they are always filled with meaning. But if you want to go and view the work simply as a dance piece, you probably can too. It's an integration, and it's an integration with the design as well. It's really important that it all comes together rather than the design being flopped on top. The design has to integrate with the ideas and the movement.

POTTER: Have you ever made a piece, or do you ever envisage making a piece, that is about dancing?

WEIR: Yes. I suppose the last piece I did for Queensland Ballet, *Jabula*, was probably the first dance piece as such that I've done in many years, and that was because Harold (Collins, artistic director of the Queensland Ballet, 1978–97) asked me to do a piece that was easy to take on tour. It didn't require a set. It was movement that showed the dancers off. I didn't find it as satisfying as I do the other work, I think, simply because I like things to have multiple meanings now, and this one didn't. The movement was beautiful but I didn't find that it worked for me. It's funny because, early in my career,

I could not have cared less about meaning or saying something, I just cared about steps. That's really been a full circle for me. It's only, like I said, in the last few works that I'm starting to get it. The movement can still be good but I'm not controlled by it. I control it to do what I want it to do.

POTTER: Even though you say you're interested in the classical vocabulary, you still seem to work with a lot of non-classical companies.

WEIR: I feel that I do work in two ways and I love working with modern dancers. I think I might even be better at it, I'm not sure. I like the physicality of the modern-trained dancers. But I think you have to be able to go between the both, otherwise there's no work here in Australia. There's only three classical companies here and not that many more modern companies lately, because of all the funding cuts. Here in Brisbane there are two companies, one's classical, one's modern. If you don't work for both of them, what are you going to do? You've got to keep artistic directors' policies in mind as well, but I never feel restricted by that. I don't feel that, because I'm working for a modern company, I can't do an arabesque or anything like that. It's just sort of an overflow of both styles. My classically based work is still far more modern than classical choreography could be, I guess. Most modern dancers are classically trained anyway. It's just that in their later training they do more modern classes, whereas in a ballet company like Queensland Ballet, they only do maybe one modern class per week.

POTTER: What happens if you revive a work? Do you rework it then because you've got different bodies?

WEIR: Generally, yes. I haven't had that happen so much. I think it would be harder to revive a work that's done on modern dancers, say a work that's done for Expressions, on a ballet company, or a work for Queensland Ballet to be done on a modern company, because the dance technique affects the choreography to a great deal. I do find classical dancers and modern dancers completely different and I find myself working in different ways. I'll go into a rehearsal with modern dancers and I'll be thinking heavier and I'll be throwing myself around onto the floor and up and down far more than if I'm working with classical dancers.

POTTER: Who do you think are the most influential people, apart from your husband, in your career so far?

WEIR: That's a hard one. Anyone who gives you a job is pretty influential, I think. I suppose, early on, Maggi Sietsma certainly was a huge influence on me in that she took me under her wing you might say. She gave me a job and always sort of helped me, kept an eye on my choreography and gave me constructive criticism. She was very, very influential in the early days and, even now, I admire her work; I think her work's very different from mine but I think she's marvellous.

I saw *Enemy in the Figure*, a work of William Forsythe's—the first work of his I'd ever seen—in Sydney last year and that had the biggest effect on me that any work ever has. I thought it was just unbelievable. In those 25 minutes I was just awe-struck. That impact has never left me. I'd love to see some more works of his. I'd certainly like to go and follow him around and say, 'How do you do it?' I think he's extraordinary. He only uses classical technique, his work's far less modern than mine, but it's just the way he manipulates it. It's just beautiful, really exciting and unusual.

Other than that, I try to sort of steer clear of being influenced by choreographers too much, because you want to develop something that's your own, not that's a bit of everyone else's—you don't want to be anyone's clone. Personally, just my parents; they are still a love of my life. And friends. Nothing terribly exciting.

POTTER: Do you teach at all?

WEIR: Yes, I do. I teach for Elsie Seguss here in Brisbane. I've been working with her for so many years now, and I sort of do it more out of love for her than anything else, and for a bit of extra pocket money. But that's all. I've given all my other teaching away. I don't think I'm a teacher. I can teach my style, I can teach my movement, but I can't teach contemporary dance as such because I wouldn't know where to begin. I've worked with children quite a lot, but it's not my love. I find it a little bit taxing and a little bit uninspiring. But then, that's not completely true either—they can be the most inspiring of all. But the sort of standard of choreography I want works better on professionals, adults obviously.

POTTER: You said you can teach your style, and I'm going to ask you what you think your style is?

WEIR: Well, it's *my* style. It's very physical, I suppose—very physical, very organic. I think my choreography is recognisable in its partner work more than anything, I think that's the thing people probably associate with me. That's what I like, doing amazing things with intertwining bodies. So I sort of see that as a very distinct part of my style.

POTTER: Even though you said you don't want to sort of get involved with other choreographers' styles, apart from Forsythe are there other choreographers whose work you find interesting?

WEIR: Yes, there are lots—I'm the sort of person that will go to a piece of dance and find something enjoyable in some way, even if it's only because I see a step that I like or an image that I think is fantastic. It only has to be fleeting for me to actually enjoy it, and because I love dance so much—I just about love any kind of dance. But that's not to say I'm not critical, but I can just about enjoy anything. I like to see people who work really differently from me. Mostly that's when you sort of go, 'I didn't think something so simple could hold your attention for so long,' or something that suddenly makes you go 'Oh', because it's not the way you would do it. That's a little bit fascinating.

POTTER: What are your aspirations?

WEIR: Well, I suppose my biggest one is to have a company of my own. That's the end of the track, I suppose—well, not the end of the track, it's the start of it all. Certainly that's what I'm working towards. That's what I want in Australia, a company, just a small company. Just six or seven dancers would be fantastic.

POTTER: Do you think companies are better companies if they're run by a choreographer?

WEIR: I've spoken to this before; I don't know, I really don't. It depends on the person obviously. If the company is run by a choreographer who is interested in seeing other choreographers develop, then that's great. But if it wasn't run by a choreographer, but someone interested in giving commissions, that would be good too. But if it's run by a choreographer who's only interested in his or her own development, then that's harder for the rest of us. So it depends on the person. If I had a company, I would largely be using it to develop my own work and to have a relationship with dance that is ongoing, not just snatched moments. But I feel that I would be keen to help people, to get people in to give them a chance.

POTTER: Is there choreographic talent emerging at the moment?

WEIR: That's a hard one. Some of the people that are coming out of the uni here work very, very differently to what I enjoy. They should almost be visual artists I think, rather than choreographers. It seems to me that the new choreographer is less interested in the dance, more interested in other things, and I think that that's upsetting for dance. Being hugely broad here, it's almost like they've forgotten that the dance can say so much that other things can't. They're not interested in developing a movement vocabulary anymore; everything's become sort of so pedestrian—I'm being very general!

POTTER: Natalie, is there anything else you'd like to say, that we haven't covered yet?

WEIR: I'll say that I choreograph because I adore it, it's sort of a passion with me, as is acting with my husband. And that's why we will continue to do it till we're bored of it—not for monetary gain, but because it's something that we absolutely love to do.

As an interviewee Natalie Weir is unassuming, blending humility with a generous, natural and open attitude to discussing her life and work. It comes as something of a shock then to realise that she has created so many works for such a variety of companies since her first student work, a four-minute piece called *Phaedra*, was performed in a Queensland University of Technology production along with other works choreographed by her lecturers. Beneath her unpretentiousness there is persistence and even a steely determination.

Choreography by Natalie Weir

1985	*Just Weight*	Kelvin Grove College
	The Players	Expressions Dance Company
1987	*Scorched Ice*	Dance North
	The Short and the Tall of It	Expressions Dance Company
1988	*The Final Move*	Kelvin Grove College
	Act of Faith	Queensland Ballet
	Colors of '88	Extensions Dance Company
1989	*The Host*	National Capital Dancers
	Elizabeth Presents, The Story of Swan Lake	Ballet Theatre
	Edge of the Precipice	Dance North
	Clutches of Sleep	Extensions Dance Company
	Snowman in the Sun	Ballet d'Action
1989–90	*Desert Magic* (with Cheryl Stock)	Dance North
1990	*To Howl at the Moon*	2 Dance Plus
	The Collector	Queensland Ballet
	Beauty and the Beast	Rockhampton Youth Ballet
	Picasso's Masque	Ballet d'Action
1991	*Fractured Canvas*	Kelvin Grove College
	Moon Song	Adelaide Performing Arts College
	Steps to Dance	Queensland Ballet (Arts in Education)/Queensland Arts Council
1992	*Medea*	Queensland Ballet
	Complex Reflections	Adelaide Centre of Performing Arts
	Down Rivers of Spine	Queensland University of Technology
1993	*The Studio*	Queensland Ballet
	Proof Sheet—Plates 1–8	Expressions Dance Company
	Jabula	Queensland Ballet
1994	*Hunger*	Victorian College of the Arts
	I am a Dancer	Queensland Ballet (Arts in Education)/Queensland Arts Council
1995	*Burning*	Queensland Ballet
	In-sight	Expressions Dance Company
	Aladdin	Rockhampton Youth Ballet
	The Collector	West Australian Ballet
	Narcissus	Queensland University of Technology
1996	*The Host*	Queensland Ballet
	The Lunatic, the Lover and the Poet	Dance North
	The Brother of Sleep	Dancers Company
	Raw	Victorian College of the Arts

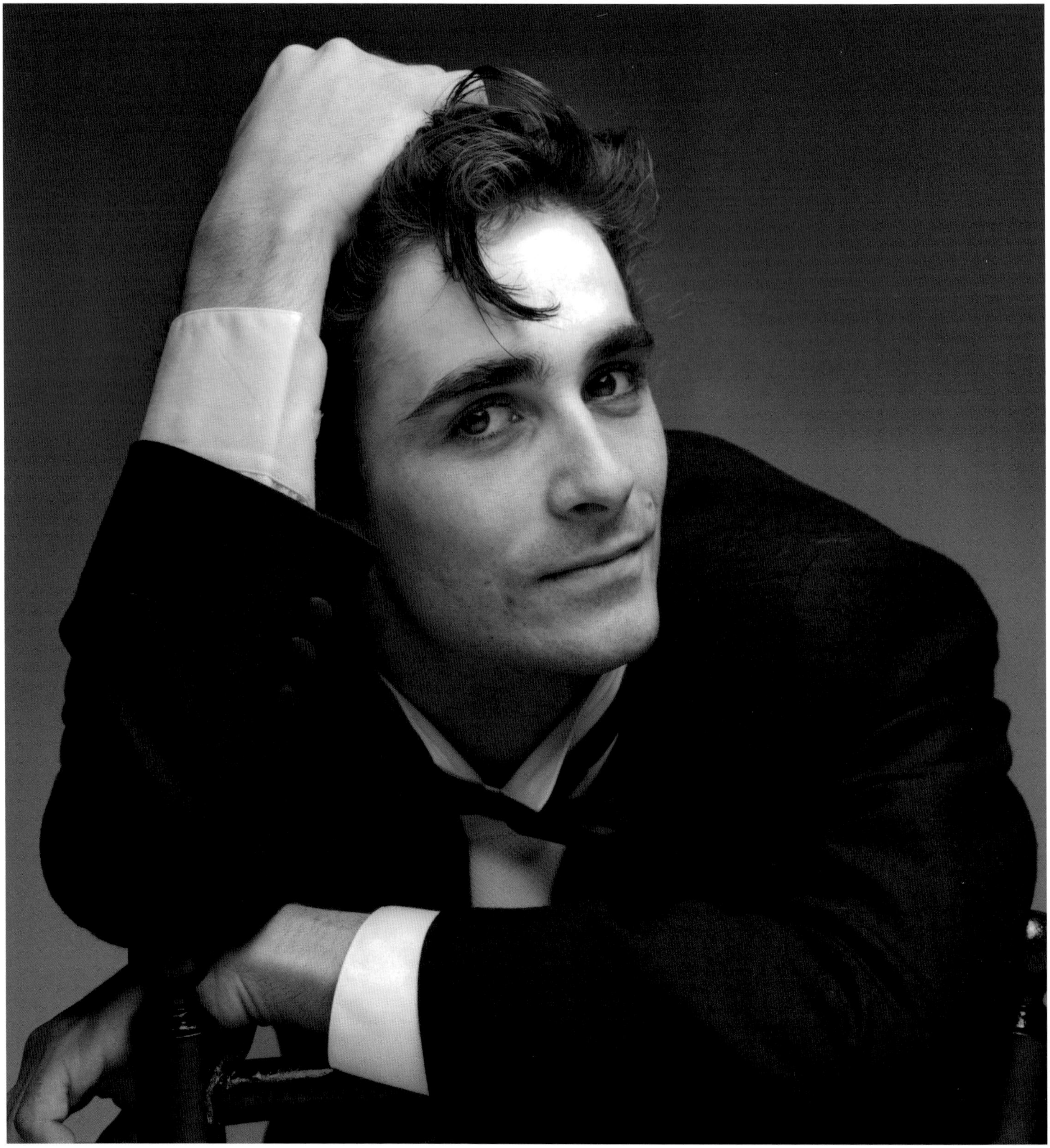

Stanton Welch

Boundless Dreams

Interview TRC 3321

Stanton Welch (born 1969), leading soloist with the Australian Ballet and since 1995 one of its two resident choreographers, was interviewed by Michelle Potter in Melbourne in August 1995

As one of two sons of renowned Australian dancers Marilyn Jones and Garth Welch, Stanton Welch was part of the world of Australian dance from a very early age, often going on tour with his parents and appearing in ballets that called for children as part of the cast. Born in Melbourne in 1969 Welch did not, however, have any early aspirations to become a professional dancer himself. He did not start taking classes until the relatively late age of 16, when he joined the Sydney dance school run by his parents. But after that initial step the development of his career was rapid. Within the space of just a few years Welch had won himself a scholarship to spend a year studying in San Francisco at the school attached to San Francisco Ballet. On his return to Australia in 1989, he successfully auditioned for a place in the Australian Ballet.

Now both a leading soloist with the Australian Ballet and one of the company's two resident choreographers, Welch appears never to have separated the roles of performer and creator. He started choreographing almost as soon as he started dance classes. Although he works from a classical base, Welch has never seen this as a limitation. His ballets often juxtapose the harmony and order of classicism with a late twentieth-century frenetic energy. Ideas, both choreographic and thematic, seem to pour out in an unending stream. His work has been made mainly for the Australian Ballet and the Australian Ballet School's Dancers Company, but he has also worked with 'the other company I call home', San Francisco Ballet.

POTTER: Tell me about your early experiences of watching people dance. Do they go back to your mum and dad?

WELCH: I don't have any memories of Dad dancing, because he'd stopped long before my memories started working. I remember sitting in the dressing room watching Dad get made up. He was performing in *Petrouchka*; he played the part of the Blackamoor for Ballet Victoria. In that show I did a little kid that walked on and had a big lollipop. But I don't actually remember him dancing. With Mum I always remember crying out the front whenever I saw her dance, not because of the beauty of it, but because she was doing *Romeo and Juliet* and she'd die. Then we'd all cry until we saw her again. Or she'd do *Sleeping Beauty* and she'd fall asleep, and we'd cry until we saw her. I just always remember being traumatised out the front watching Mum dance.

I remember more ballets than I remember individual dancers—*Romeo and Juliet*, *Onegin*, *Taming of the Shrew*; all the story ballets; *Billy the Kid*—I'd made up my own complete story to that ballet. It was completely wrong, but I had my own story and every night I'd sit there and watch my own story. I used to love making up things to ballets, especially if they were abstract. It's very easy in a ballet to create your own vision of what it's meant to mean. And that's what I think I enjoyed as a kid. You weren't strictly told what it meant, it was really up to yourself.

POTTER: Who encouraged you to choreograph in the first place?

WELCH: I guess Mum and Dad, because as soon as I started ballet I got involved with choreographic workshops. There were about 15 or 16 full-timers at Mum and Dad's ballet school—the girls had been going for a while and I joined halfway through the year in 1986. They'd had several workshops already and I was in a couple of them, and then finally I said, 'Well, it's my turn now. I'd like to do something.' I did a ballet called *Hades* and the Queensland Youth Ballet saw it and commissioned it for them. So I went up to Brisbane to put it on for them. We did it in some eisteddfods and it won some things and eventually we did it for the Sydney City Eisteddfod gala. That's when Maina (Gielgud) first saw my work. Maina and Colin (Peasley) saw it and they spoke to me afterwards and said, 'It was very good, you should keep trying.'

After I got into the Australian Ballet I went to Maina and said, 'Maina, I'm going to do a ballet for Tanya Pearson's ballet school. I'd like you to come and see it.' She saw it and then she asked me to work for the Australian Ballet. Canberra Youth Ballet had also done a ballet of mine, a pas de deux. I also choreographed for workshops at the school in San Francisco. As soon as I started ballet, at 16$^{1}/_{2}$, I started choreographing.

POTTER: Where do you look for sources of inspiration?

WELCH: From everything, I think, although I try to draw a lot on my own life. But then, too, you have to have a life to have anything come from it, and being in ballet it's really hard to have your own life. I mean, we're in here from 10.30 to 6.30 every day. Then you go home and physically you're exhausted. So I really have to push myself to try to find other interests, to go and see a play, go and see musicals. But I've really been enjoying doing that lately. And there's such a creative group of young dancers that have just come into the company. They're all good musicians. I find I get a lot of inspiration from them.

POTTER: You work with the classical vocabulary basically. Do you feel limited by it?

WELCH: No, because I don't ever think, 'Oh, I can't do that step because it's not classical.' If anything, I think it almost gives me a wider vocabulary because I'm definitely using any form of dance. I'm not just restricting myself to classical dance. I don't feel limited by it at all; I find it really inspiring actually. When I was younger and watching the ballet, I was fascinated by women's feet on pointe. There was something that finished their line or the way the feet and legs looked. Ballet has such a strong image of that for me that I can't take it away from what I imagine dance to contain.

POTTER: What do you think makes your choreography look like Stanton Welch's choreography? Do you think you have a particular look?

WELCH: There are three different sorts of ballets I like to do. I mean, the ballet I just did for the Dancers Company, *Many Colours Blue*, was distinctly for them. It was classical ballet pushing them beyond their limits. So from its conception it was aimed distinctly at these individuals. With a ballet such as *Madame Butterfly*, the story is the important thing and the dancers that come in and out of it, although they're extremely important, they're not the most important thing. It's the storyline. And you have another thing again like *Corroboree* where you're trying to branch into a different style, to try something new.

So I have these three flight plans that I like to take. So I hope I don't have something where you just go, 'Oh well, that's so typical of him.' But everyone's always said whenever they see one of my ballets, whether they like it or not, that the dancers always look good. And I'd like to think it's because I draw so much inspiration from them that I can always make them shine in their own individual talent. That's something I'd like to be able to do. If someone is really sexy, I'd like to make them look sexy on stage; I wouldn't like to make them look the opposite.

POTTER: I want just to go back to *Many Colours Blue*. It seemed to me that it was almost unclassical in the sense that you used, for example, dropped wrists and lifted elbows. It really almost subverted the classical line. Did you set out to make it look like that?

WELCH: Yes, I did. I started the ballet with the ladies doing the five positions of the arms, the classical arms. Then throughout the ballet they kept doing them, but they embellished on them gradually. If you twist a wrist or drop the elbows or take the arm slightly behind you, it can change the complete look. What I love about classical ballet is that it doesn't have to be this exact, structured thing. You can do whatever you want with it. I mean, look at Balanchine's work. It's so classical and it's just so interesting. You could take the pas de deux from *Agon* and put it today on stage with a work by (William) Forsythe or (Jiří) Kylián and you'd think it had been choreographed yesterday. But it hasn't, it's *really* old. It's just classical ballet that's *slightly* off-kilter—the hips are *slightly*

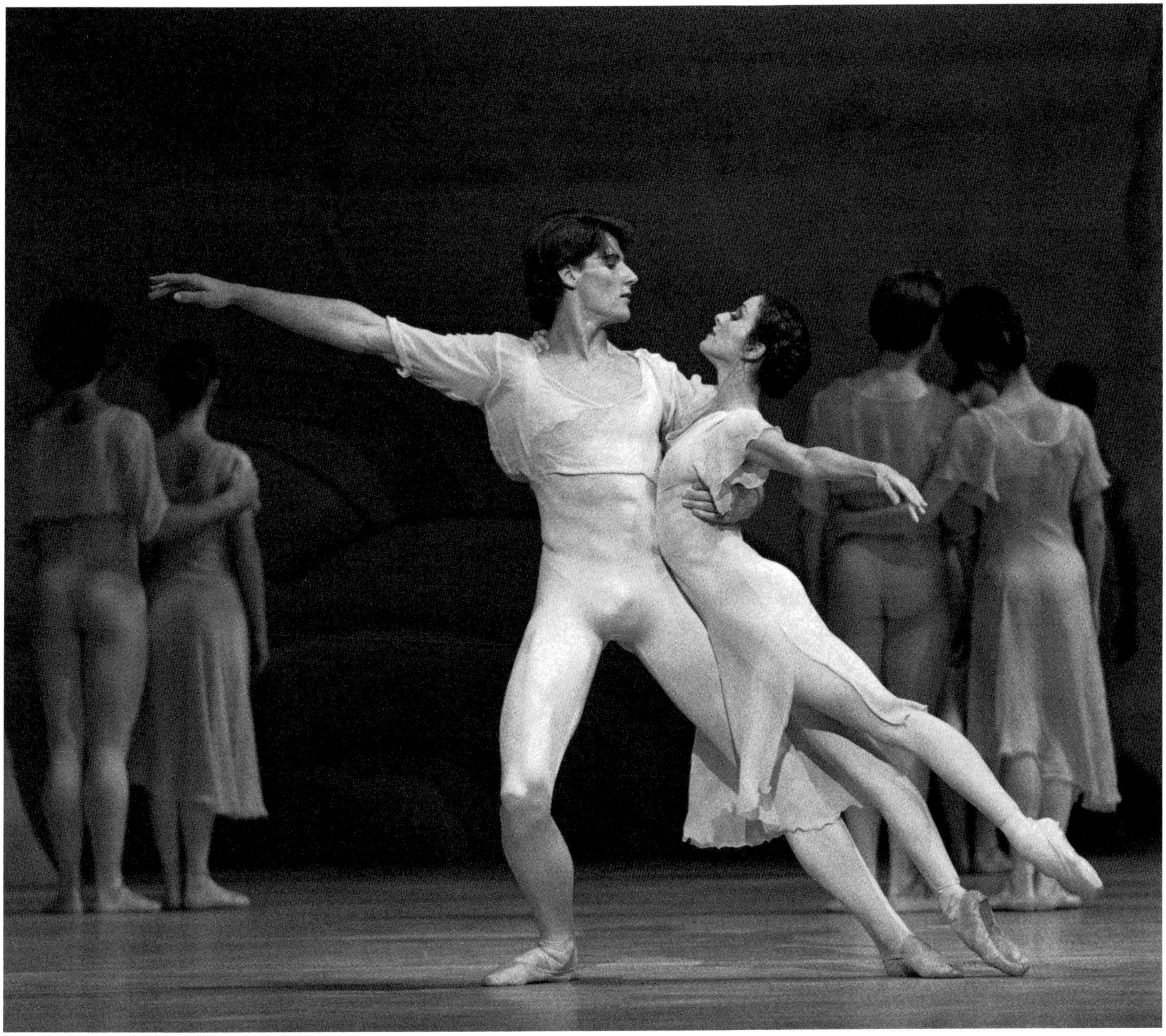

aligned in a different way, or the arms are freer. So that's what I did. I tried to make classical ballet look like it was really structured but that it also could branch off in different directions.

POTTER: Is that how you worked with *Divergence* too?

WELCH: Yes, definitely. *Divergence* was that sort of plan as well. The point of *Divergence* was that sometimes things can look a bit ugly. Classical ballet is often such a game of making everything look smooth and pretty and happy and calm. I just wanted to expose the mechanics of dance, the sexuality of dance and how the women *really* dance in ballet. Often you get the idea that they're just carried around and they're really sweet. Really they work much harder than most guys do. They're on pointe. They're exposed in a way the guys aren't.

POTTER: When you are choosing a cast, what sort of dancers do you look for?

WELCH: As soon as I find a piece of music, I pretty much cast the ballet straight away. The dancers each have their fortes. We have people that are very sexy and can be the sophisticated woman. We have people who don't mind getting grubby and are really good actors and can change their entire personality for a role. There are people who are great technicians and have beautiful style. But I think it is definitely their presence on stage that influences me. It's funny because I dance with these people as well, you see, and if we're all in, say, *Anna Karenina* and we're doing this circle step in Act I where we pass by each other and if they can look at you, if they have sparkle and they're relaxed, *that* to me is stage presence. When you sit out the front, you can pick them. So I think I look specifically for those people. They mightn't necessarily be the neatest or the most correct, but they're definitely the people who can look at you and take you away when you're in the audience. They're really comfortable with themselves and how they portray themselves on stage.

POTTER: When you go into a studio, first day, new ballet, what is your working process? How do you build up a structure?

WELCH: The first day is always the worst day. I do a lot of homework, so when I walk in on the first day I can give them a chunk of dancing which gives them something to think about. Otherwise you've got all the dancers standing around with their hands on their hips looking at you and going, 'Well, come on, what are we going to do?'

POTTER: So you have steps prepared when you go in?

WELCH: Yes, especially with big group scenes. If it's a pas de deux or a solo, then I have highlights in the music where I know on this point I want them coming in from that corner in a lift, but I like to go in and just do it in there with them. But when you've got a larger group of people, the concentration level is dreadful and you've got to be able to keep them interested. *Divergence*, for example, that whole first movement I had done before I came in, so I taught it to them on the first day. That was enough for them to think about every day for the rest of the time, so there was never a point when they were standing on the sides bored. They always had something to go through even if I changed it later.

Each day starts with a new section. I try not to come with nothing planned because of the time allowance. You have to have accomplished so many seconds or so many minutes in each day. So I try to do it that way and then you can always go back and change stuff, which you always do. But you need always to be moving forward—so you don't get panicked!

POTTER: Do you use suggestions from the dancers a lot?

WELCH: Definitely. I mean, that's what I love about it, the fact that a lot of stuff is an accident. I mean, a guy will drop someone, a girl from a lift, and she'll fall a certain way and you go, 'Oh wait, if you let her fall that way and grab her legs, she can do this.' Then it can keep building that way. I really love that.

Then you find with people they get a little complacent. You say, 'I want you to spot the back in the turn,' and they find that really hard, so they say, 'Well, I don't want to do that.' And you say, 'No, you actually *have* to do it. I know it's harder but that's what I want.' You've got to be able to draw the line between a suggestion and someone wanting to get out of doing something they find is a little bit more difficult, otherwise nothing would be done. I mean, originally with the *Butterfly* pas de deux, they said they couldn't do it, and they all can do it now. That's just the way ballet is. You rise to the occasion each time. I mean, what if the person who did

Sleeping Beauty had said that she didn't want to do the Rose Adage because it had too much balancing! Still today there are so few people that can do it well, but that's the challenge of it.

POTTER: Can you tell me about your forthcoming commission for the San Francisco Ballet—what led up to it and what you're planning?

WELCH: Okay. Well, it's still very much in a rough stage at the moment. I found a piece of music, *Maninyas* by the Australian composer Ross Edwards—I'll just go back to the beginning. When we went to San Francisco for the United Nations gala, when I did *Corroboree*, Helgi Tomasson, artistic director of San Francisco Ballet, saw it and he called me into the office on probably the last day and said he'd really like me to do a ballet for them. I didn't have any music exactly just sort of sitting around and I couldn't find anything that fitted their orchestra—they've lost their opera house due to the earthquake and they've moved into a theatre where the pit is much smaller. On the Dancers Company tour this year we went to Wagga and I went into a CD shop. There were six classical CDs and this, *Maninyas*, was one of them. So I think, in a way, that was fate. It's a great opportunity to use Australian music, too.

The piece will just be very dynamic sort of dancing. I'd like the music to start with huge silk screens and, as the dancers come through, they unveil their first screen. They're constantly taking off layers of themselves as they become more intimate with one another. Like as you get to know someone, you get more towards your true self. That's what I'd like to portray in this ballet, but it's still very much in its birthing process. And I'm really lucky because, although this is my first opportunity away, San Francisco is the other place I call home. It will be different—Americans dance very differently from us. They have different priorities, different attack levels. But as a dancer I love dancing in that style. I love their energy, their vitality, their determination. We have a 52-week contract. We are paid for our holidays. In America every State has one, if not two or three, companies and the competition level for work is extraordinarily high. They have lay-offs—periods of no pay—when they go out and become waiters, or they serve in restaurants because they love ballet so much that they're willing to do this, live in poverty for a stretch of time so they can dance these 100 shows. We complain that we do too many shows where they want more. So they're hungry for dance, which is just so exciting. That side of it I'm really looking forward to.

POTTER: Can you tell me something about *Corroboree*? You used a piece of music by John Antill that had been used before for a ballet. Did that worry you?

WELCH: No. I'd seen on video this old black and white documentary of the original *Corroboree*. And it had always fascinated me. The music is just superb, the whole thing. And it was the first ballet my mother ever saw as a child and she used to always talk about it. The first ballet impression you have is such a vivid one and, I don't know, you make it out to be so much different from what it actually ends up to be. I wanted to play with her ideas, what she'd told me, what she imagined the ballet to have in it. I wanted to make my own version of that myth.

I love wildlife documentaries, I love animal studies and nature studies, and I thought I'd love to incorporate that into a style of dance. I wanted *Corroboree* to be like a pride of lions. There was the dominant male; they had their pecking order. The females had their pecking order. It was like the struggle that we all have inside us, that's very natural to us. I think dance has that essence in it as well; it's very primitive. Originally people would have danced about things like that, to show how their tribe had succeeded, how their bloodline had succeeded. This is what I wanted to do with it.

And I'd like to do it with lots of ballets, very much. Flocks of birds, they have wonderful mating rituals; to be the strongest you have to survive this way. Maybe it's wrong, but I think in ballet it's often that way too; only the strongest survive. It's like the physically fittest survive; the people who push themselves the hardest survive. It's this constant struggle. And dancers move in such an animal-like way at times, too. Maybe that's what I look for in a dancer, some sort of totally natural movement, something that's very animalistic.

POTTER: *Of Blessed Memory* was dedicated to your mum. Has she been one of the great sources of inspiration to you?

WELCH: *Blessed Memory*—when I conceived the idea, Mum wasn't specifically going to be the person playing the role. I'd always wanted to do a ballet about leaving your mother.

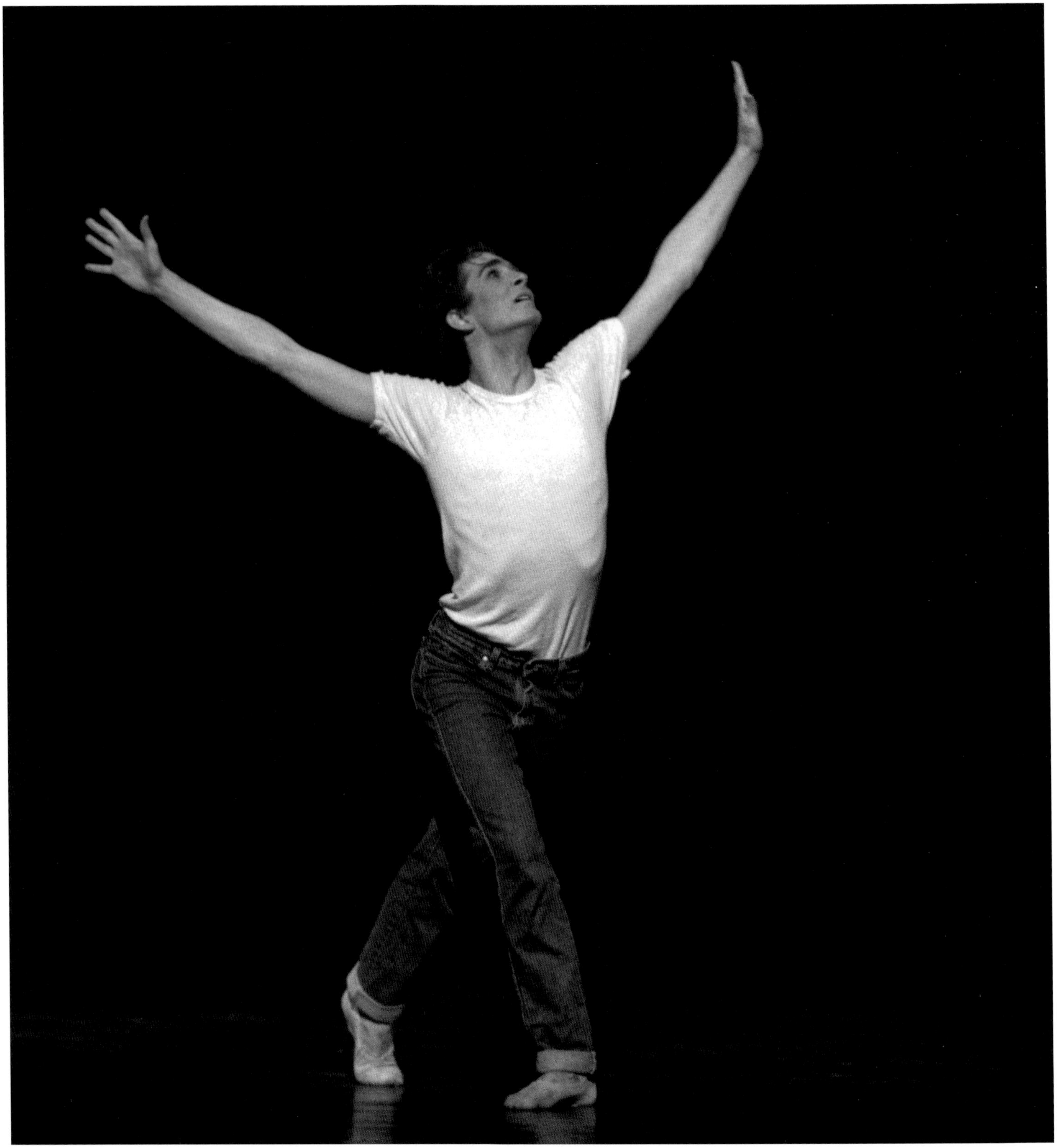

So the inspiration came from the fact that we had left our mother, but it wasn't designed for her then. It was just that she was the best female ballerina around at the time in that age group, which was great. If we do it again in ten years' time, it'll be someone else. But yes, we grew up with our mother, my brother Damien and I. And our grandmother and Dad. And they gave us so much food for our imagination. There was always a freedom to express yourself. I think that's what was important.

Welch's career has not been without its difficulties. Critics have not always treated him gently. His youth, his rapid rise to his current status as resident choreographer with the Australian Ballet, his perceived lack of choreographic training have all been the source of much debate. Much of the criticism also came at a time when the Australian Ballet was in upheaval as a result of moves to dislodge the Australian Ballet's artistic director, Maina Gielgud, from her position. Welch's first evening-length work, *Madame Butterfly*, was being rehearsed at this critical time and premiered just two months after it was announced that the then Australian Ballet Foundation would begin its search for a new artistic director. In many respects *Butterfly* was never properly examined, since few critics seemed able to disentangle it from the political events surrounding the fact that Gielgud's contract would not be renewed after 1996. But while Welch is scathing of the attacks that have been made on him, his dreams, like his ideas, are boundless.

POTTER: One of the criticisms that's been made of you just recently is that people perceive of you as never having studied the craft of choreography. How would you answer that criticism?

WELCH: I mean, really, who has? Here in the Australian Ballet we're, if anything, exposed to more choreographers than most companies in the world. We've had Jiří Kylián work with us. He came and saw my ballet for the Dancers Company. I had lengthy conversations with him. He helped. He really re-choreographed his pas de deux in *Forgotten Land* on Justine (Summers) and myself. We've had Christopher Bruce. I sat with him and talked to him for hours. He asked me if I'd like to come and watch his ballet company and work with him for an extended period of time. We had Nacho Duato come out. I worked with him, hands-on, in his ballet. I don't think I'd have had that opportunity anywhere else. Glen Tetley, first ballet I did for the company, *Of Blessed Memory*, he was there by my side, he was coaching me basically through the whole thing. I mean what more of an apprenticeship do I need? I think it's different because it's not strictly an apprenticeship with one person. But I won't come out of it the other end with people saying, 'You can see that he's influenced by so and so,' because I haven't just worked along the lines of one person. Every year we have two or three different people come here and I think that is very relevant. I mean, who has had an apprenticeship from Australia? Did Graeme Murphy? Did Sir Robert Helpmann? They were just around a lot of very influential, very talented, very artistic people, and that's how they drew their inspiration. I think that we're easily exposed to the same amount. It's just quicker. But I think that's very much the nineties. I mean it's just faster. Information is fed faster. You pick up things faster—you have to! It's not a race, but everyone's running forward.

POTTER: There was quite a lot of criticism about *Butterfly* and it seemed to centre on the idea that you weren't given enough time. Did you feel pressured and pushed for time?

WELCH: Well actually, I finished early. So, okay, as a choreographer I'd love to take four years to do *Madame Butterfly* and spend every day with every cast talking about where their heads are, but that's just not reality. And it's definitely not reality for the Australian Ballet. We're a business and if you say, 'I am going to do this ballet,' the responsibility is yours to finish it in that amount of time.

POTTER: Were *you* happy with *Butterfly*?

WELCH: Yes. I mean I've got a thousand notes. I know how I'd like to direct it and where I'd like to take things. I could refine it and change it and play with it; you could do that with all ballets. But although you can open it up and make it better, it still had some form of effect. People cried. I loved the fact that there were some people who cried—just one person would have made me happy.

POTTER: Have you found your youth to be a problem in the rehearsal studio?

WELCH: Not in the rehearsal studio at all. When I did *A Time to Dance*, which was my first piece for the Australian Ballet Foundation—it was on the School—I walked in and I was the same age as all the people that I was working with. So okay, we had some problems, but pretty soon these people realised that they wanted to be in the ballet. They worked really hard. Now I've worked with nearly every year that's come through the School. So then when they get into the company, they've already worked with me as a choreographer. So I suppose I've got a rapport with these people that have come up through the School. And the principals, right from the very beginning, were always very respectful and very helpful. This company has been based on people getting opportunities very young and they, as principals, all did, so they know what the pressure is.

The only problem is with the critics really. No-one's made me feel young; I only feel it when I read about it in the paper. The thing that's so interesting is we went to Tasmania this year with *Many Colours Blue*, which would be my eighth or ninth ballet for the Australian Ballet Foundation, and the headline was: 'Novice choreographer does ballet'. Okay, I'm 25, turning 26. That's a quarter of a century. I'm not a baby anymore. Most choreographers started choreography when they were 18, 19, and now I'm turning 26 and they're still calling me a novice. I mean that's just a catchphrase.

When we went to America in 1994, Anna Kisselgoff, dance critic for the *New York Times*, said she really loved *Divergence*. She said it was so full of ideas. Then when we got back here, every review after that said it was full of ideas—every single one! They all read what Anna Kisselgoff said and they caught the phrase and used it. It's funny that you can really see things like that travel through the press. I found that one of the most disappointing things that has ever happened to me. The critics wouldn't stand there and disagree with Anna Kisselgoff. They changed their own reviews to use her points. They can't even say, 'Okay, I have a different opinion from this person.' The Australian Ballet gets extremely harsh criticisms, especially in Melbourne. I mean, we'll go overseas with *Giselle* and they'll say it's the best *Giselle* they've seen, and we perform it here and they say why are we still doing *Giselle*? If there were more classical companies for them to compare us to, I think we'd get much higher praise. But we're the big one. We get funding and they've got to keep our egos down or I don't know what they think will happen.

POTTER: What's the future for Stanton Welch?

WELCH: This year? Sleeping is the near future.

POTTER: I had a more long-term sort of vision!

WELCH: I don't know, I don't know. Well, obviously I want to keep choreographing. I'd like to be doing a lot of ballets. If you have a group of 60 dancers, and each one has his or her own gifts and own things to give, there are ballets that you could do that are just catered to those people and their gifts. But if you're only doing one ballet a year, then you need to do something that's ballet for the sake of ballet. But if you can do a multitude of ballets, you can do a ballet for ballet's sake, you can do a story ballet, you can do a ballet designed specifically on this group of people. There's a whole group of people in this company at the moment who can sing, and play guitar, and piano. It would be wonderful to have them make their own music while they're dancing on stage. I'd love to do a ballet like that, because you could draw things from those people that might never get drawn out. They have their own special gift to give and I'd love to use that more. And to do that you need to have your own collection of dancers and you need to be doing work very steadily. So that's what I think my ideal aim would be.

POTTER: Are you saying that you'd like to have a company?

WELCH: I don't know if it's a company. I'd hate to be an artistic director after seeing everything that goes on. I'd hate to have to make those decisions and to have to make money and be aware of all that sort of stuff. But I'd love to have a very steady stream of work where I could make things individually and for specific people. I'd like to do a ballet for the company where you show the whole company off in tutus, where they're classical and strong. We do Serge Lifar's

Suite en blanc, we do Harald Lander's Études. We need our own classical showpiece. But then I'm not going to sacrifice my one ballet a year to do something like that. It's not where I want to be going. But then the dancers need that. I'd like to feed them because I draw so much from them. I'd like to give them stuff to do, a modern ballet, a story ballet, a contemporary ballet, a ballet just on them. Yes, I think that's my ultimate goal.

Stanton Welch missed his daily class to record this interview, having initially forgotten our appointment. Perhaps that was a bonus because, sitting there in practice clothes ready for a full round of afternoon rehearsals, he seemed determined to make up for his forgetfulness. If anything characterises him as an interviewee, at least on this occasion, it's his energy and enthusiasm. He talks quickly breaking off sentences in mid-stream as new thoughts take over, laughs a lot, and exudes youthful—although he would hate me using that word—charm.

Choreography by Stanton Welch

1990	A Time to Dance	Dancers Company
	Three of Us	Australian Ballet
1991	Of Blessed Memory	Australian Ballet
1992	Canon	Dancers Company
	Passion	Dancers Company
1993	Before the Rain	Dancers Company
1994	Divergence	Australian Ballet
1995	Madame Butterfly	Australian Ballet
	Corroboree	Australian Ballet, UNited We Dance Festival, San Francisco
	Many Colours Blue	Dancers Company
1996	Maninyas	San Francisco Ballet
	Red Earth	Australian Ballet
1997	Cinderella	Australian Ballet

Appendix

Oral history interviews relating to dance in the collection of the National Library of Australia

(Listed as: Interviewee; tape number; interviewer, month and year of recording)

Adams, Neil; TRC 2857; Shirley McKechnie, September 1992
Adams, Phillip; TRC 3107; Michelle Potter, August 1994
Asker, Don; TRC 2341; Hilary Trotter, October 1988
Asker, Don; TRC 2689; Shirley McKechnie, May 1991
Bain, Keith; deB 771–772; Hazel de Berg, May 1974
Bain, Keith; TRC 2649; Shirley McKechnie, November 1990
Baronova, Irina; TRC 3119; Michelle Potter, August 1994
Baynes, Stephen; TRC 3378; Michelle Potter, December 1995
Beaver, Moya; TRC 3162; Michelle Potter, October 1994
Bousloff, Kira; TRC 2627; Michelle Potter, August 1990
Boyd, Charles; TRC 3163; Michelle Potter, October 1994
Brinson, Peter; TRC 2910; Shirley McKechnie, January 1993
Cameron, Rachel; deB 957; Hazel de Berg, September 1976
Carroll, Jacqui; TRC 2646; Shirley McKechnie, November 1990
Chan, Kai Tai; TRC 2648; Shirley McKechnie, November 1990
Clapham, Eric; TRC 2818; Michelle Potter, May 1992
Coe, Kelvin; TRC 2807; Michelle Potter, May 1992
Collins, Harold; TRC 2048; Bill Stephens, August 1986, September 1991
Dalman, Elizabeth; TRC 3151; Michelle Potter, August 1994
Dean, Beth; deB 902; Hazel de Berg, December 1975
Duchesne, Mary; TRC 1981; James Murdoch, November 1985
Dupain, Max; TRC 2630; Michelle Potter, September 1990
Exiner, Johanna; TRC 3164; Michelle Potter, November 1994
Fredrikson, Kristian; TRC 2899; Michelle Potter, January 1993
Garling, Jean; deB 79; Hazel de Berg, August 1961
Gielgud, Maina; TRC 3165; Michelle Potter, November 1994, January 1995, August 1995, November 1995
Glennon, Keith; deB 958–959; Hazel de Berg, September 1976
Greaves, Donna; deB 787; Hazel de Berg, September 1974
Hammond, Paul; TRC 2394; Mark Gordon, February 1989
Hassall, Nanette; TRC 2634; Shirley McKechnie, September 1990
Haycock, Bill; TRC 3319; Michelle Potter, August 1995
Healey, Sue; TRC 2916; Michelle Potter, February 1993
Helpmann, Robert; deB 47; Hazel de Berg, March 1964
Helpmann, Robert; deB 773; Hazel de Berg, May 1974
Helpmann, Robert; TRC 22/3; Radio interview, July 1961
Ingram, Geoffrey; TRC 2372; Michelle Potter, December 1988
Jones, Marilyn; TRC 2629; Michelle Potter, September 1990
Karczag, Eva; TRC 3015; Mark Gordon, October 1992
Karin, Janet; TRC 3428; Bill Stephens, March 1996
Kitcher, Barry; TRC 3102; Michelle Potter, August 1994
Lansac, Régis; TRC 3019; Michelle Potter, February 1994
Lawrence, Bryan; TRC 2118; Bill Stephens, October/November 1986
Lowe-Henricks, Kathryn; TRC 2679; Shirley McKechnie, March 1991
McKechnie, Shirley; TRC 2517; Mark Gordon, August 1989
Martyn, Laurel; TRC 2444; Mark Gordon, May 1989

Menon, Padma; TRC 2734/3; Jennifer Gall, November 1991
Menon, Padma; TRC 3419; Michelle Potter, May 1996
Mercurio, Paul; TRC 3395; Michelle Potter, January 1996
Moreland, Barry; TRC 2642; Shirley McKechnie, October 1990
Murphy, Graeme; deB 1222–1223; Hazel de Berg, April 1981
Murphy, Graeme; TRC 2680; Shirley McKechnie, May 1990
Murphy, Graeme; TRC 3478; Michelle Potter, August 1996
Obarzanek, Gideon; TRC 3396; Michelle Potter, January 1996
Page, Stephen; TRC 3397; Michelle Potter, January 1996
Pask, Edward; TRC 2815/64; Bill Stephens, October 1993
Pask, Edward; TRC 3092; Bill Stephens, July 1994
Pelly, Noël; TRC 2799; Michelle Potter, March 1992
Powell, Ray; TRC 2941; Bill Stephens, May/June 1993
Ray, Robert; TRC 2636; Shirley McKechnie, September 1990
Reid, Rex; TRC 1982; James Murdoch, March 1986
Robinson, Roland; deB 348–351; Hazel de Berg, December 1967
Rowell, Kenneth; deB 729; Hazel de Berg, December 1973
Rowell, Kenneth; TRC 2452; Michelle Potter, June 1989
Rubinstein, Martin; TRC 3322; Michelle Potter, August 1995
Sager, Peggy; TRC 3157; Michelle Potter, November 1994
Scott, Margaret; TRC 2928; Michelle Potter, April 1993
Sietsma, Maggi; TRC 3526; Michelle Potter, November 1996
Southey, Robert; TRC 3026; Michelle Potter, March 1994
Stock, Cheryl; TRC 2578; Shirley McKechnie, May 1990
Stringer, Walter; TRC 3010; Michelle Potter, January 1994
Tait, Viola; TRC 3166; Michelle Potter, November 1994
Tankard, Meryl; TRC 2602; Shirley McKechnie, July 1990
Tankard, Meryl; TRC 3477; Michelle Potter, July 1996
Taylor, Jonathan; TRC 2690; Shirley McKechnie, May 1991
Tchinarova-Finch, Tamara; TRC 3120; Michelle Potter, August 1994
Tweedie, Valrene; TRC 2347; Michelle Potter, November 1988
van Praagh, Peggy; deB 681; Hazel de Berg, July 1973
Vernon, Janet; TRC 2650; Shirley McKechnie, November 1990
Walker, Margaret; deB 767; Hazel de Berg, May 1974
Walker, Margaret; TRC 1770; Barbara Blackman, May 1985
Warren, Leigh; TRC 2631; Shirley McKechnie, September 1990
Watson, Graeme; TRC 2600; Shirley McKechnie, June 1990
Weir, Natalie; TRC 3320; Michelle Potter, August 1995
Welch, Garth; TRC 2545; Michelle Potter, January 1990
Welch, Stanton; TRC 3321; Michelle Potter, August 1995
Whitelock, Trafford; deB 1131; Hazel de Berg, February 1980
Woolliams, Anne; TRC 2198; Shirley McKechnie, August 1987

Copies of transcripts and sound recordings can be provided on request, subject to individual access conditions. Enquiries should be directed to:

Oral History Section
National Library of Australia
Canberra ACT 2600 Australia

Phone: (02) 6262 1687
Fax: (02) 6273 6209 Email: mwoods@nla.gov.au

List of Illustrations

Dedication page (page iv)
Janet Vernon and Ross Philip in Graeme Murphy's *Some Rooms*, 1983
Sydney Dance Company
Photograph by Branco Gaica
National Library Pictorial Collection

page ix
Nik Hills (foreground) and Tracey Carrodus in Natalie Weir's *In-sight*, 1995
Expressions Dance Company
Photograph by Three Pines Studio
Photograph courtesy of Expressions Dance Company

page xii (opposite page 1)
Stephen Baynes, 1994
Photograph by Branco Gaica
Photograph courtesy of The Australian Ballet

page 4
Vicki Attard and Steven Heathcote in Stephen Baynes' *Beyond Bach*, 1995
The Australian Ballet
Photograph by James McFarlane
National Library Pictorial Collection

page 7
Justine Summers and Nigel Burley in Stephen Baynes' *Catalyst*, 1990
The Australian Ballet
Photograph by James McFarlane
National Library Pictorial Collection

page 11
Justine Summers, Steven Heathcote and Li Cunxin in Stephen Baynes' *Beyond Bach*, 1995
The Australian Ballet
Photograph by James McFarlane
National Library Pictorial Collection

page 14
Maina Gielgud, c.1990
Photographer unknown
Photograph courtesy of The Australian Ballet

page 19
Justine Summers in Stanton Welch's *Divergence*, 1994
The Australian Ballet
Photograph by James McFarlane
National Library Pictorial Collection

page 22
Steven Heathcote and Justine Summers in Stanton Welch's *Corroboree*, 1995
The Australian Ballet
Photograph by Marty Sohl
Photograph courtesy of Marty Sohl

page 29
Miranda Coney and artists in Graeme Murphy's *Nutcracker*, 1992
The Australian Ballet
Photograph by James McFarlane
National Library Pictorial Collection

page 34
Padma Menon, 1989
Photograph by Ross Gould
Photograph courtesy of Padma Menon Dance Theatre

page 37
Padma Menon performing *Yaathra—The Journey*, 1992
Padma Menon Dance Theatre
Photograph by Ross Gould
National Library Pictorial Collection

page 41
Ganesh Easwer, Caroline Bridges, Padma Menon and Diane Palmer in Padma Menon's *Relations*, 1996
Padma Menon Dance Theatre
Photograph by George Serras
National Library Pictorial Collection

page 44
Padma Menon, 1996
Padma Menon Dance Theatre
Photograph by Arunas
Photograph courtesy of Padma Menon Dance Theatre

page 48
Paul Mercurio, 1995
Photograph by Greg Barrett
Photograph courtesy of Catherine Beall Management

page 52
Paul Mercurio in Graeme Murphy's *Some Rooms*, 1983
Sydney Dance Company
Photograph by Branco Gaica
National Library Pictorial Collection

page 60
Graeme Murphy, 1996
Photograph by Greg Barrett
Photograph courtesy of Sydney Dance Company

page 64
Studio portrait of Graeme Murphy for *Poppy*, 1978
Sydney Dance Company
Photograph by Robert Hartman
National Library Pictorial Collection

page 70
Janet Vernon and Kim Walker in rehearsal for Graeme Murphy's *Kraanerg*, 1988
Sydney Dance Company
Photograph by Branco Gaica
Photograph courtesy of Michelle Potter

page 75
Graeme Murphy and Janet Vernon, 1995
Photograph by Branco Gaica
National Library Pictorial Collection

page 78
Gideon Obarzanek, 1997
Photograph by Joris Jan Bos
Photograph courtesy of Nederlands Dans Theater

page 83
Kathryn Dunn in rehearsal for Gideon Obarzanek's *Fast Idol*, 1995
Chunky Move
Photograph by Derek Biermann
National Library Pictorial Collection

page 86
Sian Stokes and Alan Mathewson in Gideon Obarzanek's *Sand Siren*, 1992
The Australian Ballet
Photograph by Simon Obarzanek
Photograph courtesy of The Australian Ballet

page 92
Stephen Page, 1995
Photograph by Greg Barrett
Photograph courtesy of Catherine Beall Management

page 96
Stephen Page, 1993
Photograph by Lynkushka
National Library Pictorial Collection

page 98
Dancers of The Australian Ballet rehearsing 'Mercury', part of Stephen Page's *Alchemy*, 1996
The Australian Ballet
Photograph by Tim Webster
National Library Pictorial Collection

page 101
Stephen Page, State Theatre, Victorian Arts Centre, 1996
Photograph by Tim Webster
National Library Pictorial Collection

page 104
Meryl Tankard in *Two Feet*, 1988
Photograph by Régis Lansac
Photograph courtesy of Meryl Tankard Australian Dance Theatre

page 109
Meryl Tankard in *Two Feet*, 1992
Meryl Tankard Company
Photograph by Régis Lansac
National Library Pictorial Collection

page 113
Roz Hervey in Meryl Tankard's *Banshee*, 1989
Meryl Tankard Company
Photograph by Régis Lansac
National Library Pictorial Collection

page 118
Grayson Millwood and Mia Mason in Meryl Tankard's *Furioso*, 1995
Meryl Tankard Australian Dance Theatre
Photograph by Régis Lansac
National Library Pictorial Collection

page 122
Natalie Weir, 1994
Photograph by Darren Jew/Living Image
National Library Pictorial Collection

page 125
Ross Hounslow, Tracey Carrodus and Nik Hills in Natalie Weir's *Proof Sheet*, 1993
Expressions Dance Company
Photograph by Three Pines Studio
Photograph courtesy of Expressions Dance Company

page 127
Dancers of the Queensland Ballet in Natalie Weir's *Burning*, 1995
The Queensland Ballet
Photograph by Phil Hargreaves
National Library Pictorial Collection

page 130
Dancers of the Queensland Ballet in Natalie Weir's *Burning*, 1995
The Queensland Ballet
Photograph by Phil Hargreaves
National Library Pictorial Collection

page 134
Stanton Welch, 1993
Photograph by Branco Gaica
Photograph courtesy of The Australian Ballet

page 137
Josef Christianson and Vicki Attard in Stanton Welch's *Of Blessed Memory*, 1992
The Australian Ballet
Photograph by Earl Carter
National Library Pictorial Collection

page 140
Stanton Welch in *Equus*, 1990
The Australian Ballet
Photograph by Earl Carter
National Library Pictorial Collection

Name Index

(Page numbers in bold type indicate illustrations.)

ABC-TV 59, 77, 103, 117, 121
Aboriginal Islander Dance Theatre 93, 94, 103—*see also* National Aboriginal and Islander Skills Development Association
ACE—*see* Australian Choreographic Ensemble
Act of Faith 133
Adelaide Centre of Performing Arts 133
Adelaide Festival 47, 121
Adelaide Performing Arts College 133
After Venice 53, 54, 66, 67, 68, 69, 77
Afterworlds 77
Agni 47
Agon 136
Aladdin 133
Alchemy 33, **98**, 103
Aldous, Lucette 6
Alonso, Alicia 25
American Ballet Theatre 17
Andante 13
Anna Karenina 138
Annear, Mark 33
Antill, John 139
L'Après-midi d'un faune vii
Arbos 89
Archer, Robyn 112
Arnold, Ronne 123
Ashton, Sir Frederick 10, 20, 27, 108
Asker, Don 108, 112
Athurs, Andy 124
Attard, Vicki **4**, **137**
Aurora 116, 117–119, 121
Australasian Drama Studies Association Conference 87, 91
Australian Ballet vi, vii, x, 1–3, **4**, 5–6, **7**, 8–10, **11**, 13–18, **19**, 20–21, **22**, 23–28, **29**, 30–33, 55, 61, 63, 65, 71–73, 77, 79, 85, **86**, 88, 90, 91, 93, **98**, 103, 108, 121, 135–136, **137**, **140**, 141–143
Australian Ballet Foundation 141, 142
Australian Ballet School 13, 20, 55, 56, 61–63, 65, 77, 84, 85, 88, 91, 99, 108, 123, 135, 142—*see also* Dancers Company
Australian Ballet Society 108
Australian Choreographic Ensemble 49, 53, 59
Australian Dance Theatre 116, 119
Australian Football League 93, 103
Australian Opera 77, 103, 121

Babicheva, Agnes 3
Bahen, Peter 15
Balanchine, George 10, 20, 136
Ballade 8, 10, 12, 13, 33
Ballet '76 65, 77
Ballet '77 77
Ballet d'Action 133
Ballet Guild vii
Ballet Imperial 10
Ballets Russes vii
Ballet Theatre 133
Ballet Victoria 135
Bangarra Dance Theatre vi, 93, 95, 97, 99–103
Banshee **113**, 115, 121
Bard Bits 77
Baronova, Irina 25
Barossa Music Festival 121
Batchelor, Adrian 100
Bausch, Pina vi, x, 108–112, 117
Baynes, Stephen vi, x, **xii**, 1–13, 18, 20, 21, 33
Beauty and the Beast 77, 133
Before the Rain 33, 143
Béjart, Maurice 18, 25, 30
Berio, Luciano 66
Beriosova, Svetlana 25
Berlin 77
Beyond Bach 1–2, **4**, 8, 9, **11**, 12, 13, 33
Beyond Twelve 18, 77
Bharatha Natyam 35, 36, 42
Billy the Kid 135
Birds behind Bars 108, 121
Birmingham Royal Ballet 17
Black River 103
Black Vine 103
Blaska, Félix 65–66, 77
Bolshoi Ballet 3, 17, 20
Bonehead **back cover**, 91
Borovansky, Edouard 72
Borovansky Ballet vii
Borzik, Rolf 111
Boston Ballet 17
Boston International Choreographic Competition 13
Bousloff, Kira vii
Boxes 77
Bridges, Caroline **41**
The Brother of Sleep 33, 133
Bruce, Christopher 141
Budapest Ballet 17
Burley, Nigel **7**

Burnett, Adrian 33
Burning **127**, 128, 129, **130**, 133
Bussell, Darcey 6

Cafe 49, 56,
Campion, Jane 114
Canadian Opera Company 77
Canberra Youth Ballet 136
Canon 33, 143
Canzona 33
Carnaval 114
Carrodus, Tracey **ix**, **125**
Carroll, Jacqui 33
Carroll, Shane 108
Carter, Andrew 1, 2
Catalyst 1, 2, **7**, 8, 9, 12, 13, 18, 33
Chandalika 47
Chandralekha 43–45
Chants de mariage I & II 105, 121
Chase, Alida 33
Choreartium vii
Christianson, Josef **137**
Chunky Move vi, 79–82, **83**, 84, 91
Cinderella 143
Clarke, Greg 129
Clutches of Sleep 133
Coe, Kelvin 85
The Collector 123, 133
Collins, Harold 87–88, 130
Colors of '88 133
The Competition 30
Complex Reflections 133
Coney, Miranda **29**
Contact 59
Cook, Rosetta 33, 87
Cool White Fridge Knocked Over 91
Corroboree **22**, 33, 136, 139, 143
Cotton, Julia 108
Court of Flora 121
Cranko, John 8, 10, 12, 27
Cross, Alan 33
Cullberg Ballet 89
Cunxin, Li **11**

Dance Collection 59
Dance Company (NSW) 61, 66, 77
Dance Horizons 108, 121
Dance North 123, 133
Dancers Company 9, 13, 20, 28, 33, 79, 87, 91, 123, 133, 135, 136, 139, 141, 143—*see also* Australian Ballet School
Dancing Daze 112
Dancing with I 59
dancing with the clown 59

Daphnis and Chloé 77
Deadly Sins 77
Dean, Christopher 61, 77
Death in Venice 67, 77, 121
de Basil ballet companies vii
The Deep End 33, 121
de Masson, Paul 8
Desert Magic 133
Diaghilev, Sergei 28
Dialogues I & II 8, 9, 10, 13
Divergence 18, **19**, 33, 138, 142, 143
Don Quixote 6, 17, 18, 20, 27
Down Rivers of Spine 133
The Dream 108
Drift Office 91
Duato, Nacho 18, 141
Dunn, Kathryn **83**
Duo for Two Boys 59
DV8 82

Easwer, Ganesh **41**
Ecco le diavole 65, 77
Echo Point 112, 121
Edgeing 59
Edge of the Precipice 133
Edwards, Ross 139
Elizabeth Presents, The Story of Swan Lake 133
Embodied 77
Emotional Disconnection 53, 59
Endicott, Jo Anne 108
Enemy in the Figure 131
Envy 59
Episodes 9, 13
Equus **140**
Études 143
An Evening 77
Evening Suite 77
Expo '92, Seville 103
Expressions Dance Company **ix**, 123, **125**, 127, 129, 131, 133
Extensions Dance Company 133

Fast Idol 81, 89, 91
La Favorita 33
Feel Good Films 59
Festival Australia 18
La Fille mal gardée 18, 27
The Final Move 133
Fire and Ice 77
Fire Earth Air Water 77
Flamenco 50–51
Flashbacks 77
Fonteyn, Margot 6, 25
Forgotten Land 141
Fornicon 73, 77

Forsythe, William 8, 10, 18, 25, 30, 81, 131, 132, 136
Four Reflections of a Quintet 13, 33
Fractured Canvas 133
Francis, Lea **back cover**
Frankfurt Ballet 17
Fredrikson, Kristian vii, 18, 68, 71, 72
Free Radicals 74, 77
Fuller, Loie 114
Furioso **front cover**, 12, 105, 116, 117, **118**, 121

Gallery 33, 77
Gamblin, Kip 8
A Gershwin Pas de Deux 33
Gielgud, Maina vi, 8, **14**, 15–33, 72, 90, 136, 141
Gillespie, Kenneth 61, 62
Giselle 6, 20, 72, 142
Glimpses 65, 77
Gordon, Timothy 33
Graham, Martha 85, 95
Grey, Beryl 25

Haara—A Garland of Pearls 47
Hades 136
Halliday, Joan and Monica 107
Hamburg Ballet 17
Hammer, Carolyn 59
Hate 77
Haycock, Bill 123, 128, 129
Haydée, Marcia 10
The Heat 87, 91
Heathcote, Steven **4**, **11**, **22**, 55
Hello? 108
Helpmann, Sir Robert x, 6, 15, 141
Herel, Dorothy 115
Hervey, Roz **113**
Hills, Nik **ix**, **125**
Homelands 77
Horsman, Greg 21
Horton, Lester 95
The Host 133
Hounslow, Ross **125**
Houston Ballet 17
Human Veins Dance Theatre 112
The Hunchback of Notre Dame 15
Hunger 133

I am a Dancer 133
Imprint 59
In Praise 43, 47
In-sight **ix**, 129, 133
In the Company of Wo/Men 56, 59, 77

In the Middle, Somewhat Elevated 30
Into Dharma 13
Into the Darkness 13
Ivanov, Lev 20

Jabarina 33
Jabula 130, 133
Johnson, Carole 100
Jones, Marilyn 15, 135–136, 139–141
Just Another Poor Boy 55, 59
Just Weight 133

Kailash Dance Company 40, 47
—see also Padma Menon Dance Theatre
Kathak 42
Kayn Walu 99, 100, 103
Kelvin Grove College 123, 125, 133
—see also Queensland University of Technology
Kibbutz Contemporary Dance Company 91
Kikimora 116, 121
King Roger 54, 77
Kirov Ballet 3, 17
Kisselgoff, Anna 142
Kontakthof 110
Kraanerg 66, 69, **70**, 77
Kuchipudi viii, 35–40, 42, 45, 46
Kuchipudi Art Academy Company 35
Kylián, Jiří 8, 9, 10, 18, 20, 25, 30, 73, 136, 141

Labèque, Katia and Marielle 66
Lander, Harald 143
Lansac, Régis 115
La Scala Ballet 9, 13
Late Afternoon of a Faun 77, 99
Lifar, Serge 142
Limited Edition 77
London City Ballet 15
Looking for Rhythm 59
Lovestruck Serenade 126
Luhrmann, Baz 49, 50, 51
The Lunatic, the Lover and the Poet 133
Lurch 91
Lytton, Ulrike 8

MacMillan, Kenneth 8, 10, 27
Macourt, Merrillee 123
MacSween, Gayrie 85–87
Madame Butterfly 18, 33, 136, 138, 141, 143

Maninyas 139, 143
Manon 27
Many Colours Blue 33, 136, 142, 143
Marinsky Ballet 17, 20
Markova, Alicia 25
The Marriage of Figaro 103
Mason, Mia **front cover**, **118**
Master Plan 59
Mathewson, Alan **86**
Maunder, Tessa 107
McLay, Grant 87
Meander 33, 77
Medea 129, 133
Melbourne Dance Theatre 91
Melbourne International Festival of the Arts, 1995 79, 80, 91
Menon, Padma viii, x, **34**, 35–36, **37**, 38–40, **41**, 42–43, **44**, 45–47, 105, 120, 121
Mercurio, Paul viii, **48**, 49–51, **52**, 53–59, 67, 77, 88
The Merry Widow 6, 30
Meryl Tankard Australian Dance Theatre **front cover**, 40, 47, 105, **118**, 119, 121
Meryl Tankard Company **104**, **109**, 112, **113**, 121
Messiaen, Olivier 66, 68–69
Metamorphosis 77
Miller-Ashmole, Petal 33
Millwood, Grayson **118**
Mohini Attam 42
A Moment of Choice 59
Moments Past 33
Monkeys in a Cage 108
Montez, Lola 114
Mooggrah 100, 103
Mooney, Graham 95
Moon Song 133
Moreland, Barry 124
Morgan, Elaine 107
Morrow, Bruce 105
Motion Pool 33
Mr Crowther and the Wallflower 87, 91
Murphy, Graeme iv, vii, x, 18, 20, 29, 33, 51, 52, 54, 56, 59, **60**, 61–63, **64**, 65–74, **75**, 76–77, 87–89, 97, 99, 100, 108, 141
My Name is Edward Kelly 33

Naharin, Ohad 89
NAISDA College 94, 95, 97–100
—see also National Aboriginal and Islander Skills Development Association

Narcissus 123
National Aboriginal and Islander Skills Development Association viii, 93–101, 103—see also NAISDA College
National Capital Dancers 59, 133
National Gallery of Australia 115
National Institute of Dramatic Art (NIDA) 103
Nearly Beloved 77
Nederlands Dans Theater 20, 77, 79, 84, 85, 88, 89, 91
Nepean Dance 59
New York City Ballet 17, 20
Niki Nali 103
1980 111
Ninni 103
Les Noces vii
North Queensland Ballet Company 123, 124
Nureyev, Rudolf 5–6, 18
Nutcracker vii, 18, **29**, 33, 71–73, 77
Nuti 115, 116, 121

Obarzanek, Gideon v, vi, vii, viii, 33, **78**, 79–91, 100
Ochres 12, 102, 103
O'Connell, John 49, 50
Of Blessed Memory 33, **137**, 139, 141, 143
Off 65, 77
Offord, Colin 115
Old Friends, New Friends 77
O Let Me Weep 121
Olympic Games, Atlanta 103
Onegin 10, 27, 135
Orphée et Euridyce 121

The Pack of Women 112
Padma Menon Dance Theatre viii, 35, **37**, 40, **41**, **44**, 45, 47
Page, David 100
Page, Russell 100
Page, Stephen vi, viii, 12, 33, 59, 88, **92**, 93–95, **96**, 97–100, **101**, 102–103
Palmer, David 16
Palmer, Diane **41**
Papillon 77
Parade vii
Parijatham 47
Paris Opera 17, 20, 26
Parker, Shaun **front cover**
Passion 33, 143
Pavane, Lisa 21
Pavlova, Anna 114

Name Index

Peasley, Colin 136
Pelly, Noël 17
Pengelly, Dale 88
Petipa, Marius 20
Petrol Head Lover 85, 89, 91
Petrouchka 135
Phaedra 126, 132
Philip, Ross **iv**
Piano Sonata 77
Picasso's Masque 133
Pineapple Poll 12
Pinkerton, Jan 59
Play Dead 91
The Players 133
Plisetskaya, Maya 25
Poppy **64**, 66–67, 77
Possessed 116, 121
Praying Mantis Dreaming 103
Les Présages vii
Pride 103
Priest, Joanna 3, 5, 10
Proof Sheet—Plates 1–8 **125**, 129, 133
The Protecting Veil 77

Queensland Arts Council 133
Queensland Ballet 65, 77, 79, 84, 85, 87, 88, 90, 91, 123, 124, **127**, 128–129, **130**, 131, 133
Queensland Dance School of Excellence 87
Queensland University of Technology 123, 124, 125, 127, 132, 133—*see also* Kelvin Grove College
Queensland Youth Ballet 136

Ramayana—A Mother Speaks 40, 42, 43, 47
Rapid Transit 108
Rasa 40, 42, 43, 47, 105, 120, 121
Raw 133
Ray, Robert 33
Red Earth 33, 143
Relations 40, **41**, 42, 43, 47
Renate Wandert Aus 108
Rhodes, Nicole 8, 10
Riabouchinska, Tatiana 25
Risks workshop, Sydney Dance Company 56, 59
Roberts, Ann 123, 125
Rockhampton Youth Ballet 133
Rococo Variations 13
The Romantics 33
Romeo and Juliet 10, 27, 87, 135
Roppola, Tuula 117

Rowe, Marilyn 15
Royal Academy of Dancing 124
Royal Ballet 6, 17, 20
Royal Danish Ballet vi, 15, 17, 20
Rumours I, II and III 77
Ryan, Michelle 117

Saccharin Suite 85, 89, 91
Le Sacre du printemps vii, 110
Sacred Dances 33
Saliba, Paul 63, 108
Salome 77
Sand Siren 33, 85, **86**, 89–91
San Francisco Ballet 135, 139, 143
Satyam, Vempati Chinna 35, 47
Scintillation 77
Scorched Ice 133
Scott, Dame Margaret 63, 65
Seascape 33
Seguss, Elsie 131
The Selfish Giant 77
Sensing 77
The Sentimental Bloke 33
Sequenza VII 65, 77
Serenade 10
Seven Deadly Sins 59, 103, 117, 121
Shadow in the Facet 12, 13, 33
Shakespeare Dances 90, 100
Shearsmith, Anthony 123
Shéhérazade 54, 77
Shimmering 77
Shining 77
The Short and the Tall of It 133
Siddhendra Yogi 36
Siesta to Dusk 90, 91
Sietsma, Maggi 123, 126, 127–128, 131
Signatures 77
Sirens 77
Siva—The Cosmic Dancer 41, 47
Skankar, Uday 43
Sketches 33
Sleep No More 85, 90, 91
The Sleeping Beauty 6, 20, 27, 28, 116, 117, 135, 139
Sloth 117, 121
Slow Me Up, Speed Me Down 91
Snowman in the Sun 133
Snugglepot and Cuddlepie 33
soft bruising 77
Some Rooms **iv**, **52**, 53, 54, 77
Sonata for Seven 33
Song of the Night 77
Songs with Mara 105, 121
Southey, Sir Robert 16
Souvenirs 13, 33

Spessivtseva, Olga 114
Spilt Milk 59
Spink, Ian 63
Stepping Stones 30
Steps, Notes and Squeaks 16
Steps to Dance 133
Stewart, Garry 79, 80
Stielow, Mary 68
Still Life 56, 59
Stock, Cheryl 133
Stokes, Sian **86**
Stomping Ground 97
Stone, Cheryl 100
Strauss Songs 1, 8, 13
Stretton, Ross 73
Strictly Ballroom viii, 49–54, 58
The Studio 129, 133
Stuttgart Ballet x, 8, 10, 17
Suite en blanc 143
Summer Nights 33
Summers, Justine **7**, **11**, **19**, **22**, 141
Swan Lake 6, 17, 20, 27, 28
Sweetheart 33, 91
Sydney City Council 103
Sydney City Eisteddfod 136
Sydney Dance Company **iv**, vii, x, 13, 49, 51, **52**, 54–56, 59, 61, **64**, 66, **70**, 74, 77, 79, 85, 87–91, 97–100, 103
Sydney Festival 91
Sydney Theatre Company 103
Symphonic Poem 33
Synergy with Synergy 77

Taahi, Alfred 100
The Taming of the Shrew 10, 135
Tankard, Meryl vi, viii, x, 12, 33, 40, 42, 43, 46, **104**, 105–108, **109**, 110–121
Tekton 77
Tetley, Glen 25, 141
There's Always Time, Always Space 59
Three Conversations 65, 77
Three of Us 33, 143
Three Sisters 33
Three Years of Your Life 13
Time Theatre 59
A Time to Dance 33, 142, 143
Tip 77, 108
To Howl at the Moon 133
Tomasson, Helgi 139
Toppe, Andris 123
Torvill, Jayne 61, 77
Toumanova, Tamara 25
Trackers of Oxyrhyncus 103

Travelling Light 112, 121
Troyens, Les 77
Turandot 77
2 Dance Plus 133
Two Feet **104**, 105, 107, **109**, 112, 114, 121
Two Men and One Woman 59

UNited We Dance Festival, San Francisco 143
Up Til Now 103

Vanderkeybus, Wim 82
van Praagh, Dame Peggy 5, 15, 63, 65, 108
VAST 77, 99
Vernon, Janet **iv**, x, 51, 61, 65, **70**, 73, **75**, 97, 100
Victorian College of the Arts 91, 116, 133
Viridian 77
Volumina 77
VX 18504 112, 121

Waiting 56, 59
Walker, Kim 49, 56, **70**, 88, 100
Walong, Bernadette 102, 103
Warren, Leigh 108
Warumpi Warumpi 101, 103
Watson, Graeme 128
The Wedding Song 103
Weir, Natalie vi, ix, x, 33, **122**, 123–133
Welch, Garth 55, 67, 99, 135–136, 141
Welch, Stanton x, 18–20, 21, 33, **134**, 135–139, **140**, 141–143
Wells, Bruce 15
West Australian Ballet vii, 13, 55, 59, 79, 91, 123–124, 133
While You're Down There 91
White Oak Dance Project 77
Wilderness 77
Williams, Peter 16
Wilson, Margaret 33
Woolliams, Anne 15, 108
World Expo on Stage, Brisbane 121
World Youth Soccer Opening Ceremony 103
Wright, Larissa 87
Wuppertal Tanztheater 108

Yaathra—The Journey **37**
You've Got Me Floating 91